Vasif Huseynov

GEOPOLITICAL RIVALRIES IN THE 'COMMON NEIGHBOURHOOD'

RUSSIA'S CONFLICT WITH THE WEST, SOFT POWER, AND NEOCLASSICAL REALISM

With a foreword by Nicholas Ross Smith

Bibliografische Information der Deutschen Nationalbibliothek
Die Deutsche Nationalbibliothek verzeichnet diese Publikation in der Deutschen Nationalbibliografie; detaillierte bibliografische Daten sind im Internet über http://dnb.d-nb.de abrufbar.

Bibliographic information published by the Deutsche Nationalbibliothek
Die Deutsche Nationalbibliothek lists this publication in the Deutsche Nationalbibliografie; detailed bibliographic data are available in the Internet at http://dnb.d-nb.de.

Coverabbildung: ID 113557567 © Andreykuzmin | Dreamstime.com

ISBN-13: 978-3-8382-1277-7

© *ibidem*-Verlag, Stuttgart 2019

Alle Rechte vorbehalten

Das Werk einschließlich aller seiner Teile ist urheberrechtlich geschützt. Jede Verwertung außerhalb der engen Grenzen des Urheberrechtsgesetzes ist ohne Zustimmung des Verlages unzulässig und strafbar. Dies gilt insbesondere für Vervielfältigungen, Übersetzungen, Mikroverfilmungen und elektronische Speicherformen sowie die Einspeicherung und Verarbeitung in elektronischen Systemen.

All rights reserved. No part of this publication may be reproduced, stored in or introduced into a retrieval system, or transmitted, in any form, or by any means (electronic, mechanical, photocopying, recording or otherwise) without the prior written permission of the publisher. Any person who does any unauthorized act in relation to this publication may be liable to criminal prosecution and civil claims for damages.

Printed in the EU

Soviet and Post-Soviet Politics and Society (SPPS)   Vol. 214
ISSN 1614-3515

General Editor: Andreas Umland,
Institute for Euro-Atlantic Cooperation, Kyiv, umland@stanfordalumni.org

Commissioning Editor: Max Jakob Horstmann,
London, mjh@ibidem.eu

EDITORIAL COMMITTEE*

DOMESTIC & COMPARATIVE POLITICS
Prof. **Ellen Bos**, *Andrássy University of Budapest*
Dr. **Gergana Dimova**, *University of Winchester*
Dr. **Andrey Kazantsev**, *MGIMO (U) MID RF, Moscow*
Prof. **Heiko Pleines**, *University of Bremen*
Prof. **Richard Sakwa**, *University of Kent at Canterbury*
Dr. **Sarah Whitmore**, *Oxford Brookes University*
Dr. **Harald Wydra**, *University of Cambridge*

SOCIETY, CLASS & ETHNICITY
Col. **David Glantz**, *"Journal of Slavic Military Studies"*
Dr. **Marlène Laruelle**, *George Washington University*
Dr. **Stephen Shulman**, *Southern Illinois University*
Prof. **Stefan Troebst**, *University of Leipzig*

POLITICAL ECONOMY & PUBLIC POLICY
Dr. **Andreas Goldthau**, *Central European University*
Dr. **Robert Kravchuk**, *University of North Carolina*
Dr. **David Lane**, *University of Cambridge*
Dr. **Carol Leonard**, *Higher School of Economics, Moscow*
Dr. **Maria Popova**, *McGill University, Montreal*

FOREIGN POLICY & INTERNATIONAL AFFAIRS
Dr. **Peter Duncan**, *University College London*
Prof. **Andreas Heinemann-Grüder**, *University of Bonn*
Prof. **Gerhard Mangott**, *University of Innsbruck*
Dr. **Diana Schmidt-Pfister**, *University of Konstanz*
Dr. **Lisbeth Tarlow**, *Harvard University, Cambridge*
Dr. **Christian Wipperfürth**, *N-Ost Network, Berlin*
Dr. **William Zimmerman**, *University of Michigan*

HISTORY, CULTURE & THOUGHT
Dr. **Catherine Andreyev**, *University of Oxford*
Prof. **Mark Bassin**, *Södertörn University*
Prof. **Karsten Brüggemann**, *Tallinn University*
Dr. **Alexander Etkind**, *University of Cambridge*
Dr. **Gasan Gusejnov**, *Moscow State University*
Prof. **Leonid Luks**, *Catholic University of Eichstaett*
Dr. **Olga Malinova**, *Russian Academy of Sciences*
Dr. **Richard Mole**, *University College London*
Prof. **Andrei Rogatchevski**, *University of Tromsø*
Dr. **Mark Tauger**, *West Virginia University*

ADVISORY BOARD*

Prof. **Dominique Arel**, *University of Ottawa*
Prof. **Jörg Baberowski**, *Humboldt University of Berlin*
Prof. **Margarita Balmaceda**, *Seton Hall University*
Dr. **John Barber**, *University of Cambridge*
Prof. **Timm Beichelt**, *European University Viadrina*
Dr. **Katrin Boeckh**, *University of Munich*
Prof. em. **Archie Brown**, *University of Oxford*
Dr. **Vyacheslav Bryukhovetsky**, *Kyiv-Mohyla Academy*
Prof. **Timothy Colton**, *Harvard University, Cambridge*
Prof. **Paul D'Anieri**, *University of Florida*
Dr. **Heike Dörrenbächer**, *Friedrich Naumann Foundation*
Dr. **John Dunlop**, *Hoover Institution, Stanford, California*
Dr. **Sabine Fischer**, *SWP, Berlin*
Dr. **Geir Flikke**, *NUPI, Oslo*
Prof. **David Galbreath**, *University of Aberdeen*
Prof. **Alexander Galkin**, *Russian Academy of Sciences*
Prof. **Frank Golczewski**, *University of Hamburg*
Dr. **Nikolas Gvosdev**, *Naval War College, Newport, RI*
Prof. **Mark von Hagen**, *Arizona State University*
Dr. **Guido Hausmann**, *University of Munich*
Prof. **Dale Herspring**, *Kansas State University*
Dr. **Stefani Hoffman**, *Hebrew University of Jerusalem*
Prof. **Mikhail Ilyin**, *MGIMO (U) MID RF, Moscow*
Prof. **Vladimir Kantor**, *Higher School of Economics*
Dr. **Ivan Katchanovski**, *University of Ottawa*
Prof. em. **Andrzej Korbonski**, *University of California*
Dr. **Iris Kempe**, *"Caucasus Analytical Digest"*
Prof. **Herbert Küpper**, *Institut für Ostrecht Regensburg*
Dr. **Rainer Lindner**, *CEEER, Berlin*
Dr. **Vladimir Malakhov**, *Russian Academy of Sciences*

Dr. **Luke March**, *University of Edinburgh*
Prof. **Michael McFaul**, *Stanford University, Palo Alto*
Prof. **Birgit Menzel**, *University of Mainz-Germersheim*
Prof. **Valery Mikhailenko**, *The Urals State University*
Prof. **Emil Pain**, *Higher School of Economics, Moscow*
Dr. **Oleg Podvintsev**, *Russian Academy of Sciences*
Prof. **Olga Popova**, *St. Petersburg State University*
Dr. **Alex Pravda**, *University of Oxford*
Dr. **Erik van Ree**, *University of Amsterdam*
Dr. **Joachim Rogall**, *Robert Bosch Foundation Stuttgart*
Prof. **Peter Rutland**, *Wesleyan University, Middletown*
Prof. **Marat Salikov**, *The Urals State Law Academy*
Dr. **Gwendolyn Sasse**, *University of Oxford*
Prof. **Jutta Scherrer**, *EHESS, Paris*
Prof. **Robert Service**, *University of Oxford*
Mr. **James Sherr**, *RIIA Chatham House London*
Dr. **Oxana Shevel**, *Tufts University, Medford*
Prof. **Eberhard Schneider**, *University of Siegen*
Prof. **Olexander Shnyrkov**, *Shevchenko University, Kyiv*
Prof. **Hans-Henning Schröder**, *SWP, Berlin*
Prof. **Yuri Shapoval**, *Ukrainian Academy of Sciences*
Prof. **Viktor Shnirelman**, *Russian Academy of Sciences*
Dr. **Lisa Sundstrom**, *University of British Columbia*
Dr. **Philip Walters**, *"Religion, State and Society", Oxford*
Prof. **Zenon Wasyliw**, *Ithaca College, New York State*
Dr. **Lucan Way**, *University of Toronto*
Dr. **Markus Wehner**, *"Frankfurter Allgemeine Zeitung"*
Dr. **Andrew Wilson**, *University College London*
Prof. **Jan Zielonka**, *University of Oxford*
Prof. **Andrei Zorin**, *University of Oxford*

* While the Editorial Committee and Advisory Board support the General Editor in the choice and improvement of manuscripts for publication, responsibility for remaining errors and misinterpretations in the series' volumes lies with the books' authors.

Soviet and Post-Soviet Politics and Society (SPPS)
ISSN 1614-3515

Founded in 2004 and refereed since 2007, SPPS makes available affordable English-, German-, and Russian-language studies on the history of the countries of the former Soviet bloc from the late Tsarist period to today. It publishes between 5 and 20 volumes per year and focuses on issues in transitions to and from democracy such as economic crisis, identity formation, civil society development, and constitutional reform in CEE and the NIS. SPPS also aims to highlight so far understudied themes in East European studies such as right-wing radicalism, religious life, higher education, or human rights protection. The authors and titles of all previously published volumes are listed at the end of this book. For a full description of the series and reviews of its books, see www.ibidem-verlag.de/red/spps.

Editorial correspondence & manuscripts should be sent to: Dr. Andreas Umland, Institute for Euro-Atlantic Cooperation, vul. Volodymyrska 42, off. 21, UA-01030 Kyiv, Ukraine

Business correspondence & review copy requests should be sent to: *ibidem* Press, Leuschnerstr. 40, 30457 Hannover, Germany; tel.: +49 511 2622200; fax: +49 511 2622201; spps@ibidem.eu.

Authors, reviewers, referees, and editors for (as well as all other persons sympathetic to) SPPS are invited to join its networks at www.facebook.com/group.php?gid=52638198614
www.linkedin.com/groups?about=&gid=103012
www.xing.com/net/spps-ibidem-verlag/

Recent Volumes

206 *Michal Vít*
The EU's Impact on Identity Formation in East-Central Europe between 2004 and 2013
Perceptions of the Nation and Europe in Political Parties of the Czech Republic, Poland, and Slovakia
With a foreword by Andrea Pető
ISBN 978-3-8382-1275-3

207 *Per A. Rudling*
Tarnished Heroes
The Organization of Ukrainian Nationalists in the Memory Politics of Post-Soviet Ukraine
ISBN 978-3-8382-0999-9

208 *Peter H. Solomon Jr., Kaja Gadowska (Eds.)*
Legal Change in Post-Communist States
Progress, Reversions, Explanations
ISBN 978-3-8382-1312-5

209 *Paweł Kowal, Georges Mink, Iwona Reichardt (Eds.)*
Three Revolutions: Mobilization and Change in Contemporary Ukraine I
Theoretical Aspects and Analyses on Religion, Memory, and Identity
ISBN 978-3-8382-1321-7

210 *Paweł Kowal, Georges Mink, Iwona Reichardt (Eds.)*
Three Revolutions: Mobilization and Change in Contemporary Ukraine II
An Oral History of the Revolution on Granite, Orange Revolution, and Revolution of Dignity
ISBN 978-3-8382-1323-1

211 *Li Bennich-Björkman; Sergiy Kurbatov (Eds.)*
When the Future Came
The Collapse of the USSR and the Emergence of National Memory in Post-Soviet History Textbooks
ISBN 978-3-8382-1335-4

212 *Olga R. Gulina*
Migration as a (Geo-)Political Challenge in the Post-Soviet Space
Border Regimes, Policy Choices, Visa Agendas
With a foreword by Nils Muižnieks
ISBN 978-3-8382-1338-5

213 *Sanna Turoma; Kaarina Aitamurto; Slobodanka Vladiv-Glover (Eds.)*
Religion, Expression, and Patriotism in Russia
Essays on Post-Soviet Society and the State
ISBN 978-3-8382-1346-0

Contents

Foreword ix
Acknowledgements... xiii
List of Abbreviations xv
List of Figures.. xix
List of Tables xx

1. **Introduction** 21
   Literature Review and Research Gap 23
   Theoretical Argument 28
   Structure of the Book.. 30

2. **Analytical Framework** 33
   Realism: Neoclassical Realism 34
   (Neoclassical) Realism on Great Power Rivalries 37
   (Neoclassical) Realism on the Foreign Policy of Regional
      States amidst Great Power Rivalries 40
   Public Opinion and Foreign Policy 43
   State Autonomy across Different Variables............. 46
   Soft Power... 48
   Historical Review on Soft Power 51
   Soft Power in Theoretical Writings 51
   Soft Power in Practice 53
   Reconceptualization of Soft Power............................. 55
   State-Managed Projection.. 58
   Soft Power vs. Hard Power 64
   Case Selection... 70
   The Russia – West Confrontation over the "Common
      Neighbourhood" 73
   The "Common Neighbourhood" States 76

Conclusion 82

3. **Soft Power in Western Foreign Policies (2004 – 2016) 85**

   Soft Power vs. Hard Power in Policies of Western Powers ... 86
   Soft Power as the Western Foreign Policy Tool 92
   Self-Projection 95
   Narratives 96
   International Broadcasting 98
   Cultural Diplomacy and Exchange Programmes 102
   Western NGOs and Support for Civil Society 104
   American Non-Governmental Organizations 105
   European Non-Governmental Organizations 108
   Foreign Aid 112
   American Assistance 112
   European Assistance 114
   Limitations of the Western Soft Power Policies 116
   Conclusion 120

4. **Soft Power in Russia's Practice (2004 – 2016) 123**

   Soft Power vs. Hard Power in Russia's Policies 124
   Soft Power as Russia's Foreign Policy Tool 131
   Self-Projection 136
   Narratives 140
   International Broadcasting 145
   Academic Exchange Programs 148
   Russia's NGOs and Support to Civil Society 151
   Economic Ties and Foreign Aid 157
   Limitations of Russian Soft Power 158
   Conclusion 160

5. **States with Relatively Strong State Autonomy: The Case of Belarus 163**

   Belarus Between the West and Russia 165

    State Autonomy *Vis-à-vis* Non-State Actors 170
    Non-State Actors under the Influence of External Powers .. 171
        Non-State Actors under the Influence of Russian Soft Power 171
        Non-State Actors under the Influence of Western Soft Power 176
        Non-State Actors and External Alignment 179
    Conclusion 182

6. **States with Relatively Weak State Autonomy: The Case of Ukraine** 185
    Ukraine Between the West and Russia 188
    State Autonomy *Vis-à-vis* Non-State Actors 196
    Non-State Actors under the Influence of External Powers .. 202
    Non-State Actors under the Influence of Russian Soft Power 203
    Non-State Actors under the Influence of Western Soft Power Projection 211
    Non-State Actors and External Alignment 217
    Conclusion 223

7. **Conclusions** 227
    The Puzzle and Theoretical Arguments 227
    Empirical Findings 230
    Implications for Theory 233

Bibliography 239

Foreword

It is a great privilege to have the task of writing the foreword for what is a fantastic book by an extremely promising scholar, Vasif Huseynov. The lingering challenge of conducting any sort of useful research is to strike a balance between novelty and importance. The trouble in a saturated field like International Relations (and its subfield of Foreign Policy Analysis) is that what can be described as novel is often not important and what is important is usually heavily examined (and thus, harder to provide novel insights). Therefore, Vasif deserves a lot of credit for producing a book that is both novel and important and, as such, makes a timely contribution to the fields of International Relations and Foreign Policy Analysis.

Few would argue that the current cooling of relations between the West and Russia is not one of the great concerns of contemporary international politics. There is the crisis in Ukraine, but also the emergence of something close to a proxy war in Syria and the apparent infiltration of Western democracies by Russia. These have been concerning developments, of course, but they have also driven a significant amount of hyperbole in the analytical discourse about where the West-Russia relationship is heading. To Vasif's credit, he does not fall into this hyperbolic trap as he lets his rich empirical findings speak for itself.

Vasif forgoes buying the inherent sensationalism of the New Cold War narrative that has come to dominate recent analyses of the West-Russia relations—especially the idea that this current cooling of West-Russia relations resembles the global struggle that characterized the Cold War proper. Vasif limits his analysis to the common neighbourhood between Russia and the West in Eastern Europe. This is important because in the current international system, a uni-multipolar system if you will, it is regional settings where competition and conflict are increasing. Thus, one of the real contributions of Vasif's book is adding insight to the current state of geopolitics in Eastern Europe, and especially how the interactions of the West and Russia has created a tense and competitive regional security complex there.

In addition, Vasif's narrowing of scope to examine the use of soft power by the West and Russia in the common neighbourhood is important for three reasons. First, it is undeniable that the information war at the heart of the cooling of the West-Russia relationship is extremely important and, as it currently stands, the most competitive (what Vasif terms "expansive") aspect of the relationship. In an age of technological advances with regards communication, winning the narrative battle has surely become a central aspect of international political competition. One of the real insights offered by Vasif in this book is his analysis of Russia's soft power. Too often, scholars in the West underestimate Russia's intentional use of its soft power capabilities—often presenting it as a blunt hard power from a bygone era—which blinds their analyses. This, thankfully, is a trap Vasif does not fall into in this book, providing a useful expose of the Kremlin's soft power capabilities.

Second, Vasif makes an interesting contribution to the soft power literature with his observation that the levels of state autonomy in a target state is an important variable in how effective a soft power strategy can be. By taking one of the core arguments of neoclassical realism (gauging state-society relations of the state under examination), Vasif adds important nuance to the soft power debate, especially as a fixation remains in the literature on examining the only state utilizing soft power, not the target state. Indeed, the relative open contest between the West and Russia in Ukraine, compared to Belarus, is convincingly explained, in part, by this observation as Ukraine's less centralization made it far more vulnerable to soft power infiltration.

Third, Vasif reinvigorates the somewhat forgotten realist observation—forged by the likes of EH Carr and Hans Morgenthau—that winning the hearts and minds of people (both internally and externally) is an important aspect of foreign policymaking. Vasif does this credibly through synthesizing neoclassical realism with the literature on soft power. Given how important this ideational battle is in the current age, the lack of incorporation of soft power (or similar concepts) by many realists in their analyses is a major limitation of the paradigm. Thus, Vasif's examination of soft power as an instrument of foreign policy within a neoclassical realist framework—adhering to the neoclassical realist mantra of "building theories"—has the potential to make a lasting contribution to realism's continued usefulness as a paradigm of International Relations and Foreign Policy Analysis.

Thanks to Vasif's watertight research design, the empirical findings of this book are of great importance to not only understanding an often misunderstood (i.e. the utilization of soft power) aspect of the West-Russia relationship but also theorizing where the relationship might head in the future. Vasif's conclusion that it is through instruments of soft power that the West and Russia are competing in their common neighbourhod—rather than through instruments of hard power—is convincing and significantly alters the way we should hypothesize about the Eastern Europe security complex moving forward. Ultimately, this book is a demonstration of how a theoretically informed, analytically focused study can produce insights and conclusions that have real-world application. And for that, Vasif should be applauded.

Nicholas Ross Smith

Acknowledgements

This book evolved from my doctoral dissertation at University of Göttingen. It would not have been possible without full scholarships of the German Academic Exchange Service (DAAD) that has generously supported my both master and doctoral studies between 2011 and 2018. I am deeply indebted to Prof. Dr. Peter Schulze and Prof. Dr. Anja Jetschke for insightful and patient supervision. I also thank Dr. Patrick Theiner and Dr. Anil Kocaman for their friendly support in the course of my doctoral studies. I am particularly thankful to my Göttingen friends, especially Elshan, Turab, Rafael, Elgiz, and Farid, whose friendship was for me a real source of inspiration and energy. I cannot thank enough to Dr. Nicholas Ross Smith whose support encouraged my decision to publish the dissertation as a book. I had also the honour to discuss the book before publication with Dr. Farid Shafiyev, Azerbaijan's ex-ambassador to Canada and the Czech Republic, whose insightful comments were extraordinarily helpful to properly revise the manuscript. Last but not least, I am deeply indebted to my parents, Maharram and Mehpara, who devoted their lives to their children in the most difficult times our family faced after the displacement from our hometown in the wake of Nagorno-Karabakh war. This book is dedicated to them.

List of Abbreviations

AA	Association Agreement
AMS	Alfred Mozer Stichting
BBC	British Broadcasting Corporation
BBG	Broadcasting Board of Governors
BOC	Belarusian Orthodox Church
CDU	Christian Democratic Union
CIS	Commonwealth of Independent States
CNN	Cable News Network
CRRF	Collective Rapid Reaction Force
CSO	Civil society organization
CSTO	Collective Security Treaty Organization
CU	Customs Union
CUFTA	Canada-Ukraine Free Trade Agreement
DAAD	German Academic Exchange Service
DCFTA	Deep and Comprehensive Free Trade Agreement
DIGIM	Digital Media Department
DoD	Department of Defense
DW	Deutsche Welle
EaP	Eastern Partnership
ECU	Eurasian Customs Union
EEAS	European External Action Service
EED	European Endowment for Democracy
EEU	Eurasian Economic Union
EFS	Eduardo Frei Stichting
EIDHR	European Instrument for Democracy and Human Rights
ENI	European Neighbourhood Instrument
ENP	European Neighbourhood Policy
ENPI	European Neighbourhood and Partnership Instrument
ERI	European Reassurance Initiative
EU	European Union
FES	Friedrich Ebert Stiftung
FLEX	Future Leaders Exchange

FSA	Freedom Support Act
FSB	Federal Security Service
FSU	Former Soviet Union
FY	Fiscal year
GCC	Gulf Cooperation Council
GCCLA	Governmental Commission on Compatriots Living Abroad
GDP	Gross Domestic Product
GIZ	German Federal Enterprise for International Co-operation
GUUAM	Georgia, Ukraine, Uzbekistan, Azerbaijan, Moldova
HSS	Hanns-Seidel-Stiftung
IDP	Internally Displaced Person
IISEPS	Independent Institute of Socio-Economic and Political Studies
IREX	International Research and Exchanges
IRI	International Republican Institute
KAS	Konrad Adenauer Foundation
KGB	Komitet Gosudarstvennoy Bezopasnosti
MAP	Membership Action Plan
MEDA	Mediterranean Economic Development Assistance
MNP	Moldovan National Platform
NATO	North Atlantic Treaty Organization
NDI	National Democratic Institute
NED	National Endowment for Democracy
NGO	Non-Governmental Organization
NIMD	Netherlands Institute for Multiparty Democracy
OSI	Open Society Institution
PCA	Partnership and Cooperation Agreement
PPS	Policy Planning Staff
NRF	NATO Response Force
RAP	Readiness Action Plan
RL	Radio Liberty
RFE	Radio Free Europe

RFE/RL	Radio Free Europe/Radio Liberty
ROC	Russian Orthodox Church
RT	Russia Today
SPD	Social Democratic Party
SU	Soviet Union
TACIS	Technical Assistance to Commonwealth of Independent States
UGRAD	Global Undergraduate Exchange Program
UNP	Ukrainian National Platform
UOC-KP	Ukrainian Orthodox Church Kiev Patriarchate
UOC-MP	Ukrainian Orthodox Church of the Moscow Patriarchate
US	United States
USA	United States of America
USAID	United States Agency for International Development
USSR	Union of Soviet Socialist Republics
VOA	Voice of America
VJTF	Very High Readiness Joint Task Force
VVD	Volkspartiy voor Vrijheid

List of Figures

Figure 1.	Soft power	57
Figure 2.	Hard power vs. soft power	67
Figure 3.	A public opinion poll in the EaP countries	138
Figure 4.	Belarussian public opinion on foreign policy	180
Figure 5.	Ukrainian public opinion on foreign policy	220
Figure 6.	Ukrainian public opinion on accession to NATO	220

List of Tables

Table 1. Public diplomacy vs. propaganda 64
Table 2. The EU assistance to the EaP countries 115
Table 3. Job approval of Ukrainian presidents 198
Table 4. The main sources of political information for Ukrainians in 2013 201
Table 5. The number of Ukrainian students studying at the universities of Russia and West 213

1. Introduction

The external alignment strategies of the post-Soviet states in the territories between the European Union (EU) and Russia – the region which is known as the "common (or shared) neighbourhood" – pose a puzzle to the students of international relations. Belarus, Ukraine and Moldova, the three states located in Eastern Europe and the three South Caucasian republics (Armenia, Azerbaijan and Georgia) have pursued dissimilar foreign policy strategies despite the similarity between them in a number of crucial aspects, including the geostrategic environment and the geo-economic structure of the region. While Belarus has opted for bandwagoning with Russia in international relations, its neighbour Ukraine is on a pro-Western path aiming to join NATO which Russia treats as its major geopolitical rival in the region. Likewise, while Azerbaijan seeks to maintain neutrality between the West (i.e. the EU and United States) and Russia, its neighbours Armenia and Georgia align with Russia and the West, respectively.

The rivalries between the West and Russia have been an influential factor in the formation of such diverse foreign policy strategies of the "common neighbourhood" states. For Russia, the hegemony over the countries located in this region are of supreme importance for its international standing as a great power. In this respect, the former Soviet countries, especially Eastern European and South Caucasian countries, are extremely important for Russia, whose leaders, on many occasions, have not refrained from openly saying that Russia would do everything possible to prevent geopolitical shifts in this region that pose threats to Russia's national security. The Kremlin's intention to reinstate its influence over the former Soviet states has been perceived as a geopolitical threat in Western capitals. Western leaders, in particular the Americans, have clearly stressed their determination to prevent or slow down Russia's regional reintegration initiatives. Over the last two decades this confrontation has dramatically evolved and exerted pressure on the foreign policies of regional states, made neutrality improbable and forced them to make a choice between the rival great powers and to align with one of them.

Both Russia and the West have made use of various means to affect the decision regional countries make in their geopolitical orientation. However, although Russia deployed military force in Georgia (2008) and Ukraine (2014) as an attempt to avert the pro-Western drift of these countries, the conflicting great powers could not militarily enforce the regional countries to join their orbit. The threat of mutually assured destruction has deterred the military escalation of the conflict between the West and Russia. It has downgraded the utility of military power to being an *ultimo-ratio* or, as Mark Galeotti (2016) points out, a "final 'just in case' option" and mostly a defensive instrument in the rivalries between the two great powers. Instead of military force, the conflicting great powers have been using non-military instruments in order to expand their influence over the regions which are also in the interests of rival great powers. Employing the instruments, which are analysed under the notion "soft power" in this research, Russia and the West have sought to reach out to the general public in target states and affect the foreign policy decisions of their respective states through influencing the masses.

Thus, this book analyses the great power rivalries as the independent variable *vis-à-vis* the foreign policy strategy of small states which are in between these rivalries. It pays particular attention to the policies of great powers to reach out to and influence non-state actors (i.e. the general public, non-governmental organizations, religious groups, etc.) in target states with the eventual aim of impacting their foreign policies. It also analyses the internal conditions in the smaller states under which the soft power policies of the great powers could wield successful outcomes. The book argues that as the internal autonomy of the state leaders decreases, the domestic non-state actors gain more scope to influence the policies of the government and the soft power policies of the external great powers find a more favourable environment in which to wield soft power and affect foreign policy decisions. The book pursues its analysis from the perspective of neoclassical realism and the concept of soft power and narrows down its empirical focus on the Russia—West rivalries between 2004 and 2014 over the "common neighbourhood" states in general, and over Belarus and Ukraine in particular.

The research employs the qualitative method of analysis to examine its hypotheses. It has explored a long range of academic works, publications of various research institutes, news media articles, official documents, public statements, reports of non-governmental organizations, etc. The materials which have been used in this process are largely in four languages: English, Russian, German, and Ukrainian. The research has used a series of public opinion surveys conducted by authoritative poll-taking institutes as an empirical basis for measurements of Russian and Western soft power in the "common neighbourhood". As conducting nationwide surveys in the case study countries is beyond the scope of this research, the results of the surveys conducted by institutes specialized in poll taking have been frequently used during the study. For instance, the results of public opinion polls carried out between 2004—2016 in Belarus by the Independent Institute of Socio-Economic and Political Studies (IISEPS), a public institution based in Lithuania, were the primary measurements used to examine the attitudes of Belarusians towards Russia and West. Likewise, the public opinion surveys conducted by the International Republican Institute (IRI) in Ukraine played the similar role in my research concerning Ukraine.

Literature Review and Research Gap

Many scholars have tried to understand the factors behind the diversity and multiplicity of approaches to the external orientation in the "common neighbourhood" states. For example, a group of scholars, namely Giorgi Gvalia, David Siroky, Bidzina Lebanidze, and Zurab Iashvili, have explored the reasons behind Georgia's shift to a pro-Western geopolitical orientation while most of the other small post-Soviet states maintain neutrality or bandwagon with Russia (Gvalia *et al.* 2013). They argue that the theories built on the external and international factors (e.g. "balance of power", "balance of threat", economic dependency etc.) fail to provide a convincing explanation for this situation. Instead, they put an emphasis on the state- and individual level of variables, especially the "elite ideas about the identity and purpose of the states", in explaining the foreign policy behaviours of these states (ibid. 99). According to them, "The idea that Georgia is a European country (and thus not a post-Soviet state) drives the elite's understanding of Georgia's place in the world" (ibid. 112). They argue that such a perception of Georgia's international standing amongst the political elites, and not the public opinion, explains the states' foreign policy strategy:

> "Although we do not wholly devalue the role of public opinion, we make the simplifying assumption that elite opinion largely shapes the foreign policy agenda, rather than the reverse, and that public opinion set the bounds of what is deemed acceptable" (ibid. 107).

Although Gvalia *et al.* rightfully examine the role of the elite perceptions as an influential variable between the international political system and foreign policy, their relegation of public opinion to elite perceptions in terms of its effect on foreign policy is problematic and cannot be easily verified. The facts that (1) Georgia's foreign policy strategy radically changed in the aftermath of the popular uprising of 2003 (Huseynov 2015), (2) the potential of the growing pro-Russian sentiments amongst the Georgians to reverse the current pro-Western political course is often recognized by the political experts (Rimple 2015; Cecire 2015), (3) Russia's anti-Western soft power projection to affect public opinion in Georgia has been officially recognized by the Georgian political elite as a threat (Rukhadze 2016) indicate that public opinion is a more influential factor than Gvalia *et al.* believe it is.

In general, the role of public opinion as a potentially influential intervening variable in the formation of the external alignment of the "common neighbourhood" states is an under-explored and largely miscalculated issue. According to conventional wisdom in scholarly studies of the region, the impact of the general public on foreign policy is rather limited in most of the post-Soviet states. For example, in 2003, Viktor Chudowsky and Taras Kuzio, prominent scholars of Ukrainian studies, wrote that "Ukrainian society is passive, atomized and its power is 'submerged' relative to that of the state" and thus "public opinion [in Ukraine] is of minimal importance in the area of foreign policy" (Chudowsky et al. 2003: 273). In less than 15 years after this analysis, Taras Kuzio, in a co-study on Ukrainian foreign policy with Paul D'Anieri, realized that in fact public opinion "has arguably had a profound effect on the country's foreign policy" (D'Anieri et al. 2017: 117). Thus, we can speak of a disinterest in and/or a misunderstanding of the public opinion — foreign policy nexus of the post-Soviet states in scholarly studies.

The scholars of international relations have also paid little attention to the fact that the role of domestic non-state actors as a potentially impactful political factor might tempt great powers[1] to reach out to and make use of them in order to affect the foreign policy of their respective state. This is advantageous when the sides are nuclear-armed great powers who cannot easily deploy military force against each other due to the threat of nuclear escalation. There is extensive literature on the policies of external actors to provoke regime change in a target state through interacting with its internal non-state players (e.g. civil society, media, political parties) (See, for instance, Muskhelishvili et al. 2009; Stewart 2009; Bunce et al. 2011; Vanderhill 2014). However, few academic studies have examined these policies from the perspective of geopolitical rivalries and political realism.

In fact, the founders of realism underscored the importance of winning power over the minds and feelings of foreign publics. The concepts developed by Edward Carr (1951) ("power over opinion") and Hans Morgenthau (1965a) ("cultural imperialism") reflected on non-hard power elements. However, the next generations of the school focused on the systemic variables as the primary determinants of international relations, conceptualized power as the combination of military and economic capabilities and disregarded its

---

1   This study subscribes to the realist classification of great powers and smaller states in accordance with their population, territory, resources, economic capability, military power, political stability, and competence (Waltz 1979: 131).

non-material dimensions. Stephan Walt's *Origins of Alliances* (1987) is one of the studies that widened its analysis beyond military and economic power. In his work, the policies of great powers to reach out to the domestic non-state actors of smaller states — what he calls "penetration" — are analysed as one of the strategies to affect their external alignment (Walt 1987: 218-262). However, he underestimates the potential of these policies:

> "[T]he importance of transnational penetration is often exaggerated and... its effect on alliance formation is usually misunderstood. The opportunity to establish informal avenues of influence with another state usually requires cordial or even close relations, which indicates that such ties are largely one result of alignment, not an independent cause... In short, penetration is not an especially common or powerful cause of alignment."

On the contrary, the advance of information and communication technologies strictly upgraded the potential of "penetration" as a foreign policy instrument. In 2004, Joseph Nye published his first major book on these policies, titled *Soft Power: The Means to Success in World Politics*. He theorized about the instruments which states can utilize to communicate with the publics of foreign countries and wield power over popular opinion abroad under the notion of "soft power". The post-Cold War developments in international relations, the pro-Western popular uprisings in post-communist states, the role of general public and non-governmental institutions in reshaping the regional geopolitical view provided empirical evidence to the growing potential of soft power. Gerald Sussman's *Branding Democracy: US Regime Change in Post-Soviet Eastern Europe* (2010) presented one of the first comprehensive analyses on the use of various public diplomacy and propaganda techniques to communicate with and influence non-state players in foreign countries in this period. However, many scholars rightfully maintain that the concept of soft power lacks "academic refinement," is "under-theorized", "misunderstood", or "difficult, if not impossible to test empirically' (Li 2009a: 58; Vuving 2009: 3). There have been numerous analyses on soft power, but neither Joseph Nye nor anybody else has provided clear answers to fundamental questions about the concept (e.g. What is soft power? How does it work? Who can produce it? Why do states need it?).

Nye (2013a) asserts that soft power is inextricably linked with Western norms and values, and therefore, states that are on different paths are bound to fail "miserably". However, this assertion implies "an obligatory respect for international norms and institutions, as well as an adherence to freedom, democracy, liberalism and pluralism" (Wilson 2015: 289). In reality, both democratic and non-democratic, liberal and illiberal states utilize soft power as part of their foreign policy toolkit and invest extensively in cultivating power over popular opinion abroad. It is often acknowledged that non-democratic great powers also reach success in these policies (Tsygankov 2005; Van Herpen 2015). Thus, Joseph Nye (2011: 82), on the one hand argues that soft power is a dimension of power and does not have any contradiction with political realism, on the other hand, as Giulio Gallarotti (2011: 19) correctly points out, presents his concept "as a subset of neoliberal logic".

In the aftermath of Joseph Nye's introduction of the notion "soft power", many academic works have been written addressing problems around the concept. One of the first major critical pieces on the soft power concept was *Soft Power and US Foreign Policy: Theoretical, Historical and Contemporary Perspectives* edited by Inderjeet Parmar and Michael Cox. In their chapter in this book, Geraldo Zahran and Leonardo Ramos (2010: 24), critically analysing the soft power concept from a Gramscian perspective and the distinction it presents between consent and coercion, argue that "disregarding hegemony, Nye creates the illusion of an aspect of power that could exist by its own only through consent, ignoring the social reality populated by intrinsic mechanisms of coercion." In response to this critique, Nye (2010: 217), in the same book, points out that "Even if Zahran and Ramos are correct that under hegemony, coercion and consent are complementary, that is not the same as saying that soft power is always rooted in hard power. Sometimes it is and sometimes it is not." The Chinese scholar Mingjiang Li (2009b: 3) suggests that the term "soft use of power" would be more appropriate than "soft power", because "soft power does not exist in the nature of certain resources of power but rather it has to be nurtured through a soft use of power." The relationship between the two types of power still remains unclear. Neither Nye nor anyone else has ever written a convincing analysis on the distinction and relationship between hard power and soft power.

The consideration of domestic non-state actors as a potentially powerful political player by neoclassical realism lays ground for its analysis of the use of soft power by great powers to affect the external alignment of states in contested regions. Neoclassical realism does not define power as only elements of material power, but includes other elements, such as the quality of government and its reputation in international politics (Ripsman *et al.* 2009: 297). The theory treats domestic political processes as an intervening variable between systemic factors and foreign policy. From this point of view, the intervening variable has the potential to "channel, mediate, and (re)direct policy outputs in response to external forces (primarily changes in relative power)" (Schweller 2004: 164).

Neoclassical Realism, the State, and Foreign Policy (2009), edited by Steven Lobell, Norrin Ripsman and Jeffrey Taliaferro, is the first comprehensive book on neoclassical realism. The authors have refined the theory and elaborated on the distinctions and commonalities between it and other branches of realism. The book serves as a useful resource to understand neoclassical realism's conceptualization of the internal political system as an intervening variable. It, however, has not explained the policies that great powers pursue to reach out to domestic non-state actors in target states and realize the desired shifts in their external alignment through the manipulation of their internal political system. Nor have other neoclassical realist scholars, some of whom have supported the incorporation of the soft power concept into the analytical toolkit of neoclassical realism (e.g. Rathbun 2008: 303-304; Berenskoetter *et al.* 2012), examined soft power as an instrument in the competition of great powers to expand their sphere of influence.

Theoretical Argument

The theoretical argumentation of the book is formed on the hypothesis that if nuclear armed great powers compete against the same type of powers to expand or sustain their sphere of influence over a populated region, they use soft power as a major expansive instrument while military power remains a tool to defend themselves and back up their foreign policies. However, the book underlines the point that the success of soft power projection by the great powers depends on the internal structure of the target states. If the leaders of a weak state, which is in between the rivalries of great powers who use soft power to expand their influence, are autonomous *vis-à-vis* the society and other internal non-state actors, they can control the inflow of soft power projection from foreign states, offset the intervening influence of the domestic non-state actors on foreign policy making, and augment their chances to more prudently and independently follow the imperatives of the international political system. Conversely, if such autonomy does not exist, then the external powers find a favourable environment in which to wield soft power, the domestic non-state actors can influence the external orientation of the state, and the state fails to offset their influence.

The non-military instruments great powers deploy and the policies they pursue to communicate with the general public and the non-governmental organizations of the target states with the aim of impacting their foreign policy strategy are analysed in this book under the umbrella of the soft power concept. The book seeks to reconceptualise soft power in the light of neoclassical realism. This approach treats soft power as a dimension of power that states make use of to reach their foreign policy goals. The book establishes a model that would allow for the study of different sources of soft power and the strategies states develop to produce it. The reason that necessitated the reformulation of the concept of soft power is related to problems and contradictions in the existing literature on the subject.

The model developed in this book follows the logic of realist scholars in its analysis of soft power. Herein the book refers particularly to the concepts "power over opinion" of Edward Carr (1951), "cultural imperialism" of Hans Morgenthau (1965a), and "transnational penetration" of Stephan Walt (1987). It examines both public diplomacy and propaganda strategies as part of great powers' policies to wield soft power. According to this model, no matter whether it is deception or truth, seduction or manipulation, foreign aid or propaganda, all types of policies to reach out to foreign publics and intentionally affect their perceptions and attitudes can be gathered under the umbrella of soft power making. As militarily powerful states can use all types of military power (air force, navy, nuclear weapons, etc.) to force the target to do what is wanted of them, the states enjoying high levels of soft power can use a wide array of instruments to wield power over popular opinion of the target state with eventually similar purposes. The model also attempts to conceptualize the hard power – soft power nexus.

Structure of the Book

The book consists of five chapters besides the introductory section and conclusions. Chapter 2 presents the analytical framework of the study. It firstly forms the theoretical framework and discusses the nexus of neoclassical realism and soft power to explain the use of soft power in great power rivalries and its impact on the formation of the external orientation of regional states. The chapter continues with the presentation of introductory information about the selected case (i.e. the Russia – West confrontation over the "common neighbourhood") and methodology used to test the research hypotheses.

Chapters 3 and 4 are focused on the analysis of the independent variable which is defined as the rivalries between the West and Russia over the "common neighbourhood". These chapters seek to defend the argument that nuclear armed great powers deploy largely soft power to expand their sphere of influence over the territories that are in the interests of rival nuclear armed great powers. Chapter 3 discusses the hard power – soft power nexus in the foreign policies of Western powers concerning the regional states. Afterwards, the chapter focuses on the use of soft power in this context. The chapter provides an analysis of different dimensions of Western soft power. Chapter 4 replicates the analytical framework of the previous chapter and applies it in the analysis of Russia's policies with respect to the "common neighbourhood" states.

Chapters 5 and 6 focus on the outcomes of the soft power competition between Russia and West. Chapter 5 discusses the case of Belarus. In this study, Belarus represents "common neighbourhood" countries with stronger state autonomy and mostly pro-Russian or neutral geopolitical orientation. The chapter tests the hypothesis on the role of strong internal autonomy of the state leaders in their foreign policy amidst the rivalries between great powers. Chapter 6, in a similar structure to the previous chapter, explores the case of Ukraine as an example of "common neighbourhood" countries with weaker state autonomy and mostly pro-Western geopolitical orientation.

The book ends with a concluding section. This section is divided into three sub-sections. The first sub-section briefly reviews the problems this book has focused on and the hypotheses it has put forward. The next sub-section presents the empirical findings of the study. It shortly overviews the discussions on the Russia–West confrontation over the "common neighbourhood" states and the cases of Belarus and Ukraine in this context. The concluding section ends with the presentation of the theoretical implications of the research for the studies of international relations.

2. Analytical Framework

This chapter is aimed at presenting the theoretical framework and case study of the research. The chapter consists of three major sections. The section following this introductory part focuses on realism and its relatively new branch called "neoclassical realism". This section will analyse the theoretical assumptions on the rivalries between great powers and their policies to communicate with the internal non-state actors of the states that are in between these rivalries. It also explores factors that impact the choice weak states make in their external alignment. The section focuses on the influence of the general public and non-governmental organizations as the intervening forces between the pressure that the international political system imposes on states (independent variable) and the foreign policy of these states (dependent variable). It also analyses the circumstances under which these non-state actors can become influential in the formulation of foreign policy. The autonomy of state leaders *vis-à-vis* domestic society is treated as the major indicator to measure the scope of the domestic non-state groups to impact state policies.

Since neoclassical realism develops theories that includes both systemic and unit level factors in its analysis of foreign policy, it has been chosen as the guiding theoretical line of the book. However, neoclassical realism, along with other branches of realism, have paid little attention to the policies of the conflicting great powers to reach out to the domestic non-state actors of states that are in between their conflict. Although neoclassical realists have acknowledged the importance of the intervening power of domestic non-state actors in the formulation of foreign policy, they have not thoroughly analysed the policies of great powers to interact with these non-state actors in target states and make use of them. The section serves also as an attempt to fill in this gap.

The second section deals with the concept of soft power which covers the major strategies and instruments great powers make use of to communicate with the non-state actors of regional states. The section provides a reconceptualization of soft power analysing it as an instrument developed by states in the pursuit of foreign policy objectives. It will be followed with the third section that presents the cases which will be used to test the research hypotheses. The section is divided in two parts separately analyzing the context of the West—Russia confrontation over the "shared neighbourhood" and the reaction of the states located in between this confrontation. The chapter ends with a brief conclusion which sums up the key points of the chapter.

Realism: Neoclassical Realism

The advocates of realism identify international politics as anarchy wherein there is no governing supranational authority. Under the circumstances of the absence of an overarching global authority, states are primarily concerned with their survival and therefore are in constant search for security. In different branches of the realist paradigm, the factors that impact and drive the struggle for power in international relations are differentiated at three levels of analysis: the individual, the state and the international system. Kenneth Waltz (2001) in *Man, State and War*, first published in 1959, characterizes these levels as three images: the first image (the individual), the second image (the state), and the third image (the international system). Mostly, adherents of realism have not limited their analyses to one image as the only determining factor of international politics. The complexity of the factors behind the behaviours of states in interstate relations has compelled realist scholars to include more than one image into their analysis. Below an overview of the three images in the realist paradigm will be presented in the discussion on the three main branches of realism: classical realism, neo- (or structural) realism, and neoclassical realism.

The first image emphasizes the impact of human nature on the conduct of international relations. Most advocates of classical realism develop their theoretical analyses on the basis of the first image. The scholars who adhere to this idea believe that human nature is inherently problematic and unchanged. Hans Morgenthau, in the beginning of *Politics among Nations* (1967: 4), asserts that "human nature, in which the laws of politics have their roots, has not changed since the classical philosophies of China, India, and Greece...." Likewise, in the thought of Edward Carr (1951), the roots of all politics and political conflicts are embroiled in man's nature. He, like Morgenthau (1965b: 192), supports Aristotle's characterization of man as a political animal, and believes that only on the basis of this view one can pursue sound reasoning about politics.

Classical realist scholars charge that the growing role of the masses in shaping foreign policy prevents states from conducting foreign policies free from the interference of public opinion and, thus, pushes the international struggle for power into relatively conflictual bounds and even into total war. They warn against the growing influence of masses on foreign policy, empowered by the nationalist and democratic revolutions of the nineteenth and twentieth centuries. For Morgenthau, the interference of the masses in shaping foreign policy brought about the disastrous conclusions (e.g. two world wars) of the first half of the twentieth century, and therefore, he advises diplomats to lead public opinion rather than follow it.

As classical realists place the primary source of conflicts and the struggle for power amongst both individuals and states in human nature, for them the impact of an anarchic environment of international relations is a rather secondary and permissive factor. Unlike them, neorealist scholars deny the determining roles of the anthropological and unit-level sources of world politics and put a primary emphasis on system-level variables. Neorealism evaluates the structure of the international system in terms of an ordering principle, such as anarchy, and a particular distribution of power. In the thought of neorealist scholars (e.g. Waltz (1979), Walt (1987), Mearsheimer (2001)), the security dilemma which originates out of the anarchic order of international politics shapes the behaviours of states in interstate relations. Out of uncertainty of each other's intentions, actions which are taken for one's own security tend to be treated by others as a threat to their security and lead to arms races, conflicts and wars. However, Waltz (2001: 238) also recognizes the importance of the other two images by underlying the interdependence of all three images to analyze world politics and predict policy outcomes.

Neoclassical realism, on the basis of the prior fundamental assumptions of the realist paradigm, emphasizes the second and third image factors and conceptualizes the foreign policies of different types of states (great, medium, and small powers). Unlike those theories which privilege either domestic (*innenpolitik* theories) or systemic factors (structural theories), neoclassical realism develops theories that integrate these two-level variables in its analysis of foreign policy. Neoclassical realist scholars highlight the significance of unit-level expertise for an accurate understanding of foreign policy, and avoid treating states as black boxes, i.e. they do not ignore their distinctive internal characteristics (Rose 1998: 166). On the basis of Max Weber's classic definition of state,[2] neoclassical realism develops its "top-down" conception of the state. In neoclassical realism, the state is treated as the central officialdom of the polity which lacks complete autonomy *vis-à-vis* society (Taliaferro et al. 2009: 27).

The advocates of neoclassical realism underscore the constraints on great powers that originate in the international system and the domestic environment. In the case of regional powers, the same are highlighted at the subsystem level (Lobell 2009: 46). In neoclassical realism, the state's relative power position in the anarchic system of international relations is considered an independent variable. Structural variables play a causal role in shaping foreign policies (Taliaferro 2009: 198). The theory positions the internal dynamics of states as an intervening variable between the constraints of the international system and foreign policy. Unlike neorealists, who see a direct translation of state leaders' apprehensions of systemic imperatives into their foreign policy, for neoclassical realists this translation is not immediate and free of obstacles (Walt 2002:

---

[2] According to Weber (1978: 904-905) "A state is a human community that (successfully) claims the monopoly of the legitimate use of physical force within a given territory. Note that 'territory' is one of the characteristics of the state."

211). Domestic political processes are treated as imperfect transmission belts between systemic pressure and foreign policy (Schweller 2004: 164). Neoclassical realism suggests that these are actual political leaders and elite who make foreign policy choices, and so their perceptions of relative power and their ability to extract or mobilize societal resources to implement foreign policy matter (Rose 1998: 147). The interference of the domestic actors (public, business and industrial sectors, labour unions, and other organized economic interest groups, media, legislature, ethnic and religious groups) into foreign policy making is another powerful intervening variable. This interference might constrain a state's autonomy from the internal society and its ability to enact policy responses to systemic imperatives (Wohlforth 1993: 2).

(Neoclassical) Realism on Great Power Rivalries

Realism underscores the struggle for power and survival as the underlying motivation of states' behaviours in the international sphere. Notwithstanding the fact that the sources of this struggle are interpreted in different ways by realist scholars, they agree on its interpretation as the guiding principle of international relations. According to realism, states are concerned about the distribution of relative power capabilities and act with "zero-sum" logic in their approaches to changes in the balance of power (Powell 1991). Therefore, states have to take care of their competitive power and maximize their probability of survival in the hostile environment of international politics. Waltz (1979: 118) asserts that those who do not follow this logic "will fail to prosper, will lay themselves open to danger, will suffer." Stephan Walt (1987: 17) defines balancing "as allying with others against the prevailing threat" and bandwagoning as "alignment with the source of danger". The expansion of a great power's sphere of influence and its growing aggregate power reinforce its perception as a threat in the eyes of other great powers. Realist-minded scholars and politicians expect other great powers to counter this threat, while smaller states are mostly expected to bandwagon (Walt 1987: 22).

From this structural realist perspective, regional hegemons — that are powerful states which dominate a certain region or regions (Mearsheimer 2001: 39) — seek to maximize their power and security by expanding their sphere of influence and undermining the bids of rival powers for regional hegemony. However, the prizes this struggle promises are limited. No great power has ever been able or is likely to be able anytime soon to become a global hegemon due to the "stopping power" of oceans (Mearsheimer 2001). This is why undermining the emergence of a regional hegemon overseas and *not* evolving into a global hegemony is considered as the uppermost objective for regional hegemons. The "fear that a rival great power that dominates its own region will be an especially powerful foe that is essentially free to cause trouble in the fearful great power's backyard" (Mearsheimer 2001: 41-42) urges the regional hegemon to seek to prevent others from dominating their respective regions.

Neoclassical realism does not depart from this realist analysis of great power politics. The primary contribution of neoclassical realism has been to put forward the intervening influence of domestic factors. Advocates of neoclassical realism argue that systemic factors alone cannot explain, for example, the US strategy of containment during the Cold War or the Iraq invasion of the George W. Bush administration (Taliaferro *et al*. 2009: 2-3). From this perspective, the impact of the internal characteristics of states (i.e. domestic non-state groups, perceptions of state leaders and their autonomy from society, the capacity of state institutions to extract and mobilize resources, etc.) need to be likewise analysed in order to provide a more complete understanding of international relations (Taliaferro *et al*. 2009: 4). According to neoclassical realism, these factors exert intervening influence on the formulation of states' foreign policy, however, the systemic variables provide permissive condition and remain an independent variable in this process (Taliaferro *et al*. 2009: 4). Thus, unlike other branches of realism, neoclassical realism combines systemic and unit level variables in its explanation of great power politics.

International relations theories, however, have paid little attention to the policies of conflicting great powers to reach out to domestic non-state actors of states that are in between their conflict. Although neoclassical realists have acknowledged the importance of the intervening power of domestic non-state actors in the formulation of foreign policy, they have not thoroughly analysed the policies of great powers to interact with these non-state actors and seek to make use of them. One of the few realist scholars who have analysed these policies is Stephan Walt. In *Origins of Alliances*, he conceptualizes such policies under the name "foreign aid and transnational penetration", and argues that great powers may use lobbyists and propaganda to alter elite and mass attitudes and to influence public perception with the ultimate goal of affecting policy decisions regarding the potential ally (Walt 1987: 46). Walt (1987: 242) defines penetration as "the manipulation of the target state's domestic political system [through propaganda, educational, cultural, and military assistance] to promote alignment". His analysis concludes that these policies play "subordinate roles" in the decision of the regional states in its external alignment (Walt 1987: 260-261).

I argue that the utility of the instruments which Walt calls "foreign aid and penetration" has been growing due to the increasingly higher costs of direct military clashes between great powers since the invention of nuclear weapons and the rapid advance of technological capabilities. It is a fact that since the invention of nuclear weapons, there have been no large-scale wars between great powers. The enormous costs of military operations and the risks of nuclear involvement have made great powers avoid using them against each other. In Waltz's words, they have faced "absolute impotence" upon their seizure of "absolute power" (Waltz 1979: 184). Thus, the possibly catastrophic consequences of a nuclear escalation make the nuclear armed great powers develop instruments to pursue their interests and expand their spheres of influence without triggering major military clashes. Soft power is such an instrument. Modern information and communication technologies raise the utility of this instrument even further.

From this viewpoint, I put forward the hypothesis that if nuclear armed great powers compete amongst themselves to expand or sustain their sphere of influence over a populated region, they use soft power as a major expansive instrument while military power remains a tool with which to defend themselves and back up their foreign policies. It is important to note that this hypothesis refers to the initial phases of the competition. Sometimes, nuclear powers may enter into proxy wars when the conflict escalates or one of the sides completely fails in the non-military dimensions of the competition. In such cases, if the stakes are too high for one or both of the conflicting sides, the escalation of conflict may even reach a nuclear level.

(Neoclassical) Realism on the Foreign Policy of Regional States amidst Great Power Rivalries

There is a consensus amongst international relations scholars that neutrality (nonalignment) is the most optimal strategy for weak states that are stuck between great power rivalries (Labs 1992: 385). This allows regional states to maintain ties with rival great powers and increases their chances of preserving their independence and security. However, most of the time, neutrality turns out impossible to be maintained, and regional states are forced to make a strategic choice. The advocates of structural realism put an emphasis on the third image analysis of international relations and assert that as the margin of manoeuvres is increasingly limited for weak states, they have to adopt to the imperatives of the international distribution of power between the great powers (Waltz 1979: 72-73; 194-195). This logic expects regional states to bandwagon with the stronger or the more threatening great power when neutrality can no longer be maintained (Waltz 1979: 127). The bandwagoning state joins regional organizations (including economic, political, and security institutions) supported by the threatening state, avoids deep engagement with rival great powers, and thus is forced to follow certain patterns of foreign policy considered acceptable by the predominant power.

Randall Schweller (1994), making an important contribution to this debate, points out that states may also bandwagon for opportunities. In this logic, aligning with the stronger state may be chosen also for economic or security benefits: "bandwagoning is not just a behaviour to avoid capitulation, but a strategy that states adopt in order to gain something without having survival at stake" (Cladi *et al.* 2016: 18). However, the history of international relations has, on many occasions, shown that weak states may also align against a stronger or more threatening power (Walt 1987: 148; Labs 1992; Van Evera 1990/91; Gvalia *et al.* 2013). In reality, not only do weaker states sometimes seek to balance against a stronger or more threatening great power, but they may even choose to fight against it alone in some cases (Labs 1992; Gvalia *et al.* 2013).

Scholars of international relations have offered various explanations to this inconsistency in the foreign policy alignment of weak states but most of them fall short of accuracy. The structural realist emphasis on the distribution of capabilities amongst great powers as the major driver in the strategic choices of weak states does not always apply in practice: the external environment and the global balance of power as an independent variable do not produce the same actions in the foreign policies of weak states which are located in a similar international environment. For example, William Wohlforth (2004: 232) points out that structural realism "is of little utility in explaining much of the variation in local responses to Russia. Even when we add conditional variables to the theory to derive more hypotheses, it fails to add much to the explanation of…why Belarus has been such a faithful bandwagoner despite relative power and a geographical position similar to the Baltics."

Stephan Walt's inclusion of factors other than distribution of capabilities that impact the formulation of foreign policy strategies cannot be applicable in many cases, either. For Walt (1987), besides aggregate power, external alignment strategies are affected by other important factors, such as: geographic proximity, offensive power, and aggressive intentions. For Walt, weak states tend to bandwagon when the threatening state is much more powerful, when other allies are unavailable or when the situation is about to transform into an armed conflict. He (1987: 25) points out that under these circumstances, attempting to balance might even be an "unwise" option. This approach fails in some cases, for instance, in the relations between Belarus and Ukraine on the one hand and Russia on the other. Although the two "common neighbourhood" states are located within the same geographic proximity of Russia, they have pursued opposite foreign policy strategies: Belarus bandwagons with Russia, while Ukraine seeks to align with Western powers against Russia. Similarly, James MacDougall's (2009: 57) study on the South Caucasus states has revealed that the regional states pursue different alignment strategies although they share a common strategic environment: "Azerbaijan and Georgia, to varying degrees, have balanced against the threat from Russia, although at times they have attempted to bandwagon. Armenia has not balanced against Russia, but rather has bandwagoned with Russia." Nor do the assumptions of the dependency theorists on the impact of economic dependence (Papayoanou 1997) provide a convincing explanation on the strategic choice of weak states in some cases. For example, the recent crisis between Ukraine and Russia took place despite economic interrelatedness between the two countries.

Neoclassical realism appears better armed than other theories to provide analyses about the foreign policy strategy of weak states. Unlike structural realism, neoclassical realism is aimed at developing theories of foreign policy. This school of realism contributes to the above-mentioned debate by highlighting the intervening influence of state level variables (Schweller 1997). Analysing domestic political processes as imperfect transmission belts between systemic pressure and foreign policy, the theory places an emphasis on the perceptions of the political elite, their ability to extract or mobilize societal resources to implement foreign policy and the interference of domestic actors (public, business and industrial sectors, labour unions, and other organized economic interest groups, media, legislature, ethnic and religious groups) in foreign policy making (Rose 1998: 147; Schweller 2004: 164).

The analysis developed in this study is focused on the intervening influence of domestic non-state actors (in particular, the general public and non-governmental organizations) on the formulation of foreign policy and external alignment. Here the research goal is to explore the impact of general public and non-governmental organizations on the formation of the external orientation of regional states in the context of the soft power projection of great powers. The book argues that these internal non-state actors can, on occasion, be impactful enough to force their governments to make changes in foreign policy which might include even the re-making of the state's external alignment strategy. In line with the expectations of realist scholars, the study finds such influence of non-state actors on foreign policy dangerous and potentially detrimental.

The book draws on the hypothesis that if the leaders of a small state, which is in between the rivalries of great powers who use soft power to expand their influence, are autonomous *vis-à-vis* society and other internal non-state actors, they can control the inflow of the soft power projection of foreign states and offset the intervening influence of domestic non-state actors on foreign policy making. Conversely, if such autonomy does not exist, then the external powers find a favourable environment in which to wield soft power; the domestic non-state actors can influence the external orientation of the state, and; the state may fail to offset their influence, and this may bring about suboptimal foreign policy decisions. The following two sections are to discuss this hypothesis analysing the nexus of public opinion, foreign policy and state autonomy across different variables.

Public Opinion and Foreign Policy

In the aftermath of World War II, a broad agreement known as the "Almond-Lippmann consensus" was formed about the public opinion—foreign policy nexus. According to the propositions developed by Walter Lippmann and Gabriel Almond:

> (1) … [public opinion] is volatile and thus provides inadequate foundations for stable and effective foreign policies, (2) …lacks coherence or structure, but (3) in the final analysis, it has little if any impact on foreign policy (Holsti 1992: 439).

Realism recognizes that public opinion can sometimes intervene in foreign policy. However, neoclassical realism, like previous generations of the realist school, supports the reasoning of the Almond-Lippmann consensus about the consequences of this intervention: public pressure on foreign policy is likely to bring about negative consequences for the whole country (Christensen 1996: 17;

Lobell 2009: 61). From this point of view, public perceptions of international threats and the subtleties of balance-of-power politics are mostly inaccurate because of a lack of proper expertise and complete knowledge. This view of public opinion is widely shared by other branches of realism. As stated above, Morgenthau (1965a: 567) warns diplomats that "the rational requirements of good foreign policy cannot from the outset count on the support of a public opinion whose preferences are emotional rather than rational." The neorealist school of realism maintains similar approach to the public opinion—foreign policy nexus. Mearsheimer (1990: 41) observes that "Public opinion on national security issues is notoriously fickle and responsive to elite manipulation and world events." Realist scholars posit that the vulnerability of state leaders to public opinion prevents them from responding to systemic incentives in a rational manner in the self-help environment of international anarchy.

Realist scholars are skeptical of the public's contribution to foreign policy. Although in some cases the demands of the general public concerning foreign policy might be more in line with national interests than the policies of state leaders, in general this interference prevents state leaders from pursuing prudent and coherent foreign policies. The world of foreign affairs a remote issue for the public and seeking detailed information on the topic is usually a secondary priority when compared to more pressing daily issues. Hence, the interference of the public threatens the quality and success of diplomacy which otherwise needs to uphold principles such as secrecy and flexibility.[3]

---

[3] The theoretical approaches that locate the major sources of foreign policy in domestic politics assume the internal factors (e.g. political and economic ideology, national character, socioeconomic structure) as the chief determinants of states' behaviours in the international system. These theories (e.g. liberal or democratic peace theories) treat foreign policy as the product of the domestic socio-political and economic environment (Doyle 1983; Russett 1993; 2009; Elman 1997; Gelpi et al. 2001; Mansfield et al. 2005). They differentiate democracies and non-democracies and argue that states avoid wars as a political tool as they become more democratic. Liberals argue that public opinion on foreign affairs is stable, rationally structured, consistent, and influences foreign policy

On the other hand, the public is not a singular body, and mostly does not speak with one voice. The public is the amalgamation of different ethnic, religious, cultural, business and other groups. Among these groups, civil society, which can be defined as non-political social groups that take an active part in public debate on issues of wider concern with no ultimate objective of political power, may exert more pressure on foreign policy making. Civil society include unions, religious groups, independent and cultural institutions, charitable organizations, professional and trade associations, women's groups, neighbourhood associations, NGOs, etc. As these groups usually pursue parochial interests, their influence on the realm of foreign policy may be contradictory to the national interests that state leaders are supposed to uphold.

Over the years since World War II, public opinion has gained a number of channels to exert influence on the management of foreign affairs. Ripsman (2009: 171) argues that "public opinion usually influences policy, when it does, indirectly through its representatives in the legislature, rather than directly through the foreign security policy executive." However, in some cases, as it happened during the "colour revolutions" in the post-Soviet countries, the public may also pose direct pressure on the government without the mediation of third actors. The domestic non-state actors find ample opportunity to directly influence the government when state leaders do not have strong autonomy with respect to society. The following section will analyse state autonomy *vis-à-vis* its surrounding society across different variables and defines the conditions which impact its level.

---

making in a way that is eventually favourable to the country. They suggest that public opinion should exert substantive influence on foreign policy. Public pressure on foreign policy formulation limits extreme elite tendencies and elite adventurism. As policy makers depend on the public to maintain their offices, they refrain from policies which are dangerously risky (Foyle 1999: 5-6). Disregarding the systemic factors in their analyses of interstate relations, these theories maintain several problematic assumptions, and often face "difficulty accounting for why states with similar domestic systems often act differently in the foreign policy sphere and why dissimilar states in similar situations often act alike" (Rose 1998: 148).

State Autonomy across Different Variables

State autonomy is the ability of public officials to translate their preferences and interests into policy and authoritative actions (Nordlinger 1981: 74; Smith 1993a: 49). This can vary radically across different states and over time within states. There are a range of variables which affect the degree of influence of a society on foreign policy making, such as regime type, the economic and political situation in the internal and external environment, socio-political composition, etc. Below, some of these factors are briefly discussed.

Regime type: In states where there is no unity amongst the governing elite, or between society and political circles, *and* the probability of a sudden *coup d'état* is high, domestic pressure on state leaders becomes more impactful. Neoclassical realists argue that as the likelihood of the domestic actors to remove state leaders from office through legal (elections or votes of no-confidence) or illegal ways (*coups d'état*) increases, the state's autonomy from its surrounding society and its political authority for the implementations of certain foreign policy decision decreases (Ripsman 2009).

In some states, the possibly grave costs of a controversy with important domestic political groups compel the state leader to seek consensus with those political actors whose pressure threatens the state leader's continued presence in office (Hagan 1987: 348-349). Compared to non-democratic regimes, in democracies state leaders' autonomy from society is usually more constrained. As the public has the legal means to remove the state leader from office through ballot boxes in the latter group of states, a state's autonomy is considerably more constrained in those states. In semi-democracies, although ballot boxes might not work out in the way they do in full democracies, non-state actors are, in general, still more capable of bringing about fundamental change than those in non-democracies.

Non-democratic leaders who have more autonomy from the society hold more political authority to conduct an autonomous foreign policy free of domestic influence. But sometimes the level of autonomy that state leaders may possess may be lower in non-democracies than in democratic states. Ripsman (2009: 189) compares the level of autonomy of state leaders of democratic and non-democratic states, and notes that a structurally constrained non-democratic leader (for example, Soviet Leader Khrushchev) might possess even less autonomy to conduct policy than a highly autonomous democratic leader (for example, the US Presidents during the early Cold War).

Domestic socio-economic and political conditions: In states, where there are relatively prosperous socio-economic standards and political stability, the influence of public opinion on foreign policy tends to be less significant. In such states, a successful domestic policy gives leeway to the political elite to pursue a relatively autonomous foreign policy. Unstable and difficult domestic conditions generate constraints on the foreign policy making. Domestic constraints become more influential in states which are not classic nation-states, and/or are a battlefield of different subnational groups competing (and sometimes fighting) on ethnic, religious, political and other grounds (Lobell 2009: 50).

The pressure that accumulates from internal variables might undermine foreign policy making and result in suboptimal outcomes to the detriment of the nation in the short or long run (Lobell 2009: 63). Neoclassical realism maintains that the state holds the highest potential to achieve optimal outcomes when "the constraints and inducements that emanate from the systemic, sub-systemic, and domestic levels" converge (Lobell 2009: 64). The policy responses of state leaders to systemic pressure emerge in a coordinated paradigm of state-society relations. The internal composition of states, the government's autonomy from its surrounding society, and the consensus amongst the elite about the nature of international threats vary across different states, and over time within states, and can significantly influence governments' manoeuvres in interstate relations (Ripsman 2009: 189).

External conditions: The situation in the external environment also affects the level of autonomy of state leaders from domestic non-state groups. During stable periods when the international environment does not pose any high-level threats to the state's national security, public opinion is expected to have greater pressure on the state's national security policy. In this period the pressure of powerful interest groups, which could potentially either assist the state leader in maintaining its hold on power or contribute to the opposition against the state leader, become more influential (Ripsman 2009: 186). However, when the international environment threatens the state's national security and its survival, or when the probability of violent confrontation with foreign powers increases, state leaders tend to ignore domestic political interests, and focus on strategies of securing national interests and the state's survival. In these periods, the possibly high costs of the interference of domestic actors into national security policy compel state leaders to ignore internal pressure on foreign policy making (Ripsman 2009: 186). A turbulent external environment gives rise to the necessity for the state leader to mobilize the public, to make it accept the decisions of the government, and in times of military confrontation — to persuade it to fight and sacrifice devotedly.

Soft Power

Power over the minds and feelings of people has long been a concept discussed by scholars of international relations and practiced by politicians. Yet it was Joseph Nye who made the first major attempts at systematizing the resources and techniques which allow states to wield attractiveness in the eyes of foreign publics, and to influence their opinions and feelings. With this intent, he coined the term "soft power" in his *Bound to Lead*, a book published in 1990. According to Nye (2004: x), soft power is "the ability to get what you want through attraction rather than coercion or payments". Nye (2004: 11) highlights three sources of soft power: culture (in places where it is attractive to others), political values (when the state lives up to them at home and abroad) and foreign policies (when they are seen as legitimate and having moral authority).

Soft power, which, according to Nye (2010: 219), is an "analytical concept" (not a theory), describes the requirements of attractive image building and successful foreign policy making. The concept explores the nature of the relationship with foreign publics and emphasizes the necessity of the inclusion of soft power elements into a foreign policy arsenal. These elements are mostly intangible resources—culture, political values, institutions and legitimate foreign policy. However, it is often stated that tangible resources (military and economic might) can generate soft power, as well (Nye 2011: 86). For example, the deployment of military resources for earthquake relief in foreign countries can produce an attractive image. It is the reason why the Chinese scholar Mingjiang Li (2009b) prefers the term "soft use of power" to "soft power".

Nye (2004: 5) considers soft power as "the ability to shape the preferences of others". According to him (2004: 31; 2011: 90), attraction, persuasion and agenda-setting are the three most important ways to build soft power. The concept treats attraction as "the currency of soft power" and defines it in terms of the behaviours and resources of a state (Nye 2004: 63). Nye (2004: 6) uses poll outcomes to measure attractiveness. According to Craig Hayden (2012: 44), attraction can play multiple roles in a soft power relationship: it is presented as a behaviour in the active approach to soft power and a resource to be leveraged to achieve an outcome.

Agenda-setting is presented as another source of soft power. It describes a situation in which certain grievances are not spoken of because "mobilization of bias" (Bachrach et al. 1962: 949) prevents these issues from becoming an issue by keeping them off the agenda. To put it bluntly, the people, aware of their powerlessness in the face of a hegemonic agenda, simply refuse to speak up and raise their concerns. According to Bachrach and Baratz (1963: 641), an agenda can be restricted with "the instruments of force, singly or in combination". However, Gallarotti (2011: 15) observes that "soft power generally eschews a strict conflict of interests…". Nye (2011: 13) argues that agenda-setting can be characterized as an element of soft power only if the agenda of action is changed through acquiescence without the deployment of threats of coercion or promises of payment.

Moreover, Nye also often mentions "persuasion" as an important constitutive of soft power. He (2004: 6) defines "persuasion" as "the ability to move people by argument" and argues that "soft power is more than just persuasion." However, Nye does not dwell on the thorough clarification of "persuasion" and its role in soft power making. In his major book on soft power titled *Soft Power: Means to Success in World Politics* (2004), the word "persuasion" is used only on three occasions, and on one of them, which is a quote from an interwar period British official, persuasion is presented as a product of propaganda (Nye 2004: 101), which Nye otherwise does not incorporate into his concept. Nye (2011: 93) states that persuasion involves some degree of manipulation and fraud. However, he does not treat manipulation and deception as part of strategies to wield soft power. In fact, Nye's attempt to include these two strategies into persuasion is at odds with many other scholars, who exclude manipulation from the set of strategies that persuasion contains (Mattern 2007; Walsh 2005: 3).

The concept of soft power treats public diplomacy, broadcasting, exchange programs, development assistance, disaster relief, even military-to-military contacts as essential instruments for soft power cultivation (Nye 2008a). Nye argues that in the modern world, in which, unlike earlier times, information is not scant, broadcasting information to the world does not suffice to wield influence on popular opinion. States, in the competitive nature of the international environment, often disseminate (dis)information damaging one another's image. Under these circumstances, credibility is more important than mere information broadcasting. Public diplomacy is presented as a tool to win credibility in the eyes of others (2008b).

According to Joseph Nye, hard power is the combination of military and economic power. He (2004: 7-8) holds a relational approach to power and maintains that hard power generally rests on coercion and inducement. For him, while coercion is based mostly on force or sanctions, bribes and payments are the most likely resources of inducement. States build their hard power on the basis of their "population, territory, natural resources, the size of the economy, armed forces [and] technological development" (Zahran et al. 2010: 17).

Historical Review on Soft Power

Nye (2004: 150; 2007: 162) often claims that he introduced the concept of soft power. However, as Baldwin (2013: 289) states, "there is a difference between coining a phrase and inventing a concept." Nye's contribution to the studies of international relations in terms of soft power was not "introducing the concept" but systematizing and synthesizing the tools and resources which are used to influence opinions, attitudes and values of the publics of foreign countries, and to shape their preferences. Elsewhere Nye (2011: 81) himself acknowledges that "though the concept of soft power is recent, the behaviour it denotes is as old as human history." In fact, not only "the behaviour it denotes", but also the ideas the concept of soft power contains have a long historical background. The historical roots of the concept of soft power date back to the political philosophy of ancient Greece. Throughout history both scholars and politicians paid significant attention to power over popular opinion along with more tangible power (i.e. military and economic might).

Soft Power in Theoretical Writings

Thucydides, who is considered a founder of classical realism makes clear in his *History of the Peloponnesian War* that hegemony solely based on coercion is doomed to fail and therefore is a dangerous strategy. This forces the hegemon to further strengthen its military and economic power, as it fears that it would face dangerous resistance if it were to be perceived as weak or irresolute. It leads the hegemon to pursue an expansionist foreign policy to demonstrate its power, a strategy which is quite risky and threatens serious military loses, and ultimately brings about the collapse of the entire empire. Thucydides states that initially, Athens' allies admired the city's courage and quality of leadership, which substantially reduced the costs of governance and leadership, as well as the maintenance of the *hegemonia*. The allies acquiesced with Athens' hegemony as long as they perceived it as benevolent and beneficial for their own states as well. When the hegemon abandoned this policy, and sought benefits solely for its own, then it became a tyrant, giving rise to its own ultimate end. Lebow and Kelly (2001: 605-606), comparing Thucydides' narrative with Nye's soft power approach, point out that unlike the latter, the former advises states to deliver tangible rewards for others in order to gain their acquiescence.

Roman political theorists also discussed the promotion of a favourable image in the eyes of foreign publics as a crucial policy tool. Marcus Tullius Cicero (107 BC – 47 BC), a Roman politician and political scientist pointed out that no power is strong enough to last if it relies solely upon inspiring fear (Korab-Karpowicz 2010: 107-108). According to Cicero, a hegemonic leadership cannot last long unless it strives to earn others' affection, confidence, admiration, and esteem through moral values and justice (ibid.).

A similar approach can be observed in Thomas Hobbes' political writings as well. Gallarotti (2010: 96), after carefully analysing Hobbes' *The Leviathan*, comes to the conclusion that according to Hobbes' vision of anarchy, "hard power resources are necessary, but soft power is just as crucial to optimize influence and achieve security in an environment without any common power to keep all actors in awe." Following these ideas, Italian communist Antonio Gramsci (1971) highlights the importance of consent along with coercion as the two pillars of hegemony. In the Gramscian sense, hegemony is established on the basis of not only economic or political spheres, but also in the ideational (cultural and moral) sphere. Gramsci argues that consent and coercion are complementary, and the latter is mobilized when consent fails to sustain the order controlled by hegemonic power.

Prominent realist scholars have also underscored the importance of image cultivation and public opinion in foreign policy management. For example, Edward Carr (1951) introduced a threefold classification of power: military power, economic power and power over opinion. He asserts that "power over opinion" is "not less essential for political purposes than military and economic power and has always been closely associated with them" (Carr 1951: 132). Noting the Catholic Church as the first totalitarian state, Carr (1951: 133) stated that the Church pioneered an understanding of the potentialities of power over the masses' opinions and established the first propaganda organization.

The significance of power over opinion was acknowledged by Morgenthau as well. He distinguishes three methods of imperialism: military, economic and cultural imperialism. For him (1965a: 61-61) while the first two aim at the conquest of territory or at the control of economic life, the latter strives for the conquest and control of the minds of men as an instrument for changing power relations. Morgenthau (1965a: 62) states that "the use of cultural sympathy and political affinities as weapons of imperialism is almost as old as imperialism itself." He emphasizes the significance of religion as a way of influencing the minds and feelings of foreign publics. Morgenthau (1965a: 61) asserts that public sympathy and an attractive image play a subsidiary role in foreign policy supporting military and economic methods. This coaxes the enemy and prepares the ground for military conquest or economic penetration. Like Thucydides, Cicero and Hobbes, Morgenthau (1965a: 63) recognizes the potential of military methods to conquer foreign territories without the support of non-military means, but he singles out its possibility to endure: "no dominion can last which is founded upon nothing but military force."

Soft Power in Practice

Throughout history the achievements of states in international politics was significantly associated with their military and economic power, as Friedrich Engels once stated, "without force and iron ruthlessness nothing is achieved in history" (quoted in Carr 1951: 102). Since the beginning of the history of civilizations, military power has been the decisive element of states' strength and existence. Likewise, as "the most obvious, the most ancient, and also the crudest form of imperialism", military assets have long been the major component of states' power (Morgenthau 1965a: 58). However, during the late Middle Ages, significant developments took place in technological, scientific and cultural spheres, including in social life and political governance. The industrial revolution, major technological advances, the increase of publishing houses, newspapers, broadcasting agencies, etc. impacted all spheres of human life. Under these circumstances, the nature of international relations did not go unchanged, and stepped into overwhelming transformations. The revolutionary changes in the character of international relations in the middle ages intensified with the French Revolution (1789). The revolution empowered the general public and granted them crucial influence on political issues. The rational-critical process of debating and weighing political issues in newspapers, speeches, meetings and other institutions of public sphere became part of the political discourse.

The importance of public opinion did not end with conferring legitimacy and influencing domestic political discourse, but also gradually gained significant leverage to impact foreign policy. This was a revolutionary change in the political nature of states and resulted in the struggle for favourable public opinion in international politics. States started to deploy instruments to influence popular opinion in other countries. For example, Simon Burrows (1997: 29), writing about the British-French confrontation in the Napoleonic era, states that the war between Britain and France "was waged at both a military and economic level, but also at the level of international propaganda." British foreign policy makers at the time paid serious attention to the production and dissemination of propaganda written in the French language by writers in Britain and aimed at "turn[ing] the French general public against the Napoleonic regime" (Burrows 1997: 29).

David Welch (2003: xvi) points out that propaganda, as a foreign policy tool historically associated with periods of wars and serious confrontation, was rarely used from the end of the Napoleonic Wars to the outbreak of World War I in 1914. The massive use of propaganda during the first total war in history, opened a path in the practice of international politics which is still being followed. The war brought the efforts of influencing public opinion as an indispensable part into the formulation of government policies. This factor played an enormous role during the war, and even some consider the weakness of Germany as a propaganda power one of the determining factors of its defeat (Welch 2003: xvii).

Prior to World War II, efforts to wield soft power reached an historical peak. Propaganda provoked a remarkable interest both among scholars and politicians. A wide array of studies were carried out to examine the ways of moulding the minds and controlling the feelings of both domestic and foreign publics. Meanwhile, special government institutions were created to project power abroad aimed at shaping perceptions of foreign publics: for example, the Ministry of Popular Enlightenment and Propaganda in Germany, the Propaganda Committee of the Communist Party in the USSR, the Ministry of Information of the United Kingdom and the Office of War Information in the USA. Nye (2008c: xiii) also points out that "Hitler, Stalin, and Mao all possessed a great deal of soft power in their heydays..."

Although historically propaganda was "regarded by almost everyone as a weapon specifically appropriate to a period of hostilities" (Carr 1951: 137), during the Cold War it gradually transformed into a foreign policy tool actively utilized in peace time as well. The changing nature of the system of international relations, the invention of weapons of mass destruction, and the increasing cost of war made great powers conduct latent wars through economic measures and propaganda tools. The world became a battlefield of a struggle for power over opinion. While since the end of World War II, a full-scale clash between the great powers has not taken place (largely because of the fear of nuclear weapons), the world has been experiencing rivalries between them in other ways: economically and ideologically.

Reconceptualization of Soft Power

This section will present a model of soft power which differentiates two sources of soft power: self-projection (attractiveness) and state-managed projection (Figure 1). Following Nye's logic, this model deals with attractiveness as a currency of soft power. The model uses the word attractiveness interchangeably with the term "self-projection". It defines self-projection as the projection of a state's cultural, political, economic, educational, military etc. accomplishments to foreign countries without the involvement of its government. Attractiveness is built on two general sources: natural endowments and human-constructed qualities. While the former denotes the natural qualities of the country, i.e. its territories, population, climate, etc., the latter characterizes policies, political values, economic standards, foreign aid, military power, technological and scientific advances, music, movies, TV channels, popular culture, ideas and customs, etc. Attractiveness empowers the state's narratives and provides arsenal against the contending narratives.

A well-endowed country acquires favourable material conditions to build strong power (both hard power and soft power). Natural endowments can allow the state to build a strong military and economic power, but do not suffice to be attractive. It is likewise important for states to have attractive human-made qualities. While natural endowments are a crucial, but neither sufficient nor necessary, condition for states to acquire attractiveness, human-constructed qualities are both a necessary and sufficient condition to be attractive. The difference in the soft power achievements of Turkey and Singapore is a telling example. In terms of natural endowments, the latter is far behind the former: Turkey with its area (783,562 sq. km) and population (78.67 million) is a far bigger country than Singapore (area: 719.1 sq. km; population: 5.535 million). Nevertheless, Singapore has been more successful than Turkey in soft power production all over the world. For example, a ranking by Monocle Magazine in 2015, considering the performances of states in business and innovation, culture, government, diplomacy and education, rated Turkey 25th and Singapore 23rd (See Monocle 2015).

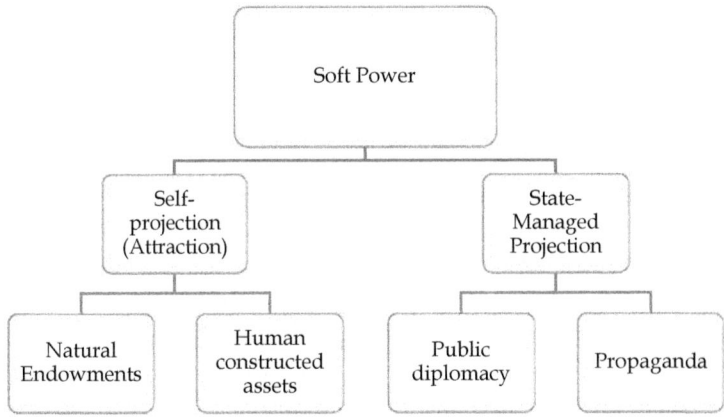
Figure 1. Soft power[4]

A state's attractive endowments and qualities can project an attractive image through informal communications, grassroots cultural exchanges, non-state actors, non-governmental organizations, (international) media, internet etc. without any state support in a way that can be theorized as "self-projection". Though self-projection happens independently, sometimes it can reach and deliver messages to foreign publics more effectively than the state-managed projection of many countries does. Nye (2011: 17) supports this belief:

> "[A] country can try to attract others through actions such as public diplomacy, but it may also attract others through the structural effects of its example or what can be called the 'shining city on the hill' effect."

---

4 Unlike Nye's model of soft power, this model does not take agenda-setting, which is defined as "raising issues to salience among the relevant community of actor" (Livingston 1992: 313), on par with attractiveness. It does not treat agenda-setting as a source of soft power, but as a possible outcome of it. This model treats soft power as power over the minds and feelings of foreign publics that can be cultivated through the international appeal of a nation's culture, values, social-political system, economic model, foreign policies, and its state-managed propaganda/public diplomacy policies. A state's soft power in a foreign country could be used for different goals by the representing country. Agenda-setting could be one of these goals, but not a source of building soft power.

If the people of state A lives in desperate poverty or chaos while its neighbour state B experiences economic prosperity and political stability, then naturally B's economic model and policies will produce attractiveness for the people of A. In such cases, country B's values, supposedly such as democracy, freedom, better living standards, and human rights may attract the people in state A, because these values "address their individual and collective desires and needs" (Roselle *et al.* 2014: 76). This attractiveness may also generate incentives among the people of state A to follow the model of the country B. Thus, self-projection, as an extension of successful human-constructed qualities, provides a favourable basis for the success of state-managed projection.

State-Managed Projection

The mounting influence of domestic non-state actors on the formation of both domestic and foreign policies encourages states to devote significant energy and resources to programmes that are designed to work with foreign publics, to inform them about the "projected" country, its values and traditions. These initiatives are formed in a way to assist the state in its pursuit of national interests through non-military means by exerting influence on foreign publics, moulding their opinions, and influencing the policies of their respective governments. In 1960s, the Director of US Information Agency, Edward Murrow (quoted in Waller 2007: 25) backed this approach by stating that "any program supported by government funds can only be justified to the extent that it assists in the achievement of national objectives."

This is why the soft power projection of external powers sometimes generates a strong backlash in target countries. If a state develops a strong amount of power over popular opinion in a foreign state with ultimately hostile intentions, it might make that state feel threatened and seek countermeasures. Pointing to this possibility, Stephan Walt (1987: 260) writes that "penetration is usually counterproductive when a state tries to alter the target's preferred alignment in an especially significant way." In some cases, the threatened state may even seek a coalition with states that share similar concerns. This approach differs from Nye's, who argues that "if a country can also increase its soft power, its neighbors feel less need to seek balancing alliances" (Nye 2012). The growing soft power of hostile states, in fact, might urge the threatened state to seek a balancing coalition. The case of the Gulf Cooperation Council (GCC) is an excellent example.

The GCC, founded in 1981, is a regional, intergovernmental union of Saudi Arabia, Kuwait, Bahrain, Qatar, the United Arab Emirates, and Oman. The Iranian regime that came to power following the Shiite Revolution in 1979 had begun to project its ideology into neighboring countries. Iran, by using a range of communicative strategies, sought to provoke the Shiite minorities in the Gulf countries to revolt against their respective states and demand transformation into a more Islamic state. The Arabian monarchies who had a considerable number of Shiite minorities felt threatened by Iran's growing soft power, its propaganda and other subversive actions. Scott Cooper (2003) writes that poor economic and social conditions amongst Shiite minorities created a favorable environment for Iran's propaganda and facilitated domestic discontent. In response to Iran's soft power projection, Gulf countries converged their counter strategies and founded the GCC to coordinate their policies. Cooper underlines that there were not any economic interests behind the formation of the Council. Nor were there military institutions within the Council to integrate military forces against a common external threat.

The GCC members cooperated, in fact, against the interference of Iranian soft power into their internal circles. Considering the state "as the intermediary between domestic society and the international system", Cooper (2003: 309) suggests that internal threats to the state can be "as serious as external threats—and may, in some circumstances, be more serious." Cooperation over the exchange of information on political dissidents, bilateral agreements involving sharing sensitive intelligence, border control, extradition of criminals served to counter domestic subversion instigated by Iran (Cooper 2003: 313-314). In this respect, some scholars and experts consider non-military interference in state's internal affairs by foreign countries through subversion, terrorism, espionage, political propaganda, or related interventions as a form of offensive power which might be as dangerous as — or sometimes even more dangerous than — conventional military actions (Walt 1987: 165, fn. 38; Priess 1996; Cooper 2003: 324).

States make use of a diverse set of strategies (persuasion, seduction, manipulation, etc.) to get their narratives through contending ones. Narratives constitute the central element of the state-managed projection, and its role in the formation of soft power is so crucial that some scholars even argue that international affairs has become a matter of "whose story wins" (Nye, 2013b) or "strategic narrative is soft power in 21st century" (Roselle et al. 2014: 71). The concept of "strategic narratives" developed by Roselle et al. (2014: 74) argues that such narratives "directly address the formation, projection and diffusion, and reception of ideas in the international system."

Roselle et al. define strategic narratives as "a communicative tool through which political actors... attempt to give determined meaning to past, present, and future in order to achieve political objectives" (2014: 3) and differentiate its three inter-related levels — international system narratives, national narratives, and issue narratives (2014: 76). While international system narratives are narratives about the structure of the international system, the players and rules in this system, national narratives set out "what the story of the state or nation is, what values and goals it has" (ibid.). Finally, issue narratives are about a state's policies, values, objectives in response to a certain national or international issue.

For example, in Russia's case these three levels of narratives can be clearly identified: Russia's calls for a multipolar world and its objections to the predominance of the USA in the international system are an example for international system narratives. Moscow's national narratives present Russia as a peace-loving country struggling to restore justice in the world which is allegedly dominated by the USA. These two levels of Moscow's narratives are complemented by its issue narratives. As in the case of the former two narratives, the issue narratives also address both domestic and foreign publics on the legitimacy of its policies and explain why a certain state action is good or just.

States employ various strategies and instruments to deliver their narratives to targeted people in foreign countries and to influence their minds and feelings: such as non-governmental organizations, international broadcasting, academic exchange programs, supporting foreign political parties and politically active groups, etc. Carr (1951: 134) noticed that, "the same economic and social conditions which... [had] made mass opinion supremely important in politics... [had] also created instruments of unparalleled range and efficiency for moulding and directing it." Public diplomacy and propaganda are two catch-all terms under whose umbrellas all the instruments and strategies utilized to wield power over popular opinion abroad can be located (Table 1).

Joseph Nye does not separately discuss propaganda as an instrument of soft power cultivation. In his concept, the policies some of which were historically considered propaganda (such as international broadcasting) are introduced under the label of "public diplomacy" (Nye 2004: 107-108). Although when talking about the policies of Western governments (including the Woodrow Wilson administration) during World War I, Nye (2008b: 96-97) names the initiatives of these governments to influence domestic and foreign public opinion "propaganda", he (2004, 2008b, 2011) uses the term "public diplomacy" when talking about the similar policies of the United States in the modern period. Nonetheless, a deeper analysis of these two concepts indicates that although the term propaganda is disregarded in Nye's concept of soft power, in fact this is still an integral part of policies to wield power over opinion.

The term "public diplomacy", which emerged in the second half of the twentieth century, does not have a single definition all scholars subscribe to. Paul Sharp (2005: 106) defines it as "the process by which direct relations are pursued with a country's people to advance the interests and extend the values of those being represented." According to Nye (2008b: 95), it is an instrument that governments use to mobilize its soft power arsenal to communicate with and attract the publics of other countries. Nevertheless, according to Edmund Gullion, who allegedly coined the term "public diplomacy" in the mid-1960s, the new term emerged as a result of their attempts to avoid the word "propaganda" about the policies of the United States. He (quoted in Vincent 2007: 237) pointed out that although the activities in question could be called "propaganda", because of its pejorative connotation a new term "public diplomacy" was preferred to "to describe the whole range of communications, information, and propaganda".

Propaganda is mostly defined as "the dissemination of ideas intended to convince people to think and act in a particular way and for a particular persuasive purpose" (Welch 2003: xix). Propaganda is historically associated with the Latin term propagate (*propagare*) denoting the activities of religious circles spreading the Christian faith during the Middle Ages (Sussman 2010: 14; Vincent 2007: 234). Historically the term was not at all suggestive of the dissemination of disinformation aimed at goals which were to the detriment of the original interests of the receivers. However, currently it is mostly conceived as a tool used to mislead people about various domestic and international issues (Miller *et al.* 2010: 4).

Welch (2003: xix) points out that propaganda functions through the transmission of ideas and values for a specific purpose which serve the interests of the propagandist directly or indirectly. Propaganda denotes the dissemination of not only misleading, but also true information which does not simply intend to inform the receivers, but to direct their minds and feelings into a specific direction pre-determined by the propagandist (Sussman 2010: 12). For example, as opposed to the assumptions of propaganda as mere lies, and the conviction that the dissemination of true information cannot be propaganda, French philosopher Jacques Ellul (1973: 53) asserts that the best propaganda operates with some degree of truth on the basis of which it gives the greatest results. He rightly states that propaganda does not only aim to change opinions, but much more importantly, it seeks to reinforce existing beliefs and attitudes. A few decades before Ellul, writing in 1936, Aldous Huxley (quoted in Taylor: 1979: 22) also pointed out that "The propagandist is a man [who] canalizes an already existing stream; in a land where there is no water, he digs in vain."

Preserving the ultimate goals of propaganda, public diplomacy included elements into its range of activities which look much less objectionable, and even altruistic. As opposed to propaganda that was historically conducted through broadcasting via radio, television or newspapers, public diplomacy developed two-way communication. The public diplomacy tools generate the possibility of communicating with foreign publics face-to-face which is arguably "the most effective" communication method (Nye 2004: 111). Unlike propaganda, it allows for deeper engagement with foreign publics. As Nye notes, "the best propaganda is not propaganda" (Nye 2014). Non-governmental and civil society institutions are of paramount importance for the success of soft power policies. Hence, as Jan Melissen (2005: 4) names soft power a "postmodern variant of power over opinion", we can assuredly call public diplomacy a "postmodern variant of propaganda". In a similar vein, for the definition of public diplomacy Geoff Berridge and Alan James write that it "is a late-twentieth-century term for propaganda conducted by diplomats" (Berridge *et al.* 2001: 197).

Propaganda vs. Public Diplomacy		
Commonality		
Strategies	Deception	
	Persuasion	
	Manipulation	
	Seduction, etc.	
Objectives	To influence the opinions and feelings of the people in other countries	
	To reinforce or change their attitudes	
Dissimilarities		
Propaganda	Public Diplomacy	
Mostly a wartime weapon	Mostly a peacetime strategy	
Pejorative connotations	Less objectionable	
Mostly no direct engagement	Deeper engagement	
Conducted through mostly international broadcasting	Conducted through NGOs, academic exchange programs, cultural diplomacy, civil society actors, etc.	

Table 1. Public diplomacy vs. propaganda

Soft Power vs. Hard Power

The distinction and relationship between hard power and soft power is one of the most debatable questions in the concept of soft power. While a group of scholars, including Nye, consider soft power independent of hard power, there are others who claim the opposite. According to Nye (2004: 9), "soft power does not depend on hard power." In his defence of this statement, Nye mentions the Vatican as an example claiming that it has soft power even though it has no hard power. Afterwards, Nye defends this view with the consequences of the Soviet invasions of Hungary (1956) and Czechoslovakia (1968) to Soviet soft power, stating that these invasions led the USSR to lose much of its soft power despite its growing economic and military capability. In contrast, Colin Gray (2011: 46) states that "soft power flows to the owner of hard power." In a similar vein, Christopher Layne (2010: 57) argues that Nye's concept wrongly assumes that foreign policy is controlled by public opinion. In general, vagueness regarding the hard power – soft power nexus is often mentioned as one of the flaws of Nye's concept of soft power (Zheng *et al.* 2012: 22).

Another contradiction regarding soft power and hard power in Nye's concept is about the nature of their sources. Nye (2003: 10) is well-aware of the fact that military and economic power can generate soft power as well. However, as Zheng and Zhang (2012: 24) write, he does "not provide a clear, logical and persuasive explanation to this contradiction in his soft power theory." Zheng and Zhang (ibid.) argue that Nye prefers a simple partitioning of the policies and behaviours of two types of power: "For instance, the policies and actions of military power include coercive diplomacy, war and alliance; those of economic power include aid, bribes and sanctions; and those of soft power include public diplomacy and bilateral and multilateral diplomacy."

As an attempt to settle this contradiction I propose an analysis of the soft power – hard power nexus based on the following four assumptions (Figure 2):

1. The possession of hard power (i.e. economic and military power) is a precondition to develop strong soft power;
2. Diminishing utility of military power in international politics compels great powers to develop their soft power capacity in the pursuit of their foreign policy goals;

3. Soft power is not a substitute for hard power, and, therefore, states need and must pay adequate attention to the development of their hard power;
4. The possession of strong, hard power elements (e.g. economic power) does not automatically produce soft power; states need to take appropriate measures to wield soft power.

Below these arguments are discussed in more detail.

1. The possession of hard power (i.e. economic and military power) is a precondition to develop soft power:

Nye's above-mentioned description of the negative consequences of the Hungary and Czechoslovakia invasions to Soviet soft power is a good point to start. As a matter of fact, a similar image crisis — which the USSR underwent in the aftermath of these invasions — happened also to the USA following the Vietnam invasion (1960s). However, both the USSR and the USA managed to recover their soft power by the virtue of their growing economic and military resources. Otherwise they would have failed to regain attractiveness if they had lost their military and economic power. Elsewhere Nye (2004: 14) himself acknowledges this fact: "When the policy changed and the memories of the war receded, the United States recovered much of its lost soft power" during the Vietnam war.

Strong hard power backing creates a favourable basis for international soft power projection to be effective and successful. Edward Carr in *Twenty Years Crisis* asserts that military and economic strength makes the success of international propaganda possible. He (1951: 139) observes that "The Third or Communist International enjoyed little influence until the power of the Russian state was placed behind it." On the contrary, Trotskyism, which theoretically was not less influential, remained without influence, as it was not supported by the power of any state.

The importance of hard power for a soft power campaign is also acknowledged by many contemporary scholars. For example, Chinese scholar Hongyi Lai (2012: 12) portrays economic clout "as a bedrock for a nation's soft power". Lai (2012: 9) observes that Germany, Canada, and Japan, the countries that emerged as the top three most respected nations in polls which were conducted by GlobeScan for BBC World Services in 21 countries in different parts of the world between 30 November 2009 and 16 February 2010, are also among the most economically developed nations and among the top benefactors of foreign aid in total and especially in terms of the ratio of aid to GDP. He (2012: 11) rightfully concludes that the importance of economic resources, foreign aid, and technological and scientific capacity for soft power cannot be underestimated.

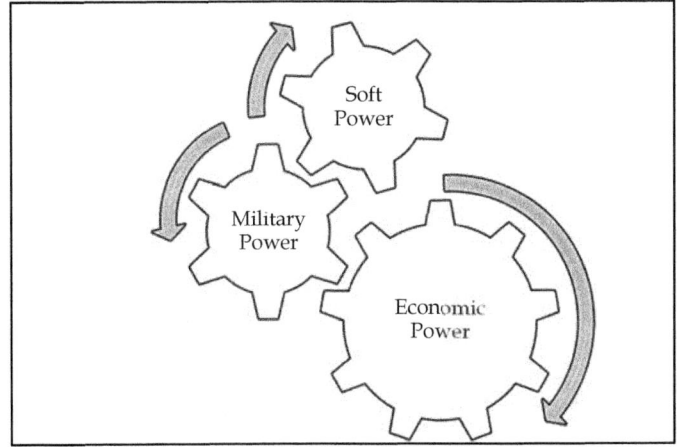

Figure 2. Hard power vs. soft power

2. Diminishing utility of military power compels great powers to develop their soft power capacity:

The evolution of soft power in the policies of great powers is also a result of the diminishing utility of military power (Huseynov 2016). It is a fact that since the invention of nuclear weapons, the international political environment has not experienced any large-scale war between great powers. The enormous costs of military operations and the risks of nuclear involvement have made great powers avoid using them against each other. They have faced "absolute impotence" upon their catch of "absolute power" (Waltz 1979: 184).

The decline in the utility of military power and, against this background, the rise of soft power, has also been affected by a series of other developments in recent decades. On the one hand, the information revolution which has rendered worldwide communication cheap and easy, is a crucial factor thanks to which soft power has gained more importance in foreign policy. For some, even the rapid developments in technology and communications are the most central driving force in this process (Mattern, 2007: 101-102; Nye 2014). On the other hand, even though the world community has not managed to establish an international Leviathan that can oversee and control international affairs, the world has gone a long way in this direction since World War II. The establishment of numerous international organizations, non-governmental organizations, conventions, international courts, etc. has dramatically affected the *modus operandi* of international relations.

Thus, information technology, the relatively more effective role of international organizations and law in the management of interstate relations, but arguably most importantly, the growing destructive capability of military power, have contracted its efficiency while increasing the costs of its usage. Its diminishing utility makes great powers import soft power into their primary foreign policy toolkit. Nevertheless, this does not mean that the utility of military power has disappeared; on the contrary, military power still plays the primary role in international politics as *ultimo ratio*.

3. Soft power is not a substitute for hard power, and, therefore, states need and must pay adequate attention to the development of their hard power:

The shrinking utility of military power between great powers does not necessarily give grounds to perceive soft power as a substitute for hard power. First, a state's soft power cannot guarantee its independence and sovereignty unless the state secures its economic and military security. Hence, states cannot and should not rely on soft power resources for national security. Strong military power or, in the case of smaller states, participation in a military bloc (i.e. bandwagoning) is a more serious and prudent security measure both in regard to non-state threats and rival great powers. Therefore, military capability will long remain an essential part of states' power (Gray 2011).

Second, nobody would admire a country which sinks in economic problems or shakes under the weight of threats of others. A state needs an economic and military basis to a certain extent in order to be able to pursue further foreign policy goals which would include cultivating an attractive image abroad. Nye (2003: 10) himself contends that "a country that suffers economic and military decline is likely to lose its ability to shape the international agenda as well as its attractiveness." For instance, Russia enjoyed attractiveness in the first decade of this century by the virtue of its growing economy, military power and rising influence in international affairs. In late 2014, following the Ukraine crisis, Moscow faced an economic and financial crisis. This badly affected Russia's attractiveness. Although, Russia's aggressive foreign policies and anti-Russian narratives of Western institutions have also played a role in it, economic and financial downturn was ultimately not less influential. In fact, Russia experienced a similar situation after the dissolution of the Soviet Union when Moscow had lost a considerable part of the military and socio-economic capacity it once enjoyed. The 1990s were a period during which Russia suffered military and economic backwardness, and under these circumstances the production of soft power was improbable (Shubin 2004: 110). On the contrary, the country enjoyed rising soft power between these two periods- from the beginning of 2000s until 2014 (Rutland *et al.* 2016). Thus, states tend to lose their soft power when they fail to successfully handle their economic and political challenges. Conversely, they develop soft power when they are exemplarily successful in these spheres.

4. The possession of strong hard power elements (e.g. economic power) does not automatically produce soft power; states need to take appropriate measures to wield soft power:

It is, nevertheless, incorrect to consider soft power to be completely dependent on hard power. Soft power is not a given power. States (including great powers) do not enjoy a favourable image abroad immediately after they achieve strong military or economic capability. This dimension of power can be produced on the basis of given cultural resources (such as popular traditions, literature, music, unique architecture and so on.) and political values through well-prepared and accordingly implemented soft power doctrine. For instance, until the late 1990s China was devoid of strong soft power despite its growing economy and military might. In the beginning of the new millennium, after having achieved dazzling economic growth, Chinese officials started thinking about broadening their influence internationally. Beijing became able to invest a huge amount of money on various projects which have been projecting Chinese soft power globally. For example, the number of Confucius institutes, of which the first one was established in 2004, rose up at an impressive speed to 440 institutes and 646 classrooms serving 850,000 registered students worldwide by the end of 2013. Around $278m was spent on the institutes which serve to project Chinese cultural values worldwide along with providing Chinese-language courses. Additionally, a long range of other projects, such as hosting the Olympic Games in 2008 and the Shanghai Expo in 2009, were initiated, and millions were spent on expanding China Central TV's broadcasts in English and other languages etc. Arguably, China would not have been able to achieve its current popularity around the world without these efforts. Most Chinese scholars and politicians find soft power and hard power mutually complementary within the correlation in which soft power can facilitate the growth of hard power, whereas hard power can demonstrate and support the increase of soft power (Li 2009b: 27-28). Therefore, the acquisition of strong hard power does not lead automatically to strong soft power. It demands efforts to build power over hearts and minds across the globe.

Case Selection

The hypotheses developed above will be tested in the study of the Russia—West confrontation over the post-Soviet states (Belarus,

Ukraine, Moldova, Azerbaijan, Armenia, and Georgia) of the "common neighbourhood". This study examines rationale behind the formation of dissimilar external alignment strategies of these states despite their location in a similar geo-strategic environment. It found that the existing theories of political realism do not provide convincing tools to explain this divergence in the foreign policy strategies of the regional states and the policies of conflicting great powers to affect their foreign policy choices. The rest of this book will explore this case in the light of the theoretical assumptions presented in the previous sections.

Two of the regional states—Belarus and Ukraine—are going to be more deeply analysed in order to test the hypothesis about the foreign policies of weak states which are caught in between the great power rivalries. The empirical analysis here is particularly focused on the timeframe spanning from 2004 till 2016. This period has been chosen because the rivalries between Russia and the Western powers, unlike the expectations of many observers (e.g. Bremmer *et al.* 2004), evolved to a very critical level during this period. The Georgia war of 2008 and the international crisis over Ukraine of 2014 have affected international relations in the region and across the globe. Following Crimea's annexation, Russia—West relations reached such a critical state that many observers warned against an all-out war between the two sides (Shlapak *et al.* 2016; Brewster 2016). However, the confrontation remained limited to non-military means and none of the sides dared to militarily attack the other side.

A number of other existing and past international rivalries between great powers in various regions across the world, such as the Cold War rivalries between Western powers and the Soviet Union over the Third World countries, the slowly growing Russia—Chinese competition over the Central Asian countries and the Chinese—American confrontation over the Pacific countries can serve as relevant case studies to test the hypotheses of this research. As delineated in Hypothesis 1, the rival sides in these examples are nuclear-armed great powers seeking to expand or secure their influence over the mentioned territories. Although they are (or "were" as in the case of the Cold War) highly keen to expand their sphere of influence over the contested regions and prevent the advance of the rival power's influence, they do (did) not dare to make a direct military attack.

Although US—Soviet tensions rose to dangerous levels on a number of occasions because of their rivalries over the countries in Asia, Africa, and Latin America, they had to look for ways to pursue their interests through methods which did not include a head-on superpower confrontation. Their projection of non-military, ideological power produced different results across different countries and regions. While in some cases they managed to push desired changes in the external orientation of the target states, they also failed in other cases and had to engage in proxy wars at times. The outcome of their policies was not only affected by the international distribution of military capabilities, but also by ideological/cultural components of their power, as well as by the internal processes in the regional states.

Similarly, the slowly growing Russia—China competition over the Central Asian countries includes elements that may be analysed from the perspectives of the soft power concept and neoclassical realism. Russia's longstanding military presence in the region and its historical cultural dominance do not suffice to avert the increasing Chinese influence, which includes both economic and cultural expansion (Pantucci 2015: 275-276). While, as expected by realist scholars, neutrality between Russia and China could benefit the regional countries more both in terms of security and economic dividends, the competition between the rival great powers makes the neutrality challenging to be maintained. This book intends to provide tools which can also be employed to look into the nature of the confrontation between Russia and China in Central Asia, analyse how the internal structures of the regional states would affect their alignment strategies between the two surrounding great powers and predict the outcomes of this confrontation.

The Russia—West Confrontation over the "Common Neighbourhood"

In the aftermath of the dissolution of the Soviet Union, the states located between the EU and Russia, the region which is often called the "common neighbourhood", found themselves in an international context that was entirely different from the Cold War years. The Kremlin lost its control over these territories that had been under Moscow's rule for a significant part of recent history. Russia was unwilling to reconcile with the loss of its former vassals and tried to reinstate its supremacy over these territories through various channels including economic and political reintegration. Russian leaders were adamantly against any economic or political rapprochement between regional states and the rival great powers (in particular, Western powers). They warned against the potentially grave consequences of any expansion of the Western military and political structures into the region which the Russians treated as their "near abroad".

The region remains a priority for Russia's foreign policy a quarter of a century after the collapse of the Soviet Union. The establishment of unchallenged dominance in these territories is considered of existential importance for the Russian political elite and is regarded pivotal to its international standing and foreign policy perspectives (Jackson 2003: 69-70). For the Kremlin's geopolitical vision, the hegemony over the "near abroad" is a prerequisite for Russia to become a global player. This approach, developed in a similar manner to the US treatment of the Western Hemisphere, is often analyzed as "Russia's Monroe Doctrine" (Smith 1993b; Skak 2010: 139). Russia sees the region as its periphery and claims the right to control the geopolitical manoeuvres of regional countries (Igumnova 2014: 48). Russia's leaders, on many occasions, have not shied away from openly saying that Russia would do everything possible to prevent geopolitical shifts in this region that pose threats to Russia's national security. During the Georgia war of 2008 and the Ukraine crisis of 2014 the Kremlin demonstrated that it was ready to take military actions towards this end.

Western powers are also interested in this region, especially in preventing Russia's plans to re-integrate the regional countries under its hegemony. Many analysts consider former Soviet Eastern Europe and the South Caucasus as "the most important neighboring region of the European Union" (Fischer 2011). The region as a transport corridor between the EU and China and as a transit route for European energy supplies bears geostrategic importance. Above all, for the EU, the central question of its policy toward this region is the security of its eastern frontiers (Skålnes 2005; Dannreuther 2004). The Union's foreign policy approach with regard to its eastern neighbourhood is a prominent example of its policies which are often characterized as "far more Machiavellian than Kantian" (Smith 2016: 43). Zimmermann (2007: 815), in similar vein, has written that:

> "The European Union is often seen as the very antithesis of realism and the extent of co-operation achieved among its Member States is frequently cited as one of the strongest real-world cases refuting realism. However, this interpretation refers to the integration process itself. It is not necessarily a given that this would be also reflected in EU external behaviour."

The EU seeks to establish Western-controlled stability in its eastern neighbourhood. It is believed that the maximum possible economic, political, and normative convergence with the neighbouring countries would contribute to the stability of the region (Missiroli 2004; Lavenex *et al.* 2009; Hagemann 2013; Smith 2015: 6). It is therefore not a coincidence that NATO's eastward enlargement was also first proposed by German policymakers in 1993, and later supported by the United States and other NATO members (Skålnes 2005: 231). For example, German Defence Minister Volker Rühe was convinced that "if we do not export stability, we will import instability" (quoted in Brown 1995: 37).

The endurance of "frozen conflicts" in the former Soviet Eastern Europe and South Caucasus is also one of the most serious security challenges to European security. In recent years, these conflicts have erupted into bloody clashes that have killed thousands of people in Ukraine and the South Caucasus and displaced more than a million people. Thus, economic and political stability in the eastern neighbourhood is a particular concern for the EU, as instability, chaos, and abandonment of reform in those countries would ultimately constitute various threats, for instance illegal immigration, smuggling, organized crime, and terrorism. On the other hand, Eastern European and Baltic members of the European Union are pushing for the deeper integration of former Soviet members into the Euro-Atlantic military and political structures to "constitute a buffer zone ("our backyard") against the unfriendly Big Other" (Makarychev 2013: 5). Against this background, in its foreign policy the EU is focused on two particular goals with regard to the countries of former Soviet Eastern Europe and the South Caucasus:

1. Extending the EU's influence over the regional countries through transferring *acquis communautaire* to the regional countries, a process which is often characterized as "external governance" (Missiroli 2004; Raik 2006a; Lavenex *et al.* 2009; Hagemann 2013; Smith 2015: 6).
2. Preventing rival powers (first and foremost, Russia) from (re)establishing supremacy over the countries situated in this region (Smith 2015);

Despite the fact that the United States is not geographically related to the post-Soviet countries located between the European Union and Russia, it has also been heavily involved in the geopolitical mapping of the region since the very beginning of the post-Cold War years and sought to establish its influence in the region (Haas 2007). The interests of the United States with respect to former Soviet Eastern Europe and the South Caucasus overlap partly with the interests of the European Union: like its European allies, the USA seeks to avert the re-integration policies of Russia, whom some American politicians consider the "number one geopolitical foe" (Willis 2012) of the United States. The emergence of Russia as a regional hegemon in Eurasia could entail dramatic geopolitical consequences which would threaten the interests of the USA. Thus, the United States tries to prevent the revival of Russia's influence over the former Soviet countries and Moscow's regional re-integration policies (Sakwa 2015: 30). Washington is interested in distancing the countries of the post-Soviet region from Russia's orbit economically, politically, and culturally. US leaders also openly oppose and criticize the integration projects of the Kremlin as imperialist moves akin to the Soviet invasion of the region. For example, in 2012 then-Secretary of State Hillary Clinton called Russia's push for a Eurasian Customs Union "a move to re-Sovietize the region", and warned, "we are trying to figure out effective ways to slow down or prevent it" (RFE/RL 2012).

Thus, while the maintenance of its dominant role in the region is for Russia a matter of survival as a great power, for Western powers the expansion of their influence over the common neighbourhood is a measure to ensure the security of eastern borders and prevent re-emergence of a strong regional hegemon (Lavenex *et al.* 2009; Hagemann 2013; Smith 2015: 6). Leonid Kuchma, Ukraine's second president (1994–2005) later wrote in his memories that for Russia's leaders "The loss of former influence, particularly in the borders of the former Soviet Union is a catastrophe" and a "life-and-death matter" (quoted in Trenin 2011: 88). By deploying military power in the conflicts with Georgia and Ukraine, Russia has shown that it would risk even a military escalation with the West to prevent the expansion of the Western military and political institutions into its backyard. The reserved reaction of the Western powers to Russia's military interventions in the regional countries indicated that the region was of a greater importance for Russia, and its leaders were ready to take more risks for it. These circumstances define the nature of the great power rivalries as the independent variable in this study. From the perspective of the regional states, Russia is closer, stronger, more determined, and a more threatening power than the EU and the United States. The confrontation between these two geopolitical centres exerts pressure on the foreign policy making of the "common neighbourhood" states and pushes them to the either/or choice between the two.

The "Common Neighbourhood" States

In the early years of the post-Soviet period, the states located in the "common neighbourhood" sought to minimize Russia's influence and strengthen their newly gained independence. Towards this end, they either prioritized neutrality as their foreign policy strategy or tried to align with the Western bloc against Russia (Wolczuk 2002; Makili-Aliyev 2013; Szeptycki 2014: 37, Fesenko 2015: 134-135; Huseynov 2015). However, the international context presented in the preceding section, in particular Russia's persistence to preserve its influence over these states at all costs, made balancing impossible for the regional states. Consequently, the regional states tried to either maintain neutrality or align with the stronger and more threatening power (i.e. Russia).

Two of the regional states, Armenia and Belarus, as expected by structural realism, bandwagoned with Russia, which complicated their relations with Western powers and gradually pushed the two to deeper economic and military dependence on Moscow (Van der Togt 2017: 10; Bosse 2009). Although according to the state constitution (adopted in 1994), Belarus is supposed to be a neutral state (Nice 2012), this was not possible to be upheld in practice. The isolationist policies of the Western leaders with respect to the Belarusian leader Aleksander Lukashenko have further complicated Belarus's international position (Bosse 2009). The country regularly participated in Russia's regional integration projects, including the Collective Security Treaty Organization (CSTO) and the Customs Union (CU) as a founding member, while its cooperation with Western military and political organizations remained very limited or non-existent.

Up until the outbreak of the "colour revolutions" in the region, the other four regional states (Azerbaijan, Georgia, Moldova, and Ukraine) tried to keep neutrality between the two surrounding great powers and maintain economic and political relations with each of them. Moldova's constitution (adopted in 1994), in a similar vein with Belarus's constitution, declared the country "neutral". Although these states, together with Uzbekistan, founded an organization (GUUAM) that was widely seen as "pro-NATO" and "anti-Russian" (Kuzio 2000; Splidsboel-Hansen 2000), they avoided making real steps towards NATO membership. In this period (i.e. up until the occurrence of the "colour revolutions"), GUUAM dealt mainly with economic cooperation, and geopolitical issues were largely downplayed in the agenda (Landry 2011: 22). Similarly, although the leaders of Georgia and Ukraine publicly declared membership in the EU and NATO as their priority in foreign policy, neither President Leonid Kuchma of Ukraine nor President Eduard Shevardnadze of Georgia made tangible steps towards this end (Rondeli 2001: 197-203; Wolczuk 2002; Szeptycki 2014: 37, Fesenko 2015: 134-135; Huseynov 2015: 120-121). At the same time, all of these four "common neighbourhood" states cooperated with Russia within regional integration projects (e.g. the Commonwealth of Independent States (CIS)) initiated by the Kremlin.

This international status-quo in the region began to partially change after the popular uprisings known as "colour revolutions" in the beginning of the XXI century. However, this change was not in line with the expectations of structural realist scholars: Georgia and Ukraine, departing from neutrality, sought to align themselves with Western powers against an increasingly stronger and more threatening Russia, while Moldova, although did not depart from its constitutional neutrality, began to deepen its economic and political cooperation with the EU notwithstanding the threats from the Kremlin (Kuzio 2011; Samokhvalov 2015; Huseynov 2015: 126-230). The pro-Western shifts in external orientation in the early 2000s turned out costly for these states, particularly for Georgia. In the aftermath of the Rose Revolution, relations between Tbilisi and Moscow gradually deteriorated and eventually resulted in a war over the breakaway regions of Abkhazia and South Ossetia of the small South Caucasian republic. The five-day Russian-Georgian war in August 2008 ended disastrously for Georgia. On the contrary to Tbilisi's expectations, the West did not declare a war against Russia to protect Georgia (Huseynov 2015). Russia established its unequivocal control over Georgia's breakaway regions, recognized the independence of the republics of Abkhazia and South Ossetia and underlined the irreversibility of this decision.

The rivalries between Russia and the West challenged the external orientation of the "common neighbourhood" states again after the announcement of regional integration projects by the EU and Russia. The EU's Eastern Partnership Programme (EaP) and Russia's Customs Union project complicated geopolitical affairs in the region. The integration calls by these great powers came to the table of regional state leaders as an either/or issue. In the face of such a geopolitical dilemma, they behaved differently. One group of states (Armenia, Azerbaijan, and Belarus) did not risk a confrontation with Russia. The second group of states (Moldova, Ukraine, and Georgia) that had already experienced "successful" "colour revolutions" eventually signed or initialized the AA with the EU. One of these states, Ukraine, in which the state leader brought to power by the "colour revolution" left office in 2010 and the new administration chose non-alignment as the guiding strategy in foreign policy, initially found the deal with the EU not "in the national interest" (Traynor *et al.* 2013) and refused to sign it. However, another "colour revolution" took place and again changed the course of the state. The 2014 protests brought to power the political elite who opted to balance with the West against Russia and thus signed the AA and DCFTA.

Building its analysis on the hypotheses presented in the previous sections, this book will look into the role of domestic non-state actors in the formation of the external orientation of these states. The foreign policy choices of these states and the role of the internal non-state actors in this process against the backdrop of the Russian and Western soft power projection will be analysed exclusively in Chapters 5 and 6. The fact that the region hosts countries that have different levels of state autonomy increases its relevance as the case study in this research. The level of state autonomy in the regional countries is identified by considering the political processes that took place in these countries over the period under study (2004-2016). The existence of a different type of political systems allows the study to identify variations in the autonomy of state leaders in these countries *vis-à-vis* their respective societies. With this purpose, the book has categorized them into two groups: (1) countries with relatively strong state autonomy (Armenia, Azerbaijan, and Belarus) and (2) countries with relatively weak state autonomy (Georgia, Moldova, and Ukraine).

Armenia, Azerbaijan, and Belarus are the "common neighbourhood" states where the state leaders have relatively more autonomy *vis-à-vis* their respective society. This has been possible by minimizing the influence of internal non-state groups on the management of foreign policy in a consistent and decisive manner. Unlike the leaders of Ukraine, Moldova, and Georgia, the political leadership in these three states have been able to manage the relevant stability of the political systems established in early 1990s. For example, in the wake of massive anti-government protests the Georgian President Shevardnadze stepped down in 2003 and the Ukrainian President Yanukovych stepped down in 2014 without demonstrating resistance to maintain power. Anti-government protests in Moldova have usually followed a similar line. On the contrary, the political elites in Armenia, Azerbaijan, and Belarus proved themselves more unwavering in the face of similar acts in the examined period (2004-2016).

The above discussed similarities between these states allow the study to categorize them in the same group and focus on only one state to test the hypothesis concerning the foreign policy of the states whose leaders obtain stronger autonomy *vis-à-vis* internal non-state players. In this book, only the case of Belarus is going to be discussed in detail which is meant to provide helpful insights to make inferences about the cases of Armenia and Azerbaijan as well. The particular reason for my choice of Belarus as the case study is that the location of Belarus is strategically more important for both the West and Russia than the relatively faraway South Caucasian countries. Together with Ukraine, Belarus forms the critical buffer zone between Russia and Western powers. The fact that the country borders the EU members Poland, Latvia, and Lithuania, who feel more threatened by Russia, makes Belarus supremely important for the West. Any instability in Belarus could pose threats to the European Union. This is why both Russia and the West seek to possess control over this landlocked former Soviet state.

Georgia, Moldova, and Ukraine, known as the most revolutionary nations in the "common neighbourhood", have made successful revolutions and numerous popular uprisings over the last two decades. They differ from the other three states that have been discussed above in terms of both their internal political structure and foreign policy priorities. The frequent change of governments in these three countries has entailed unavoidable implications for their foreign policies, too. Their leaders have been structurally more restricted than their counterparts in Belarus, Armenia, and Azerbaijan. This internal pressure has limited their ability to independently deal with the imperatives of the international political system. When they have attempted to disregard public opinion in making fateful decisions in the past, they have faced, on many occasions, overwhelming domestic discontent and popular upheaval.

The similarities discussed above make it possible to focus on Ukraine alone to test the hypothesis concerning the foreign policy of the states whose leaders are weakly autonomous *vis-à-vis* internal non-state players. The particular reason for my choice of Ukraine as the case study is similar to the one that I declared about Belarus. Like Belarus, Ukraine's geopolitical importance for Russia is immeasurable: "it is an existential imperative" (Bogomolov *et al.* 2012). Ukraine has been invariably the primary target of Russia's integration projects. It is a country without which Russia's plans to re-integrate the post-Soviet states under the Eurasian Union would lose most of its value. This is why it is also of a great geostrategic importance for Western powers.

Ukraine and Belarus, along with other "common neighbourhood" states, receive similar pressure from the Russian side to refrain from Euro-Atlantic integration. Simultaneously, Western powers seek to tear these countries away from Russia's sphere of influence. These conditions make their geostrategic environment largely similar. The recent historical background of the two states is also amongst the conditions which make them comparable: both of the countries were part of the Soviet Union being amongst its official founders and disintegrators. They declared themselves independent after the collapse of the Union in 1991. Existence under Soviet control for long years has had a series of implications for these countries. For example, it has made their economies inherently tied with the Russian economy. In 2016, the exports to Russia accounted for 46,5% of Belarus's total exports, while imports from Russia were more than 55% of its total imports (See National Statistical Committee of the Republic of Belarus 2017). Russia was also the major trade partner of Ukraine until relations deteriorated in the aftermath of the Euromaidan revolution (2014). In 2013,

Ukraine's exports of goods to Russia amounted to 50,6% of its overall exports of goods, while its imports from Russia were below 40% (See State Statistics Service of Ukraine 2013). In spite of these similarities, they opted for different strategies in their external alignment over the period under study (2004-2016). The research aims to explain this variation in their foreign policy choices by putting an emphasis on the (non)intervention of domestic non-state groups in foreign policy.

Conclusion

This chapter has presented the hypotheses that will be tested in the case of the Russia—West rivalries over the post-Soviet states located between the EU and Russia. This study has found that international relations scholars have not thoroughly examined the policies of the rival nuclear-armed great powers to reach out to the domestic non-state actors of the targeted regional states in order to affect their external alignment. The realist scholars (e.g. Walt 1987: 218-261) who have paid attention to these policies have underestimated their potential to be effective and focused more on the distribution of material capabilities. In contrast to them, this chapter put forward the hypothesis that if nuclear armed great powers compete to expand or sustain their sphere of influence, they attempt to affect the external orientation of the regional states by affecting their domestic political system through influencing the attitude of the masses and the perceptions of the elite. In this process, great powers make use of various instruments which I have analysed under the umbrella of soft power. In this context, they use soft power as a major expansive instrument while military power remains a tool of defence and a method of backing up their foreign policies.

The chapter has also explored factors which impact the decision of the regional states in their external orientation when neutrality (non-alignment) turns out impossible to be maintained and the international system forces them to make a choice between bandwagoning and balancing. The chapter concluded that approaches emphasizing the role of the distribution of material capabilities in international relations, geographic proximity, aggressive intensions, offensive power, and economic dependence fail in many cases. It was argued that the analytical toolkit of neoclassical realism, recognizing the causal influence of systemic pressure and including the intervening influence of state-level variables, provides more convincing assumptions to explain the foreign policy strategy of weak states.

The chapter narrowed down its focus on public opinion and state autonomy as the intervening variable in its analysis. It explored the theoretical foundations of the great powers policies to affect the external alignment of weak states through influencing their publics. It formed the hypothesis that if the leaders of a weak state, which is in between the rivalries of great powers who use soft power to expand their influence, are autonomous *vis-à-vis* the society and other internal non-state actors, they can control the inflow of the soft power projection of foreign states, offset the intervening influence of the domestic non-state actors on foreign policy making, and augment their chances to more prudently and independently follow the imperatives of the international political system. Conversely, if such autonomy does not exist, then the external powers find a favourable environment in which to wield soft power, the domestic non-state actors can influence the external orientation of the state, the state fails to offset their influence, which may result in suboptimal foreign policy decisions.

In the next section, the chapter aimed at exploring the concept of soft power, its fundamental assumptions and shortcomings. After having reviewed the works of a series of scholars, the chapter presented its reconceptualization of soft power. The model it presented differentiated two sources of soft power: self-projection (attractiveness) and state-managed projection. It argued that a state's attractive self-projection is built on the superiority of its natural endowments and human-constructed assets. However, this is not a sufficient condition on which to build strong soft power in the target states. For that, great powers need to develop a complex set of strategies which the chapter called "state-managed projection". Public diplomacy and propaganda have been analysed as the two terms that include the instruments (e.g. international broadcasting, scholarly exchanges, etc.) used in this process. Hard power was also analysed in the chapter and presented as an important type of power which cannot be easily substituted with soft power.

The chapter has finally introduced the cases which will be used to test the hypotheses. It opted for the Russia—West competition between 2004—2016 over the states which are located between the EU and Russia—the region which is known as the "common (or shared) neighbourhood". It categorized the regional states in two groups in accordance with some of the political events happened in these states in the target period: states with relatively strong state autonomy (Armenia, Azerbaijan and Belarus) and states with relatively weak state autonomy (Georgia, Moldova and Ukraine). One state from each group will be subject to more thorough analysis of the book: Belarus and Ukraine.

3. Soft Power in Western Foreign Policies (2004 – 2016)

As outlined in Chapter 2, the hypothesis on rivalries between nuclear armed great powers predicts that if these great powers compete to expand or sustain their sphere of influence, they use soft power as a major expansive instrument while military power remains a tool with which to defend themselves and back up their foreign policies. This chapter tests this hypothesis along with some of the assumptions developed by the soft power model of this book in the case of the policies of Western powers (i.e. the EU and the United States). It analyzes their rationale of using soft power and hard power in the policies concerning the post-Soviet region. The chapter particularly explores how Western powers make use of the instruments which I have analysed under the notion "soft power" to communicate with and influence domestic non-state players in the "common neighbourhood" states.

The chapter's discussion on Western soft power policies is based on the analytical framework of the soft power model presented in Chapter 2. This model differentiated two sources of soft power as self-projection (attractiveness) and state-managed projection. Self-projection is built on the basis of natural endowments and human-constructed assets, while state-managed projection is conducted through propaganda and public diplomacy. The model presented propaganda as a one-way communication strategy (e.g. international broadcasting). On the contrary, public diplomacy is considered as a two-way communication strategy that includes face-to-face interactions with the people of the target states. The model also presented a reconceptualization of the distinction and relationship between hard power and soft power highlighting *inter alia* the importance of hard power to produce strong soft power.

The chapter consists of two major sections. The first section that follows this introduction briefly examines the policies of Western powers to draw the "common neighbourhood" states into their orbit. It will be followed by a larger section on the soft power policies of the West with respect to this region. The section explores elements of both self-projection and state-managed soft power projection of Western powers in the regional states. A short conclusion in the end briefly reviews the findings of the chapter.

Soft Power vs. Hard Power in Policies of Western Powers

The previous chapter's analysis of the interests of Western powers with regard to the "common neighbourhood" states concluded that the region is of lesser importance for the West than it is for Russia. However, the fact that the subordination of the regional states to Russia's control could have entailed a range of geopolitical implications forced Western powers to think about drawing them into their own orbit and preventing Russia's plans to pursue regional re-integration. Below, three main directions of Western policies which are aimed at this end are discussed: (1) European integration; (2) Transatlantic integration; (3) the reinforcement of the defensive capabilities of the Alliance along its eastern borders.

European Integration: A few years after the dissolution of the USSR, the EU started to make inroads into Eastern Europe and the South Caucasus, which had until then been under Soviet control. In a relatively short period of time three members of the former Soviet Union (Latvia, Lithuania, and Estonia) and most of the other formerly communist Eastern European states (Czech Republic, Hungary, Poland, Slovakia, Slovenia, Romania, and Bulgaria) were admitted to the EU and NATO. This process went rapidly, largely thanks to the impressive attractiveness of these organizations for the regional states. Prior to the EU's 2004 enlargement, this fact was specifically stressed by Romano Prodi, the then chairman of the European Commission: "The EU looks certain to remain a pole of attraction for its neighbours. For many of the countries in our future 'backyard' the EU is the only prospect" (European Commission 2002a). Prodi also underlined the importance of "attractiveness" as the fundamental pillar of the new proximity policy of the EU with its new neighbours in the Eastern neighbourhood.

In 2002, Prodi announced that a "ring of friends" would be formed around the borders of the EU in the aftermath of the enlargement of 2004-2007. He pointed out that this policy "must unlock new prospects and create an open and dynamic framework," and "it must motivate... [the EU's] partners to cooperate more closely with the EU" (European Commission 2002b). Outlining the future perspectives of the proximity policy, Prodi fleshed out that the EU should neither promise nor exclude eventual membership to the countries involved in this policy. These ideas were encapsulated in the "European Neighbourhood Policy" (ENP), which was announced in 2004 and viewed all periphery countries in the Middle East, North Africa, Eastern Europe, and the Southern Caucasus as external partners. As an attempt towards differentiation between Southern and Eastern neighbours within the ENP, in 2009, at the initiative of foreign ministers Radoslaw Sikorski of Poland and Carl Bildt of Sweden, the EU and six post-Soviet states (Armenia, Azerbaijan, Georgia, Belarus, Moldova, and Ukraine) launched the Eastern Partnership Programme (EaP), based on a commitment to fundamental values (including democracy, the rule of law and respect for human rights and fundamental freedoms), a market economy, sustainable development, and good governance. The programme sought to reproduce the internal model of the EU in the target countries without granting membership, bring them under the normative influence of the EU, and ensure stability of the eastern boundaries of the EU.

The EaP envisioned two primary integration targets with the partner countries: (1) the signing of an Association Agreement (AA), an integral part of which would be accords on a Deep and Comprehensive Free Trade Agreement (DCFTA), and (2) full visa liberalization, meaning a visa-free travel regime with the EU. Initially, some of the former Soviet states opposed this project. For example, the Moldovan President Vladimir Voronin characterized the initiative as "a ring around Russia", and questioned the need for a new, anti-Russian CIS under the leadership of the EU (Sputniknews 2009). However, eventually they all joined it.

The EaP reached some successful results in the ensuing years: Above all, Ukraine, Republic of Moldova, and Georgia signed AAs, including DCFTAs. The agreements comprise four general chapters: Common Foreign and Security Policy, Justice and Home Affairs, the Deep and Comprehensive Free Trade Area (DCFTA), and a fourth chapter covering a range of issues including the environment, science, transportation, and education. They create mechanisms for reform in a variety of fields in the respective countries, cut import tariffs, open EU markets to them and vice versa, and thus strengthen cooperation between the sides.

Likewise, the DCFTAs deal with principles on environment, transportation, science and education that are not typical to classic trade agreements. They also seek to harmonize the trade-related legislation of these countries with EU standards and the *acquis communautaire*. The countries that sign these agreements commit themselves to adopting some 350 EU laws within a ten-year timeframe. The three countries have also gained visa-free access to the Schengen zone. They also joined the Energy Community that was created by the EU in 2006 for the Western Balkans countries to incorporate them into the EU's electricity and gas markets.

Transatlantic Integration: The end of the Cold War generated a cooperative international environment between NATO and Russia. Particularly, the 1997 Russia–NATO Founding Act and the 2002 NATO–Russia Council formalised relations between former Cold War foes and created a basis for cooperation. The Alliance underscored that it had "no intention, no plan and no reason to deploy nuclear weapons to the territory of new members" and the integration of new members into NATO would not follow with "additional permanent stationing of substantial combat forces" on their territory (See NATO 1997). In the following years, the Alliance expanded its borders eastward and integrated the Baltic States and most Central and Eastern European states. It also declared the door of the Alliance open to all European democracies, including the post-Soviet states in Eastern Europe and South Caucasus, that meet the standards of membership. Thus, the US demonstrated that it was unwilling to stop the enlargement of NATO's sphere of influence at the border of the former Soviet Union, despite the fact that it was clear that these policies might be confronted with Russia's military counteractions. The US leaders made clear that they would not recognize the right of any external power to impose limitations on the external alignment choices of regional states.

Encouraged by such declarative support, two of the regional states, Georgia and Ukraine, decided to knock at the door of the Alliance. Their leaders, Mikheil Saakashvili and Viktor Yushchenko respectively, who had been brought to power by "colour revolutions", asked the Alliance for the Membership Action Plan (MAP), a program designed to help aspiring countries prepare for eventual membership. The Alliance debated the MAP issue for the first time at the NATO summit in Bucharest, Romania (2–4 April 2008). Due to French and German opposition, the Alliance refused to launch the MAP process. The final declaration of the summit indicated in an obscure manner that Georgia and Ukraine would, one day, become members of NATO.

The discussion of the membership of the neighbouring post-Soviet states at this high level outraged the Russian leadership. However, it failed to deter the Euro-Atlantic aspirations of the regional states, in particular of the Georgian leadership. President Saakashvili erroneously believed that the EU and the US would stand by Georgia in a military clash with Russia over the tiny breakaway regions of Abkhazia and South Ossetia. Ronald Asmus in his *A Little War That Shook the World: Georgia, Russia, and the Future of the West* aptly characterizes Saakashvili's pre-war foreign policy as what Richard Nixon once called the 'madman theory' of foreign policy—threatening to act irrationally in order to get someone's attention (Asmus 2010: 10).

The reluctance of the Alliance members to militarily support the regional states against Russia's military operations, despite their regular declarative support, happened again in the aftermath of Crimea's annexation. Although Western powers imposed economic sanctions on Russia and provided support to Ukraine, they did not militarily stand against Russia. The threat of the escalation of the conflict and its transformation into a nuclear war again determined the fate of the region. Under the existing circumstances, the West cannot benefit from its military superiority and does not seem willing to militarily intervene to avert Russia's efforts to allegedly "re-Sovietise the region". Although both the EU and United

States support some of the regional groups who try to make pro-Western changes in their respective countries, none of them has shown a serious determination to put all their resources at stake to materialize those changes in the region. Thus, this observation allows us to argue that since the collapse of the Soviet Union, the primary goal for the West has not been to draw post-Soviet countries into their orbit and to get them to join the EU and NATO which would lead to an all-out military clash with Russia; rather the goal has been to minimize Russian influence in the region and to impede upon the Kremlin's re-integration efforts at relatively little cost.

Reinforcement of Defence: Although Western powers did not deploy military force against Russia's military intervention in the "common neighbourhood", they strictly reinforced their defensive capabilities along the eastern borders. In the aftermath of the Georgia—Russia war of 2008 and the Ukraine crisis of 2014, NATO members reinforced the Alliance's military presence along the Eastern borders. This was principally remarkable because up until those events, the role of NATO in European security was gradually declining as Europe was becoming increasingly more capable of providing regional security on its own (Dannreuther 2004: 2). Some analysts also claimed that "NATO [was] destined for a greatly reduced role in Europe's security architecture" (Hyde-Price 2007: 4). As opposed to those expectations, as Richard Sakwa (2015: 4) aptly points out, "NATO's existence became justified by the need to manage the security threats provoked by its enlargement." The wars between Russia and its former allies were used by the Alliance as a reason for further reinforcement in the region, as the regional NATO members appealed for a stronger NATO presence in their lands as a security guarantee against potential Russian aggression. Thus, although Western powers deployed non-military power to expand their influence inwards in the post-Soviet region, they reinforced their military force in order to counter any backlash of this expansion.

The Ukraine crisis entailed "the most significant reinforcement of NATO's collective defence since the end of the Cold War" (NATO 2017). At the 2014 Wales Summit, the member countries came to terms with the Readiness Action Plan (RAP) to strengthen the capacity of the Alliance to respond swiftly and firmly to new security challenges in an increasingly hostile environment. The RAP considers "continuous air, land, and maritime presence and military activity in the eastern part of the Alliance (...) on a rotational basis", deployment of increased weaponry, including fighter jets and multinational maritime forces, and the reinforcement of the NATO Response Force (NRF) (NATO 2014). The personnel of the NRF were increased to 40,000 in the aftermath of the Ukraine crisis from 13,000; moreover, the Very High Readiness Joint Task Force (VJTF) of around 20,000 troops, of which about 5,000 are ground troops, has been founded. Even though Russia's military budget (nearly $69 billion in 2014) is far lower than those of NATO members ($852 billion in 2014), the Alliance leaders also called for increasing the defence budget to counter Russia's growing military budget. All in all, Moscow's reaction to NATO's enlargement initiatives has led to more efforts on the part of the Alliance to strengthen its defencive capabilities along its borders with Russia.

In June 2014, the White House proposed a European Reassurance Initiative (ERI) with the declared goal of "reassuring North Atlantic Treaty Organization (NATO) allies and partners of the US commitment to their security and territorial integrity" (See Office of the Under Secretary of Defense 2016). The ERI funds the exercises, trainings, and rotational presence in Europe, particularly Central and Eastern Europe. It seeks to increase the capability and readiness of US allies within NATO and its partners (Georgia, Moldova, and Ukraine), to show "a quick joint response against any threats made by aggressive actors in the region" (ibid.). The Telegraph reported that the initiative was aimed at "deter[ring] Russia from carrying out additional land grabs after its 2014 annexation of the Crimean Peninsula" (Telegraph 2016). The spending through ERI amounted to $985 million in 2015 and $789,3 million in 2016. For the fiscal year (FY) 2017, this amount quadrupled to $3,4 billion. The FY 2017 ERI funding is expected to support projects of the Department of Defense (DoD) seeking "to reinforce the defences of NATO members and non-NATO partners in the region that feel most threatened by Russian aggression" (Office of the Under Secretary of Defense 2016).

Additionally, the Pentagon confirmed that it plans to deploy fully manned combat brigades to Europe in response to "an aggressive Russia", in addition to the presence of more than 60 thousand US troops in Europe (Telegraph 2016). In June 2015, the US announced to pre-position 250 armoured vehicles (M1 Abrams tanks, Bradley fighting vehicles and M109 howitzers) and their associated equipment in Central and Eastern Europe. The Polish Institute of International Affairs reports that "For the first time in NATO's history, such equipment will be stored on territories of "new" members: Estonia, Latvia, Lithuania, Poland, Romania, and Bulgaria" (Kacprzyk 2015: 7). In 2016, the alliance organized its biggest ever joint military exercises in Poland where some 31,000 Polish, American and other troops participated in land, sea and air exercises. Despite Russia's consistent warnings, NATO is set to strengthen its eastern flank with new multinational battalions in Poland and the Baltics and open communication centres in Bulgaria and Romania.

Soft Power as the Western Foreign Policy Tool

The importance of reaching out to foreign publics as a way of ultimately influencing the foreign policy actions of their respective governments was recognized by the US foreign policy makers at the very beginning of the Cold War. In the late 1950s, a report prepared by the State Department's Policy Planning Staff (PPS) mentioned the changing character of foreign policy making. The report noted that unlike previous times, now diplomacy did not only target foreign policy elites and professional diplomats but sought to reach out to the general public as well. The report explained that "Convincing a foreign official is often less important than carrying an issue over his head to his people, to public opinion in the country he represents... The people will influence the official's action more than he will influence theirs" (Osgood 2002: 89). With these intentions in mind, the USA set up a number of institutions to connect with the people of the Soviet Union and its satellite countries.

Radio Free Europe (RFE) and Radio Liberty (RL), Voice of America (VOA), United States Agency for International Development (USAID), numerous cultural and academic exchange programs, scholarships, etc. played a crucial role as an alternative source of information for millions of people behind the Iron Curtain. RFE and RL, which were founded in 1949 and 1951 respectively and were financed by the CIA for a long time, served as a primary instrument of US foreign policy to inform and influence the public of the rival bloc. Michael Nelson (1997: 163) reports that VOA reached 14-18 percent of the Soviet adult population during an average week prior to 1985, followed by Radio Liberty with 8-12 percent, the BBC with 7-10 percent, and the German broadcaster Deutsche Welle with 3-6 percent. The remarkable aspect of these broadcasters was that they were mostly broadcasting in the local languages of the countries they targeted. For example, in 1980s RFE/RL broadcasted in 21 languages to the Soviet Union and Eastern Europe (Mickelson 1983: 3). They were trying to inform people living under communist regimes about the high living standards in the West and make them rebellious against the material deficiencies and political repression of the communist governments.

Cultural diplomacy and educational exchanges have also long been an essential tool for Western governments to project favourable images into foreign countries. Exchange programs played an essential role in combating communism at the height of the Cold War. Unlike the Soviet Union, Western countries were not reluctant to send their own nationals and to bring the nationals of communist countries through these exchanges. The West was eager to project a tempting and attractive image of abundance of material wealth, consumer culture, technological know-how, individual freedom, and political democracy to both communist and non-communist countries. For example, in response to the offers of the US government to accept a hundred students each year from the Soviet Union in the late 1950s, for a long-time the Soviets agreed to send only 20 students and mostly over the age of 30 who had already advanced in their career (Richmond 2003: 22).[5] In later years, the number of Soviet students who studied in Western universities gradually increased.

The exchanges in culture, education, information, science, and technology between the Soviet Union and the West over the thirty-five years that followed the death of Joseph Stalin in 1953, are often analysed as one of the important factors that brought down communism (Richmond 2003). The role of educational exchanges in the fall of the Soviet Union has been confirmed by many Soviet participants of exchange programs in the United States. For example, Oleg Kalugin, one of the very first Soviet exchanges who studied in the USA and later became a KGB General likened the exchanges to "a Trojan Horse in the Soviet Union… that played a tremendous role in the erosion of the Soviet system" (Richmond 2003: 32).

The information war between the West and Russia did not come to an end with the collapse of the Soviet Union. The gradual deterioration of relations between the sides in geopolitical affairs also found its way into the information space. In the wake of the dissolution of the Soviet Union, the focus of US broadcasters shifted gradually towards countries that were still under Russia-supported governments. RFE/RL completed its mission in and terminated its broadcasting to Hungary in 1993, Poland in 1997, and Estonia, Latvia, Slovakia, Croatia, Montenegro, Bulgaria, and Romania in 2004. However, it continued and enlarged its broadcasting to the post-Soviet world. Unlike the Cold War years, in the new era the European countries also actively participated and assumed a major role in the soft power competition with Russia over the "common neighbourhood" countries. A long range of non-governmental institutions, exchange programs, international broadcasters, think-tanks, etc. were deployed in the fight to win approval amongst the peoples of the post-Soviet regional states.

---

5 As a matter of fact, initially President Eisenhower suggested that that ten thousand Soviet students would be invited to the United States, all expenses covered. However, Eisenhower's proposal was not made public, as the State Department warned that this would alarm the Soviet officials and problematize the negotiations. Therefore, eventually only a hundred students were offered to the Soviet Union to be sent to the United States (Richmond 2003: 22).

Self-Projection

Western powers (i.e. the European Union and the United States), being some of the most developed states in the world, have acquired wide-ranging capabilities to develop effective self-projection. The USA and the EU are the world's first and second largest economies, respectively. They together ($34,176 trillion) produce more than 45% of the global gross domestic product (World Bank 2017a). The countries look like paradise for millions of people across the world with a GDP per-capita $38,442 and $54,629, respectively (World Bank 2017b). Besides, this economic basis also allows the West to be militarily second to none: NATO's total budget is over $904 billion (SIPRI 2016). Around 32% of this budget is covered by the European members of the alliance (ibid.). A 2015 ranking by Monocle Magazine, considering the performances of states in business and innovation, culture, government, diplomacy and education, ranked 13 EU Member States in the top 25 globally in terms of soft power, with Germany ranking number one and the United States ranking number two (Monocle 2015).

The enormous economic advance has been possible thanks to their natural endowments (e.g. geographic location and climate) but more importantly thanks to the brilliant policies these countries have historically developed. This is why the socio-political and economic model of the West has been admired by millions of people across the world and in the countries of the Former Soviet Union (Portnov 2014: 13; Ostrovs'kyj 2014: 21; Onuch 2014: 48). Although the image of the liberal democracy model of the Western community was tarnished by the rise of right-wing populism towards the end of 2016, until then (in the period under study — 2004-2016) this model had been a major soft power asset of the EU and the USA in their policies with regard to the "shared neighbourhood". The ideals that are attached to the West — freedom of speech, human rights, the rule of law, accountability — have been a major motivation for the post-communist countries in aspiring to join the European Union.

It is due to these ideals that many observers consider the EU's soft power as "unrivaled", although, according to others, US soft power surpasses that of Europe. The latter refers particularly to the worldwide fame of American cultural products. A leading French specialist, Frederic Martel (2010), on the basis of his research in 30 countries, concluded that American cultural exports (movies, music, books, broadcasting, etc.) has captured a leading position in the formation of global entertainment, shaping tastes and views over the world. Criticizing the European cultural industry, which he argued fails in producing equally attractive cultural goods, Martel fleshed out that this strength gives America "a capacity to influence other cultures and societies" (in an interview to Basil Maudave (2010)). But, in this research, no differentiation is made between the EU and the USA, and their soft power projection is treated as a unified unit in competition against Russia in the "shared neighbourhood".

Narratives

In their policies to wield power over the minds and feelings of the people of the "common neighbourhood", Western powers do not build their narratives on the basis of religious affinity, historical past or ethnic bonds. The narratives which they arm their soft power policies with have been overwhelmingly future-oriented proposing "an attractive vision of the future" (Chatham House 2011: 10). They address the existing socio-economic and political problems the people in "common neighbourhood" countries struggle with. European integration has been presented by pro-Western forces and seen by many local people as "a promise of wealth and development as well as better governance and public sector reform" (Lang 2015: 37; Fesenko 2015: 132-133). For example, the former communist member states of the EU formulated their narratives within the framework of their post-communist journeys. Referring to their own experience following the collapse of the Soviet Union, they argued that European integration was the proven way of success to overcome dictatorships and to embark on political and economic development based on liberal and free market principles (Sadowski 2015: 66).

For the most part of the period under study (2004-2016), democracy promotion, which was defined by the European Council of Ministers as "the full range of external relation and development cooperation activities which contribute to the development and consolidation of democracy in third countries" (quoted in Burnell 2007: 1) was a buzzword for Western policies with regard to post-Soviet countries. The EU and United States called upon regional states to foster democracy and promote the right of citizens to choose their own leaders in a free and fair process. Western powers also criticized leaders who built up dictatorial rule through corruption and clampdown on independent voices. However, this criticism was applied selectively depending on its relevance from the perspective of the regional geopolitical and economic interests of the Western powers. Some political figures like President Lukashenko and his entourage were *personae non-grata* in the US and EU, while others never experienced similar reactions (Ioffe 2004: 96). While anti-Lukashenko critics were provided by the West with financial and logistics support on significant scales, Western powers demonstrated disinterest towards those oppositional forces that fought against the leaders of friendly countries to the West (Landry 2011: 21).

On the other hand, the EU and the USA criticised Russia's regional integration projects and accused it of harbouring new imperial ambitions. From this point of view, Russia's Eurasian Union was a mere reconstruction of the Soviet Union in a new form which Hillary Clinton famously described as "a move to re-Sovietize the region" (RFE/RL 2012). They condemned Russia's policies of obstructing access to the Euro-Atlantic path of regional countries by deploying military force in a strictly asymmetric manner. Western leaders repeatedly stressed that no external power could veto the foreign policy choices of the regional countries or undermine their right to chart their own future path. Declaring that "We may not give in to external pressure, not the least from Russia" or "the times for limited sovereignty are over in Europe," they opposed Russia's attempts to maintain control over the external alignment options of the regional states (Marszal 2013).

International Broadcasting

The renewed confrontation between the West and Russia brought back rivalries between the former foes in the information space as well. Many Western politicians, academicians, and experts sounded the alarm about Russia's information war. In response to these developments, the EU reinforced its support for the development of "free" and "independent" media in "common neighbourhood" states. The EU Commission states that between 2011 and 2015 it invested €15.5 million for (i) journalist training and networking, (ii) information and communication campaigns, (iii) opinion polling and media monitoring in the regional countries of the Regional Communication Programme (See European Parliament 2014). In 2011, then US Secretary of State, Hillary Clinton warned that "We are in an information war and we are losing that war" (Warrick 2011). Similarly, in 2013, in her testimony before Congress, she criticized the performance of the Broadcasting Board of Governors—which oversees several international broadcasting institutions, including the Voice of America and Radio Free Europe/Radio Liberty—as "practically defunct" (Schadler 2013).

These concerns even grew in the wake of the breakout of the Ukraine crisis. Enders Wimbush, a former Broadcasting Board of Governors (BBG) governor and director of Radio Liberty, asserted that the Ukraine crisis was "the most serious challenge US international broadcasting has faced since the fall of the Soviet Union" (Strobel 2015). Western leaders feared that their counterarguments did not have a sufficient degree of persuasion. These developments urged the EU and NATO to take a series of measures to combat Russian propaganda in the Eastern Neighbourhood. In March 2015, the European Council stressed the necessity to challenge Russian propaganda in neighbouring post-Soviet region, to persuade the people of the region that deeper engagement with and implementation of reforms backed by the EU could improve their lives over time. The Council also initiated the establishment of the East StratCom Task Force that is functional within the EU's diplomatic corps, the European External Action Service (EEAS). The institution was tasked with developing communication products and campaigns focused on explaining EU policies and promoting European values in the Eastern Neighbourhood. The EU also began debating the possibility of broadcasting in local languages in these countries.

A similar institution, named the "Strategic Communications Centre of Excellence", was founded by NATO in Latvia's capital, which Russian media described as a "propaganda centre". In 2015, the EU, with the support of NATO, launched a Russian language TV channel named ETV+ in Estonia. The channel focuses mostly on Estonia's Russian-speaking minorities and is the first Russian-language TV channel in the country where more than a quarter of the population speaks Russian as their native language. The channel's Deputy Director noted the Ukraine crisis and Russia's impressive capabilities of spreading disinformation across the region among the factors that necessitated the establishment of the Russian-language broadcasting service (Tagesschau.de 2015). It is financed by the Estonian government, but its regional office in Narva, a city close to the Russian border where Russian speakers constitute 97% of the population, is technically supported by the NATO. But the channel reports that the Alliance does not have any influence on the content of the programmes. Similar channels have been planned to be opened in the other two Baltic States, as well.

One of the primary goals of the establishment of the channel was mentioned as "counterbalancing Russian propaganda". German Foreign Minister Frank-Walter Steinmeier stated that the channel was not meant to be a counter-propaganda tool arguing that "You cannot combat propaganda with counter-propaganda in a democratic society" (ibid.). Thus, in a similar vein with other international broadcasters, Western communication channels broadcasting to the post-Soviet region strictly reject the word "propaganda" to describe their own activities. For example, Peter Limbourg, the Director General of German broadcaster Deutsche Welle (DW), responding to questions about DW's involvement in EU's policies to counter Russia's narratives in the post-Soviet region, argued that "We do not see ourselves in the role of creating counter-propaganda. We do journalism on the foundation of democratic values" (Luther *et al.* 2015).

Deutsche Welle (DW), Germany's government-financed international broadcaster, is also actively involved in the establishment of media outlets to counter Russian narratives in the Eastern Partnership countries. In the aftermath of the Ukraine crisis, DW built up its Russian and Ukrainian editorial office providing 24-hour service. DW also cooperates with Estonia's Russian language TV channel ETV+, supporting them in technical issues, building the content of the programs, and offering trainings for its workers. The other EU member states are also contributing to international broadcasting in the "shared neighbourhood". For example, Poland provides financial (€4 million annually) and technical support (with equipment and trainings) to the Poland-based Belarusian language TV satellite station "TV Belsat" (Sadowski 2015: 72). There are also two Poland-based radio stations ("Radio Ratsya" and "Euroradio") and a series of information websites that reach out to Belarusians (ibid.). The Polish government also provides ample support to TV stations, information agencies and journalists in other common neighbourhood countries, particularly in Ukraine and Moldova.

The US's BBG reported in early 2016 that the agency had created or expanded 35 programs, mostly in the Russian and Ukrainian languages, since Russia moved into Crimea in February 2014. Additionally, the agency asked Congress for additional funding, arguing that while Russia spends $400 million to $500 million a year on foreign information efforts, the United States only spends about $20 million annually on the broadcasting services in the Russian language (Strobel 2015). $15.4 million from the 2016 budget of the BBG was allocated "to Russian-language TV programming" alone (BBG 2015). In October 2014, the BBG started a daily, 30-minute Russian language television news program called *Current Time* that has since then been broadcasting in the post-Soviet countries bordering Russia. In Ukraine, Moldova, Georgia, and Lithuania the program is broadcasted on domestic television stations, while in Russia it is available on a video-based news site. The BBG fights against Russia on social media as well: in 2015, Radio Liberty opened a Digital Media Department (DIGIM). It was reported that the department would serve the main purpose of "using social and digital tools to enhance RFE/RL overall digital presence with a focus on the Russian language sphere" (RFE/RL 2016).

In June 2016, the US Assistant Secretary of State for European Affairs Victoria Nuland, reported before the US Senate Foreign Relations Committee about the work the USA had done to combat what she described as "Russian propaganda" since the outbreak of the Ukraine crisis. She said that:

> "Since 2014, the total appropriation now, the State Department, USAID [US Agency for International Development], BBG (Broadcast Board of Governors) on the US side is about $100 million to counter Russian propaganda. The money goes… from clean honest Russian language programming that BBG is now putting out every day, the expansion of Radio Free Europe/ Radio Liberty, VOA [Voice of America] to about $88 million that we use in State Department and AID to support civil society, independent media, journalists training, including outside Russia for those Russian journalists who have fled" (Sputniknews 2016a).

In her speech, Nuland compared the budget of Russia's RT channel and the US spending on information warfare with Russia. Despite the fact that the budget of BBG for international broadcasting operations in 2016 was over $749 million (See BBG 2017), she complained that:

> "[Our spending of $100 million to counter Russian propaganda] … pales in comparison to the $400 million at least that Russia spends and frankly to the levels that we spent during the Cold War on such activities, which was over $1 billion a year" (Sputniknews 2016a).[6]

In addition to already existing media channels, new legislation has been adopted since the start of the Ukraine crisis in both the EU and the USA, which called for more measures to combat Russian propaganda. For example, an act adopted by the US House of Representatives in September 2016 called on the Secretary of State to "develop and implement a strategy to respond to Russian Federation-supported disinformation and propaganda efforts di-

---

6   On the other hand, Nuland's comparison disregards the fact that the USA is not the only Western country that fights against Russia's international broadcasting.

rected toward persons in countries bordering the Russian Federation" (Official Website of the US Congress 2016). The strategy which is going to be developed in the upcoming months is required also to establish a partnership with governmental and private-sector entities "to provide Russian-language entertainment and news content to broadcasters in Russian-speaking communities bordering the Russian Federation" (ibid.).

Cultural Diplomacy and Exchange Programmes

With the end of the Cold War and the fall of the Soviet Union the Western community accomplished a fateful victory. The disappearance of the Soviet Union also marked the decline in Western soft power projects addressing the former Soviet region. In the 1990s the United States began to cut expenses on cultural and educational exchanges with the regional countries. Nevertheless, Western powers still have a multitude of exchange programs that bring students from these countries to study at Western universities. Particularly, the USA remains the pole of attraction in academic and research spheres, and many students worldwide, including from the former Soviet countries, see the United States as an attractive destination for academia.

The United States Department of State offers a number of exchange programs for nationals of the former Soviet states. This includes most prominently the Fulbright Program, Humphrey Fellowships, the Future Leaders Exchange (FLEX) Program, Global Undergraduate Exchange Program (known also known as the Global UGRAD Program), the Benjamin Franklin Program, Title VIII Grant, etc. These programs are quite popular in the "common neighbourhood" states. For example, the FLEX Program that reaches secondary school students from former communist countries has supported one-year undergraduate exchange studies of over 24,000 high school students (including nearly 8,000 from Russia) at United States universities since its inception in 1993. During the 2012-2013 academic year, the selection rate of the program in Russia was 1.4 percent: Only 239 out of over 17,000 applicants were admitted (Koshkin 2014). In comparison, Harvard's selection rate was 5.9 percent in 2012 (ibid.). Another popular American exchange program that is exclusively focused on the post-Soviet region is the Edmund S. Muskie Graduate Fellowship Program. Established by Congress in 1992, the program supports one to two years of graduate studies of emerging leaders from the former Soviet countries at the universities of the United States. Nearly 5,000 Muskie fellows have participated in the program since its inception in 1992. The program's publication celebrating its 20 years of service in Eurasia claims that 75% of its alumni are in a professional leadership position.

In the framework of the Eastern Partnership, the EU also pursues cultural diplomacy to facilitate durable cultural exchanges, people-to-people activities, and cross-cultural communications. These goals are encapsulated in the EU's Eastern Partnership Culture Programme. The first phase of the programme ran between 2011 and 2015. In this period, the programme invested €12 million in grants and technical assistance to help build the capacities of public administration and non-governmental cultural operators. The second phase of the program, which run until 2018, implemented similar projects with a budget of €5 million. In early 2016, the EU also launched a Cultural Diplomacy Platform to enhance its engagement with third countries and their citizens. Several prominent public diplomacy institutes of the member countries, including the Goethe-Institute, British Council, the Centre for Fine Arts Brussels (Bozar), the European Cultural Foundation, EUNIC Global, and Institut Français, have been involved in the project. A scholarship programme of the EU called Erasmus Mundus, starting in 2004, has selected hundreds of students from Eastern Partnership countries to study in exchange programs (master's and doctoral degrees). The programme opens up opportunities for young people to study, train, volunteer and do youth work abroad. It also supports staff exchanges and cooperation with universities in third countries to create lasting academic and cultural ties.

Educational exchanges constitute an important part of the policies of the German government to maintain and reinforce its image abroad. Germany invests in exchanges more than any other country and is seen as a place for plentiful opportunities for students, both during the study period and after graduation. The exchange programs offered by the German Academic Exchange Service (DAAD) are particularly popular in the post-Soviet countries. Each year thousands of students apply for different degree programs offered by the DAAD. Its budget of over €400 million is derived mainly from federal funding for various ministries, primarily the German Federal Foreign Office, but also from the European Union and a number of enterprises, organisations and foreign governments (See DAAD 2017). The Institution regards the "Central- and Eastern-Europe, Community of Independent States" as a priority in its activities: For example, in 2013 it supported the education of 16,000 people from this region (Lang 2015: 51).

Western NGOs and Support for Civil Society

Civil society has long been recognized in Europe as a crucial instrument for change and has been at the front lines of the anti-government protests in the post-Soviet countries. Prior to the "colour revolutions" in early 2000s, the US and the EU began to pour a significant amount of financial resources into the civil society activists in the regional countries. Western NGOs became a channel to deliver the earmarked money in forms of grants and various projects to local NGOs and social movements (Beissinger 2007: 261). Western organizations also supported coordination between local non-governmental organizations. The representatives of local NGOs came together in the framework of different international meetings and training projects which are mostly supported by Western foundations. These trips have been especially productive and significant at the time of "colour revolutions". For example, the Centre for Non-Violent Resistance, founded by Serbia's OTPOR, an NGO that played a key role in overthrowing Serbian Leader Slobodan Milosevic, organized trainings for activists from post-Soviet states and shared their experiences with them on how to charter a movement, recruit people, and develop mass actions (Beissinger 2006: 20; Beissinger 2007: 262). Thanks to this cooperation the NGOs in post-Soviet space were able to emulate the successful practices of their foreign colleagues. Analyzing the diffusion character of "colour revolutions", Mark Beissinger (2007: 261) writes that it was NGOs and local social movements that emulated and spread anti-government revolutions in the region. Beissinger lists external support amongst the top six common elements of the "colour revolutions" (ibid.).

Thus, Western-supported NGOs have already proved themselves as effective instruments in the promotion of Western agenda in the former Soviet Union. Their role in the formation and spread of "colour revolutions" in the territories of the former Soviet Union has been well documented (Beissinger 2007; Brucker 2007; Lane 2009; Welt 2010; Wapinski 2014: 49). Over the years since the first wave of the "colour revolutions", the European Union and United States have established various institutions and programmes to reach out to non-state actors in the region and strengthen and promote their role in their respective societies. The USA and the EU are present in post-Soviet countries with so many non-governmental organizations and foundations that it is beyond the scope of this book to provide detailed information about all of them or their activities. The following section will talk about some of the largest of these organizations. However, the list of non-governmental organizations to be presented below is by no means exhaustive.

American Non-Governmental Organizations

The "behind-the-scenes roles" of American non-governmental organizations (such as NDI, IRI, Freedom House, and Soros Foundation) in pro-Western political developments in the former Soviet region has been documented by many Western observers and scholars (Carothers 2006a: 56; Beissinger 2006; Sussman 2010). These non-governmental organizations usually portray themselves as "independent" and deny the influence of any government on their activities.

The Eurasia Foundation: The organization was founded and incorporated as a non-profit organization in Washington, DC in early 1990s. Its declared mission is to empower people to take responsibility and affect change for social justice and economic prosperity through hands-on programs, helping them to improve their communities. The organization addresses every former Soviet state, including Russia. Over the last decade, the foundation has established separate branches for the sub-regions within the FSU: (1) The New Eurasia Foundation was launched in Russia as a joint Russian-American-European partnership in 2004; (2) The Eurasia Foundation of Central Asia was founded in Bishkek and Osh (Kyrgyz Republic), Almaty (Kazakhstan) and Dushanbe (Tajikistan) in 2006; (3) The Eurasia Partnership Foundation, serving Armenia, Azerbaijan and Georgia, and the East Europe Foundation, serving Ukraine, Belarus and Moldova, were launched in 2007. Between 1992 and 2005, the Eurasia Foundation invested nearly $275 million through more than 7,700 grants and technical assistance projects in the countries of the former Soviet Union, including Central Asia (See Eurasia Partnership Foundation 2017). Its activities are supported by a range of donors, particularly the United States Agency for International Development (USAID), and the Foreign & Commonwealth Office.

In a similar vein to other Western organizations, the Eurasian Foundation also operates as a soft power agent of the West in the region and seeks to help Western narratives defeat contending narratives. For example, during the Ukraine crisis, the Eurasia Partnership Foundation held a roundtable discussion on the topic of "Crisis in Ukraine and Its Influence on the Nagorno-Karabakh Process: Perspective from the West" in Baku, Azerbaijan, on March 17, 2014. The event was attended by representatives from diplomatic missions, Azerbaijani government officials, members of parliament and local experts in the field. The report of the event, which is uploaded to the organization's website, is full of statements condemning Russia's aggression against Georgia and Ukraine, its annexation of Crimea, its massive use of propaganda both for internal and external purposes and calls for serious Western presence in the region and a stronger response to Russia's actions (See Eurasia Partnership Foundation 2014). Some of them are worth reading:

> "The West needs to be serious about taking care of the Crimea case, otherwise the former Soviet States may lose confidence in them."

"Azerbaijan must make a choice in favour of the US and its European partners, as it is not the neighbours to the North or South who will support Azerbaijan."

The National Endowment for Democracy: The NED is active in the post-Soviet region with its four "core institutes" — the National Democratic Institute for International Affairs, the International Republican Institute, the American Centre for International Labour Solidarity and the Centre for International Private Enterprise — which represent the two major American political parties, the labour movement and the business community, respectively. Although it is mostly financed by governmental institutions, the NED claims to be "independent from the US Government" and points out that this status "allows it to work with many groups abroad who would hesitate to take funds from the US Government" (NED 2016). The spectrum of activities of these four institutes are so large that it is beyond the scope of this book to cover all of them. These activities include cooperation with civil society organizations, local election monitoring organizations, business associations, grassroots business communities, providing support to reforms of governmental institutions, programs for involving women and youth in political activities and conducting opinion surveys.

Since the early 1990s, the National Endowment for Democracy has also been engaged in providing assistance to political "democratic" parties in some post-Soviet countries through the International Republican Institute (IRI) and the National Democratic Institute for International Affairs (NDI). The political party assistance of these institutes includes a wide range of activities, such as training seminars and conferences, targeting party leaders, elected representatives, and candidates who represent different political parties. The political party assistance provided by these institutes is funded mostly by the USAID and to a much lesser scale by the NED, the State Department, international organizations such as the World Bank and private institutions (Bader 2010: 37; Sussman 2010: 87). However, it has not been possible to access statistics about the expenses of these organizations on party assistance in the post-Soviet region. Nor was it possible to find this information for comparable European organizations.

The Open Society Institution: The Open Society Institution (OSI) of George Soros has passed a noteworthy evolution process since it was founded in 1984 and become an important force with an annual budget of hundreds of millions of dollars, more than 30 separate foundations and sub-organizations (Sussman 2010: 102-103). Like many other non-governmental organizations, the OSI also portrays itself as an independent agency. Regional authoritarian leaders have very often blamed the foundation (along with many other Western non-governmental organizations) of supporting anti-government forces and interfering in the internal affairs in the region. For example, Georgia's former President George Shevardnadze acknowledged the shortcomings of the elections that led to the Rose Revolution but protested the Soros Foundation's involvement[7] in the process asking "why are international forces getting involved? What does Soros want?" (Ó Beacháin 2010: 209). The contribution of the foundation to the collapse of communism through supporting dissident activities and civil society groups across the Eastern Europe and the "colour revolutions" of recent years in the Former Soviet Union is also acknowledged by George Soros himself (CNN 2014).

European Non-Governmental Organizations

In the aftermath of the launch of the European Neighbourhood Programme, in 2006, the EU founded the European Instrument for Democracy and Human Rights (EIDHR) to work with non-state actors in non-EU countries. The EIDHR is focused particularly on civil society actors who make up 90% of the partners of the programs (the rest are international organizations) (Dobreva 2015). It is reported by a publication of the European Parliament that the EIDHR "does not require the consent of national authorities" to provide funding

---

7   Beissinger (2006: 20) reports that the local Georgian branch of the Soros Foundation supported Kmara (the NGO that spearheaded the Rose Revolution) out of its $350,000 election support program.

for civil society organizations (CSOs). The budget of the programme for the period 2007-2013 was €1,1 billion; although there was some rise for the next 6 years (2014-2020) but it did not make more than €1,3 billion. Support for civil society in the "common neighbourhood" countries has also been considered within broader assistance programmes. For example, 5% of the €15.433 billion budget of the European Neighbourhood Instrument (ENI) is to support civil society in the ENP partner countries.

EU support for civil society actors in the countries of the "common neighbourhood" gradually increased following the inception of the EaP in 2009. A Civil Society Forum was established for "promot[ing] contacts among civil society organisations and facilitat[ing] their dialogue with public authorities" (See European Commission 2011). Afterwards the forum built National Platforms in each EaP country. The platforms bring together almost all the pro-European civil society organizations in their respective countries. The tools they utilize for this purpose are wide-ranging. For example, the Moldovan National Platform (MNP), which brings together at least 35 non-governmental organizations, reports that:

> "[Between October 2013 – October 2014] [a] considerable number of pro-European promotional materials were published and distributed, including more than 6,000 leaflets about the DCFTA and AA, 1,000 brochures about the EaP CSF, 800,000 postal cards about the benefits of the EU Association Agreement, 12 posters and 40,000 EU binders. Additionally, 8 editions of the 'European Objective' newspaper in Romanian and Russian with approximately 100,000 copies were published and distributed as supplements to many national and local newspapers and 10 informative filters were intensively broadcasted on TV stations with national coverage" (eap-csf.eu 2014).

They also fight against Russia's soft power projection. The promotion of national culture and values, local languages, narratives against the domination of Russia, etc. has been on the top of the agenda of these National Platforms. Coordinating civil society actors, the national platforms also take a leading role in protesting the misdeeds of the public authorities, even when the EU leaders avoid publicly confronting regional governments.

The European Endowment for Democracy (EED): The EED, a brainchild of the Polish government that aims at supporting pro-

Western activities in the Eastern Neighbourhood, was established in October 2012. Originally the geographic focus of the EED was exclusively Eastern Partnership countries. Although in December 2014 the foundation began to support projects from Russia, the Arab world, and Central Asia, it is still mainly focused on the EaP region. With the motto "supporting the unsupported", and with flexibility and minimal bureaucracy, the foundation provides support to civil society groups, pro-Western media, political parties, non-registered NGOs, trade unions and other social groups. The organization, according to its executive director, is specifically aimed to provide alternative to Russia's state media that meddle in domestic affairs of the regional countries (Dempsey 2015). It is reported that the fund provided by the European Commission to the EED has been doubled to €12 million for the period 2016-18 following the positive evaluation of the work the institution had done in previous years (European Parliament (2015).

German Foundations: Germany, as the largest economy of the European Union, plays a principal role in the soft power projection of the EU. Key actors in Germany's strategic communication in the post-Soviet world are party-affiliated political foundations (*Stiftungen*). The internationally active party-affiliated actors from other countries are usually smaller and represented abroad with non-permanent agencies. But the German party foundations are represented with permanent offices in many countries around the world, including in the former Soviet Union. Many scholars have pointed out that the work of these party institutes was part of the official foreign policy of their respective countries, despite the fact that they were autonomous in formal terms (Bader 2010; Carothers 2006b; Pogorelskaja 2002; Sussman 2010).

The largest *Stiftungen* operating in the region are the Konrad Adenauer Stiftung (KAS), the Friedrich Ebert Stiftung (FES), and the Hanns-Seidel Stiftung that are affiliated with the Christian Democratic Union (CDU), Social Democratic Party (SPD), Christian Social Union, respectively. The "non-governmental" status of the *Stiftungen* gives them more space to operate than diplomats are usually given. "Their informal face as an NGO-like organization" also allows them to establish contacts with groups and individuals who do not have contacts with diplomats (Lang 2015: 46; Brucker 2007: 304). The foundations, declaring democratization as their goal (Brucker 2007: 308), are particularly specialized in the promotion of European values, culture, policies and institutions. The foundations also award scholarships for Ph.D., bachelor's and master's degree students from regional countries.

Some other Non-Governmental Organizations: In addition to the above mentioned non-governmental organizations, some of the other EU member states are also actively involved in soft power projection into the EaP region through similar institutions. For example, Dutch party institutes — Eduardo Frei Stichting (EFS), Alfred Mozer Stichting (AMS), and the International Bureau of VVD (Volkspartiy voor Vrijheid en Democratie or People's Party for Freedom and Democracy) provide support to civil society organizations and liberal-minded political parties in the regional countries. These institutes are also engaged in political party assistance in the EaP countries, albeit in a considerably more limited scale than the above-mentioned six actors. The three institutes together or in cooperation with other institutions organize trainings for political parties, "leadership academies" for youth from the most relevant parties. These activities are aimed at familiarizing local parties with the political platforms of Western countries, developing their media skills, providing platforms for reflecting on the problems and shortcomings of their respective parties, and involving young people and women in politics. These party institutes are supported by the Matre programme of the Dutch Ministry of Foreign Affairs. The program was established in 1993 and aims "to support democratisation in Central and Eastern Europe" and "to contribute to EU enlargement policy and the European Neighbourhood Policy (ENP)". Through the Matre programme Nederland spent €44.3 million on various projects in the Eastern Partnership countries between 2008-2014. The programme also supports Netherlands Institute for Multiparty Democracy (NIMD), another Dutch non-governmental organization that works also in the FSU (particularly in South Caucasus). Established in 2000, NIMD has a regional office for the Eastern European Neighbourhood which covers Georgia, Armenia, Azerbaijan, and Ukraine and is one of the six organizations (the others are NDI, IRI, KAS, FES) that offer the largest assistance to political parties in the EaP countries.⁸

Foreign Aid

The civilian aid of the USA and the EU countries to the "common neighbourhood" states has played a pivotal role in the formation of pro-Western sentiments amongst many people across the region. Although the aid provided by the Western community might not always pursue geopolitical objectives, this has truly affected the image of the West in the regional countries and consequently boosted its soft power. Many Western governmental (such as USAID, the embassies of the USA and some EU members) and international non-governmental organizations (such as the Open Society Foundation, World Vision, and Oxfam) have been involved in this process at different times since the very beginning of the post-Cold War period. Below a quick review is given about the activities of these organizations and the consequences of their work.

American Assistance

In 1992, the US Congress passed the Freedom for Russia and Emerging Eurasian Democracies and the Open Market Support Act (FSA). A US Congress report states that between 1992 and 2007 the United States provided more than $28 billion in assistance to the former Soviet states (excluding the Baltic States, including Russia and Central Asia) (Tarnoff 2007). The American assistance to regional countries is largely assumed to have planted seeds of change for anti-government upheavals in Ukraine, Georgia, and Kyrgyzstan (ibid.). These three countries, prior to the "colour revolutions" since the collapse of the Soviet Union, had received a substantial amount of US assistance, a part of which was earmarked to civil society and political party trainings. The above-mentioned report points out that before the "colour revolutions" the United States

---

8   Max Bader (2010: 36) estimates that "these six organizations probably account for over ninety per cent of expenditures on party assistance worldwide."

had sent $807 million in aid to Georgia, $2.1 billion to Ukraine, and $408 million to Kyrgyzstan (including $138 million, $453 million, and $94 million respectively in democracy aid) (Tarnoff 2007).

USAID is the leading American government agency that is responsible for administering civilian foreign aid. The organization began operating in the post-Soviet region after the collapse of the Soviet Union. Since the early 1990s it has been involved in a very wide range of activities throughout regional countries with strong financial backing. It is involved in supporting various initiatives to stimulate economic growth, develop democratic institutions, enhance energy security, and improve health and education. It helps improve social services, ensures the integration of disadvantaged, vulnerable groups and women in social and political activities, amongst other activities. Initially this aid made an important contribution to the success of pro-Western anti-government forces in Eastern Europe and the former Soviet region. It is reported that the US government spent $41 million on Serbian civil society groups that were in the forefront of the Bulldozer Revolution in 2000 (Bessinger 2006: 20).

In 1990s, amidst economic decline, political instability, war and chaos, the aid provided by these donors was gratefully embraced by local people. Particularly the aid for people in war-torn zones and internally displaced persons (IDPs) was of immeasurable value for thousands of people in the region. As an IDP family in Azerbaijan, my family was one of the recipients of the aid after having fled our home in Kalbajar leaving behind everything we had in the wake of the Armenian occupation of the town in 1993. Living in desperate conditions in a yard of a hospital many of us looked forward to monthly aid (particularly food) brought to us by USAID. As a child in those years I first came to know about USAID when I read its name on the packages we were given.

The agency also supports educational initiatives. For example, with a USAID grant, a master's degree programme in property management with European-based course offerings was launched at Belarusian State Technological University, in partnership with Lithuania's Vilnius Gediminas Technical University. Although the program is open to Belarusian, Lithuanian and foreign students, in the 2014-2015 academic year only Belarusian students were enrolled in the program. The agency pays special attention to people-to-people contacts between regional countries and the USA. Such a program called "Community Connections" is in operation in Belarus. The website of USAID reports that since 2006 the program has provided over 340 Belarusian professionals in business, education, law, civil society and government the opportunity to gain practical experience in the United States from their American counterparts within their respective fields (USAID 2016).

The aid provided by the organization is particularly important for empowering the civil society institutions in the regional countries. It helps civil society organizations increase civic engagement, supports the oversight of local governance and decentralization reform at central and local levels, supports independent media, helps targeted media outlets to improve their professional capacity to produce fact-based, quality content as well as act as effective media watchdogs, etc. The agency carries out more projects in Georgia, Moldova, Ukraine, Armenia and at lesser extent in Belarus and Azerbaijan.

European Assistance

Over the years since the collapse of the Soviet Union, the EU, the largest aid donor in the world, has initiated three broad projects to coordinate its assistance to the former Soviet States in their transition to market economies and democratic political reforms: (1) The Technical Assistance to Commonwealth of Independent States (TACIS) in 1991-2006; (2) The European Neighbourhood and Partnership Instrument (ENPI) in 2007-2013; (3) The European Neighbourhood Instrument (ENI) in 2014-2020 (Table 2).

The Assistance of the European Union to the "Common Neighbourhood" Countries			
The Programme Name	Focus Countries	Time Period	Budget
TACIS	Former Soviet Countries (excluding the Baltic States, including Russia and Mongolia)	1991-2007	€ 7,3 billion
ENPI	ENP partner countries and Russia	2007-2013	€11.2 billion
ENI	ENP partner countries and Russia	2014-2020	€15.43 billion

Table 2. The EU assistance to the EaP countries

TACIS was the first initiative of the EU to engage with the post-Soviet countries and deliver technical support to their political and economic transformation policies. A publication of the European External Action Service (EEAS) distinguishes two phases of the programme: demand-driven (1991-1999) and dialogue-driven (2000-2006). While in the former period the EU organized its assistance in accordance with the requests of the ministries of the partner countries, in the last seven years it began to uphold conditionality in its cooperation with those countries. During the second phase the EU expected the partner countries to demonstrate commitment to policy reforms in order to further the cooperation and allocate resources.

In the next long-term assistance programme following TACIS, post-Soviet countries were merged with the Mediterranean countries which previously were addressed within the Mediterranean Economic Development Assistance (MEDA) programme—a twin initiative to TACIS. The European Neighbourhood and Partnership Instrument (ENPI) coordinated EU assistance with those countries between 2007-2013. In 2014, the third phase of EU assistance to the neighbourhood countries started with the announcement of the European Neighbourhood Instrument (ENI). The assistance to the partner countries is formed separately within comprehensive multi-annual single support framework agreements. The priority areas of the instrument are boosting small businesses, civil-society engagement, climate change action, easier mobility of people, energy cooperation, gender equality promotion, gradual economic integration, people-to-people contacts, transport connections, youth and employment.

Apart from these assistance programmes, the EU has allocated loans and aid to the "common neighbourhood" countries on a bilateral basis. For example, in the immediate aftermath of Yanukovych's fall, the EU Commission announced a large support package for Ukraine. The package included overall support of €11 billion over the next seven years from the EU budget and international financial institutions, including up to €1.4 billion in grants from the member states (European Commission 2014). EU member states themselves are also involved in development aid to many countries around the world. For example, Germany's development aid in total amounted to €10.7 billion in 2013 and was delivered to many countries around the world primarily by the German Federal Enterprise for International Cooperation (GIZ). The GIZ is, with an annual turnover of €1.9 billion (2013) and more than 16,000 employees in 130 countries, the main public institution in implementing Germany's development aid (Lang 2015: 47). It has been operating in the "common neighbourhood" since the early 1990s. Besides Germany, other EU member states also provide development aid to countries in this region (Sadowski 2015).

Limitations of the Western Soft Power Policies

Western powers had to pursue these soft power policies in a regional and social context which had had historically few cultural and political links with the West. On the one hand, the historical ties, cultural and linguistic proximity between Russia and regional countries, the existence of Russian minorities in those countries, and on the other hand the restricted space for free and independent media, have made it hard for Western soft power channels to effectively operate in the region and triumph over contending narratives. Although the appeal of European narratives and the desire for closer relations with the West are quite strong amongst the regional people, Russia is also considered by many as an indispensable and/or strategic partner (Lang 2015: 37). Due to this vagueness, the pro-European sentiments in the region, though widespread, are "shallow and confused" (Popescu *et al.* 2009a: 324; Lang 2015: 37). Moreover, not everybody is enthusiastic about Western values. Although pro-Western liberal groups glorify the political and civil liberties the West promotes, traditional segments of societies oppose some of these liberties, for example LGBT rights. The observation of Nicu Popescu and Andrew Wilson (2009b: 4) concludes that:

> "The EU is comprehensively outplayed by Russia in the neighbourhood media. Few people in the neighbourhood read or watch EU media, and other than Ukraine, none of the six states has a free media market. Russian media both takes an active role in domestic politics in the neighbourhood and shapes the way citizens see international events."

Towards the end of 2016, the challenges the EU faced in its internal politics, particularly the disintegration crisis, financial crisis, growing right-wing populism among others shook the foundations of the liberal democratic model of the West and affected the perception of the EU and United States in the "shared neighbourhood" (Qasimov 2016a). A publication by European Parliament lamented that:

> "It is difficult to deny that the Union's 'soft power' has suffered considerably in recent times: internal divisions, inadequate policy delivery, and mounting populism have all contributed to creating an environment (even inside the EU itself) significantly more receptive to their messaging – which, in turn, further undermines that 'soft power' and, more generally, EU influence" (See European Parliament 2016).

This observation is confirmed by a political analyst from the South Caucasus, who writes that:

> "… the increase of centrifugal tendencies within the EU have dealt a crushing blow to the reputation of the Union in the post-Soviet region and given ammunition to Kremlin propaganda; the internal challenges of the EU are

used by Russian propagandists to portray Western integration projects as a perilous alternative to a Russia-led Eurasian Union... Russian-sponsored news outlets convincingly argue that an EU that is stuck in several crises and at the verge of collapse cannot be a worthy economic and political bloc to trust in" (Qasimov 2016a).

Western self-projection has also been damaged by its failure to successfully handle the challenges the EU and the USA encountered in their policies concerning the post-Soviet region. This has been reflected in its policies with respect to the ethno-territorial conflicts in the region and in a number of shortcomings in the EU's and the USA's engagement with regional conflicts. The West appears to have limited leverage to seriously affect the ethno-territorial conflicts in the "shared neighbourhood" — a region which is embroiled in many such conflicts (only one country — Belarus — has not been inflicted with such a conflict). It is rather important for the West to be influential in its conflict resolution policies in order to overhaul its image. However, this has not happened yet. Particularly in the South Caucasus, neither the EU nor the USA can exert effective influence on frozen conflicts. It is due to this fact that voices have recently started to be heard from the region questioning if "the West [in fact] recognizes the South Caucasus as a de-facto Russian sphere of influence" (Qasimov 2016b). This threatens to erode the credibility of European projects among the publics of the Eastern Neighbourhood.

On the other hand, the fact that the West cannot back its soft power projection in the "common neighbourhood" states with equally strong hard power, damages its image in the region. In Georgia (2008) and Ukraine (2014), the transatlantic alliance, in general, demonstrated its reluctance to confront Russia militarily. This makes the regional people reconsider their geopolitical strategies and refrain from provoking Russia into military action.

The EU's reluctance to promise membership perspective to the countries in the EaP has also been regularly criticized by pro-Western groups in the region (Nielsen *et al.* 2013). Many commentators rightfully argue that "the membership perspective is the EU's biggest soft power asset and removing it reduces its leverage" (Nielsen *et al.* 2013: 16). Although for the countries (Azerbaijan, Armenia, and Belarus) that are not enthusiastic or hopeful about this perspective this situation is not a serious concern, for the ones who have been traditionally seeking to join the Union it causes a depressive effect and disillusionment. It might be difficult to say how much positive difference the existence of this perspective would make in the policies of the governments (Nielsen *et al*. 2013: 16), but it would definitely be a great incentive for the people of those countries. The lack of this incentive discourages regional countries to undertake "overly costly" political and economic reforms on their Euro-Atlantic integration path (ibid.). For example, while the EU allocated €120.4 million to Georgia between 2007-2010 within the ENPI, it was reported that the costs of the Georgian criminal law reform alone, which was one of the priorities of the EU-Georgia Action Plan, was estimated to be almost €130 million (Rinnert 2011: 8).

The underfunding of Western soft power projects with regard to the "common neighbourhood" countries has been another shortcoming that is often criticized by political experts from the region (Nielsen *et al*. 2013). As the previous section concluded, neither the EU nor the USA has ever demonstrated a serious and consistent interest to pull the "common neighbourhood" states into their military and political structures and as such has not invested significant resources in policies with regard to this region. Rather they have tried to block Russia's policies to build EU or NATO-like organizations with those countries. This has been reflected in the EU's and the US's regional soft power policies, as well. The projects that address the "shared neighbourhood" countries have been often underfunded. For example, the EU's Eastern Partnership programme, which has been the major framework of relations between the EU and regional states since 2009, has been regularly criticized for its limited budget (Makarychev *et al*. 2012) and for being "stingier… compared to the pre-accession aid" provided to the Central and Eastern European candidates following the end of the Cold War (Nielsen *et al*. 2013: 17).

Despite this type of problems, public opinion polls conducted in the "common neighbourhood" have demonstrated that these problems have not strictly deteriorated the image of the West in this region. For example, 90% of the Georgian people supported the country's joining the European Union in a March 2017 poll conducted by the International Republican Institute (IRI 2017). Although the other regional countries were not as enthusiastic about the EU, they still had a sizable number of EU supporters. For example, despite extensive anti-Western propaganda by pro-Russian groups (See next chapter), in a late 2016 poll, more than half of the respondents (51%) in Ukraine supported admission to the EU which was significantly higher than the supporters for the Customs Union with Russia, Belarus and Kazakhstan (19%) (IRI 2016).

Conclusion

This chapter explored the soft power—hard power nexus in the case of Western policies concerning the "common neighbourhood" in accordance with the principles of the soft power model presented in Chapter 2. It indicated that, as expected by the hypothesis about the use of soft power as an expansive instrument and the use of hard power as a defensive tool, the EU and the United States have sought to draw the regional countries to their orbit through the use of soft power. Although they have demonstrated strong declarative support for the Euro-Atlantic aspirations of the regional countries, they have not become militarily involved in the region when these aspirations encountered Russia's military response. However, in spite of the reliance on soft power in regional intervention and the choice not to confront Russia militarily, the West has strengthened its military force along the Eastern borders, as predicted by the assumption of the model about hard power: Soft power is not a substitute for hard power, and, therefore, states need and must pay adequate attention to the development of their hard power.

The chapter also explored the soft power potential of Western powers (i.e. the EU and the United States) and their policies to wield power over popular opinion in the "common neighbourhood" countries. The chapter firstly focused on Western self-projection. It found that the attractive human-constructed assets of Western powers (i.e. economic prosperity, higher living standards, high ranking universities, culture, political values, etc.) effectively armed their state-managed soft power projection to the post-Soviet space during the period under study (2004-2016). As expected by the soft power—hard power nexus of the model, the possession of strong hard power resources allowed the EU and United States to establish a long range of propaganda and public diplomacy instruments to communicate with the "common neighbourhood" countries. The chapter also concluded that the policies to reach out to the domestic non-state actors of the target countries with the intention of affecting the policies of their respective governments have been used by Western powers ever since the early years of the Cold War. Analysing Western propaganda and public diplomacy projects, it concluded that although the EU and United States sought to wield soft power in the "common neighbourhood", their projects were usually underfunded. The chapter claimed that this could be because of their reluctance to accept these countries into the Western political and military structures as fully-fledged members. The EU and United States appeared more interested in preventing Russia's regional integration projects rather than opening the door of the EU and NATO to the regional states which *inter alia* could have led to disastrous consequences in relations with Russia.

4. Soft Power in Russia's Practice (2004 – 2016)

This chapter replicates the structure and goals of the preceding chapter and applies them in the analysis of Russian soft power policies with respect to six post-Soviet states (Azerbaijan, Armenia, Georgia, Moldova, Ukraine and Belarus). Its analysis aims to test the hypothesis that amidst the rivalries between nuclear armed great powers, soft power serves as an expansive instrument, while military power is used by the conflicting sides to defend themselves and back up their foreign policies. In its analysis of Russian soft power, the chapter follows the principles of the soft power model presented above. This model differentiates two primary sources of soft power as self-projection (attractiveness) and state-managed projection. It describes self-projection as based on the natural endowments and human-constructed assets a state possesses.

The model points out that a state which is well-endowed with rich natural resources obtains favourable conditions in which to a build successful economy and attractive culture. These human-constructed qualities have been designated as a necessary condition to build an attractive image to project to the foreign publics. Thus, the model argues that states need appropriate policies in order to deliver their narratives to foreign countries and wield power over the minds and feelings of their people. These policies have been categorized as propaganda and public diplomacy. While propaganda is presented as a one-way communication strategy conducted through mostly international broadcasting (television, journals, newspapers, online media channels, etc.), public diplomacy has been conceptualized as a two-way communication strategy using instruments such as non-governmental organizations, scholarly exchange programs, cultural diplomacy, etc. The chapter also tests the soft power – hard power nexus of the model which *inter alia* argues that soft power is not a substitute for hard power, and, therefore, states need and must pay adequate attention to the development of their hard power.

The chapter proceeds as follow. The next section explores the soft power—hard power nexus in Russia's policies concerning the "common neighbourhood". This is to be followed by a broader section on Russia's soft power policies with respect to this region. The section analyses Russia's self-projection, strategic narratives, international broadcasting, academic exchange programs, non-governmental organizations, economic ties and foreign aid. The chapter ends with a short conclusion. The chapter by no means provides an all-inclusive coverage of all dimensions of Russian soft power. Due to time and space limitations, it will only briefly review key elements of Russia's soft power *vis-à-vis* the regional countries.

Soft Power vs. Hard Power in Russia's Policies

Russia has developed a complicated strategy to keep the regional post-Soviet countries in its orbit and prevent "the perceived erosion of its 'sphere of influence'" due to EU and NATO expansion (March et al. 2006: 351–52). The Kremlin launched several integration projects to retain the regional countries under its control and prevent their drifting away from Russia's orbit towards competing projects, particularly Western-led integration projects. In the 1990s, projects such as the Collective Security Treaty, the Commonwealth of Independent States (CIS), the Economic Union Treaty (1993), the Free Trade Agreement (1994) failed to achieve most of their declared goals. Ukraine never signed the charter of the CIS, Turkmenistan declared itself neutral at the outset, and Georgia left the organization in the aftermath of the 2008 war. In the early 2000s, Russian policymakers decided to establish a Common Economic Space that would integrate Russia, Belarus, Ukraine, and Kazakhstan in a common economic union. It was supposed to be an EU-like institution and was predicted by the Kremlin to be formed by 2008-2010. However, the eruption of the "colour revolutions" in the region complicated these plans.

Following the Orange Revolution in Ukraine (2004-2005), the Kremlin sought to build a fundamentally new integration regime—the economic union of Eurasian independent states, or the Eurasian

Economic Union. In January 2010, Russia, with Belarus and Kazakhstan, launched its Customs Union (CU), which was framed in a way that excluded the participation of its members in any other free-trade agreement which the EaP had declared as one of its objectives. In the following years, Kyrgyzstan, Ukraine, and Armenia announced that they would cooperate with the CU. In October 2011, two weeks before the second Eastern Partnership Summit was to be held in Warsaw, then Prime Minister Vladimir Putin presented the plan to upgrade the CU into a Eurasian Union. In May 2014, in a move forward towards the Eurasian Union, Russia, Belarus, and Kazakhstan signed the treaty establishing the Eurasian Economic Union (EEU), which extended the provisions of the existing Eurasian Customs Union (ECU) and came into existence in 2015. Armenia and Kyrgyzstan became members of the ECU in 2015. The Union was envisioned by Moscow as a project which would enable the Kremlin to challenge the attractiveness of the EU in its neighbourhood and "to create an alternative power centre for integration to the EU's normative power" (Vilpišauskas et al. 2012: 11).

However, the underlying problem regarding Putin's new initiative is that like previous generations of Russia's regional integration projects, the ECU is first and foremost a political project with vague economic benefits for participating states. Although the declared goals of these projects were economic, they were in fact pursuing predominantly political objectives. The countries that these projects target do not hold weighty shares in Russia's overall trade. Thus, regional economic trade, which has steadily declined over the past twenty years, is of less significance for Russia. The share of CIS states in total Russian exports dropped from 22 per cent in 1994 to 14 percent in 2013. Their share in Russian imports dropped from 27 to 12 percent in the same period (See Federal Statistics Service of Russia 2017). The declining role of the neighbourhood countries in Russia's foreign economic activities can also be seen in the share of the CIS countries in Russia's external investments: these countries' share in Russia's total investment abroad was around 22 percent in 2003, but this figure went down to a mere 2.5 percent in 2013 (See Central Bank of the Russian Federation 2017).

Alongside economic and political integration, Russia has also pushed NATO-style military integration in its neighbourhood. The Collective Security Treaty, which was signed back in early 1990s by Armenia, Kazakhstan, Belarus, Russia, Uzbekistan, and Tajikistan, Georgia, and Azerbaijan, transformed into fully-fledged organization (the Collective Security Treaty Organization (CSTO)) in 2002.[9] The treaty aimed at providing a common defence system if one member were to fall under attack, and promoted cooperation among member states against terrorism, extremism, separatism, organized crime, drug trafficking and so forth. Although the principles remained the same, transformation into an organization strengthened its structure and enlarged the responsibilities and competence of the Council of Ministers of Foreign Affairs, the Council of Ministers of Defence, and the Committee of Secretaries of the Security Councils. The CSTO created its Collective Rapid Reaction Force (CRRF) in February 2009, which, according to then Russian President Medvedev, would be *on par* with NATO (Oldberg 2011: 38). The CRRF was largely a response to NATO's plans to consolidate its forces in Eastern Europe through enlargement and the deployment of a missile defence system. It was formed based on Russia's 98th Airborne Division and the 31st Airborne Assault Brigade.

Although Putin noted the European Union as a model to emulate in its regional integration projects, his methodology of integrating the neighbouring countries has been different from that of the EU. As opposed to the "soft power" approach of the EU, the Kremlin policies to discipline those countries contained more hard power elements including economic power, military, and energy (Hagemann 2013; Bugajski *et al*. 2016). The display of military force takes a central place in Russia's policies against the EU and NATO enlargement. At the 43rd Munich Security Conference in 2007, President Putin made clear that Russia would no longer tolerate any further expansion of NATO towards Russia's borders. He stated that in the territories of the former Soviet Union Russia's opposition

---

9   In 1999 Azerbaijan, Georgia, and Uzbekistan left the treaty. In 2006 Uzbekistan re-joined and in 2012 left again.

to NATO's enlargement would not be limited only to verbal protests as it was in Eastern Europe and Baltic states but would potentially cause a geopolitical crisis.

Soon after the Munich Security Conference, in August 2008 Russia deployed military power against Georgia. Prior to the war, Georgia, under the leadership of President Mikheil Saakashvili, was advancing on the road to NATO membership and "Russia [was] gradually being forced to retreat from this region" (Haas 2007). Therefore, Moscow started to militarize the breakaway regions of Georgia in the hopes that Georgian leader Saakashvili would respond with a military attack that would provide a reason for Russia to intervene (Van Herpen 2014). Svante Cornell (2009: 134) observed that "Russia 'set a trap' for Saakashvili, and... [he] stepped into it."

It is reported that Western leaders regularly warned the Georgian leadership against a military venture and called them to "avoid a direct military confrontation with Russia at all costs..." saying that "You cannot prevail. It simply is not possible" (See Reuters 2008). Nevertheless, Saakashvili decided to counter Moscow's heavy militarization of the breakaway regions with a sudden attack. The five-day Russian-Georgian war in August 2008 resulted in a devastating defeat for Georgia. Despite Saakashvili's expectations, NATO did not launch a war against Russia to protect Georgia. Consequently, Russia established its control over Georgia's breakaway regions, recognizing the independence of the so-called republics of Abkhazia and South Ossetia and underlining the irreversibility of this decision. As Washington's envoy to the Caucasus, Matthew Bryza, reportedly warned Tbilisi before the war that a military clash with Russia would destroy any chance Georgia had of entering NATO (Spiegel 2010).

In Georgia, Russia demonstrated that it would not refrain from using military force if its control over the geopolitical posture of the countries in its sphere of influence is at stake. However, although the consequences of the war became a serious obstacle for Georgia's pro-Western path and alarmed NATO states, it failed to completely banish Western influence from the post-Soviet space. In

2009, the EU launched its Eastern Partnership programme and offered regional states deeper European integration. The constituents of the programme, particularly the agreements (i.e. Association Agreements and Deep and Comprehensive Free Trade Deal) it offered, outraged Russian officialdom. The establishment of the DCFTA process between the regional states and the EU would single out their participation in Russia's Customs Union which was to form the basis of its Eurasian Union.

Prior to the EaP summit in Lithuania's capital Vilnius in late 2013, Russia threatened the countries (Moldova, Ukraine, Georgia, and Armenia) that were preparing to sign or initialize the agreements with the EU. Russia's Deputy Prime Minister Dmitry Rogozin explicitly warned Moldova that the country's pro-European choice might cause them "to freeze in winter" and to lose its control over the breakaway region of Transnistria (See Moscow Times 2013). In a later move the Kremlin imposed some trade restrictions on Moldova and generated problems for the inflow of labour migrants. Similarly, the Kremlin threatened Ukraine that signing the agreement would turn out to be catastrophic for the Ukrainian economy and generate political and social unrest mentioning specifically the possibility of separatist movements springing up in the Russian-speaking east and south of Ukraine (Walker 2013). Like Armenian President Serzh Sarkysan, who abruptly opted for the Customs Union in return for lower prices in natural gas imports and a security guarantee against Azerbaijan and Turkey, in a surprising *volte face* the Ukrainian President Yanukovych made an abrupt about-turn in favour of the Customs Union under Russian pressure in return for $15 billion counteroffer and discount in gas prices (from $400 to $268 per 1000 cubic meters) (Rutland 2015: 137). Although the Armenian president managed to fulfil the agreement, Yanukovych failed due to the sudden outbreak of massive popular upheaval, which became known as the "Euromaidan revolution" supported by the European and American leaders (Müllerson 2014).

In the aftermath of the Euromaidan revolution, Russia's leaders declared their readiness to intervene in post-Soviet countries when Western-backed anti-regime protestors threatened the existing governments. For example, the head of the Russian Federal Security Service (FSB), Aleksandr Bortnikov, in a meeting with the representatives of CIS intelligence services, unequivocally stated that the FSB "considers that there can be in [the CIS] countries forces with definite intentions concerning the overthrow of the authorities" (Newsru.com 2014). Pointing to the Euromaidan revolution, he said that the attempts of the oppositional groups and foreign forces to "overthrow the authorities with the goal of changing the constitutional system" is unacceptable and "we will act harshly in the framework of the law not to give an opportunity to destructive forces to influence the situation in our countries" (ibid.). Apparently, following the ousting of President Yanukovych, Russia became more assertive in declaring the possibility of using military intervention to prevent anti-government protests of a similar scale in territories of allies (McDermott 2015). Such protests or "colour revolutions" were mentioned along with other security threats that Russia encountered in the recent Military Doctrine of December 2014 and National Security Strategy of December 2015.

Likewise, in the other former Soviet countries in its shared neighbourhood with the EU, Russia sees the existing interstate or intrastate territorial disputes or ethnic conflicts (e.g. the Nagorno-Karabakh conflict between Armenia and Azerbaijan and the Transnistria issue in Moldova) as a tool of influence. These conflicts have problematized the Euro-Atlantic path of the parent states, as neither the EU nor NATO would recruit a new member that cannot exercise full control over its territory, is involved in internal conflicts with breakaway regions, or has Russian troops on its soil (Siddi *et al.* 2012: 7). When the geopolitical situation of the regional states develops to the dislike of Russia, Moscow escalates those conflicts, and through this leverage has so far been able to reach its objectives. For example, many observers have concluded that "The 'de-freezing' and rapid escalation of the conflicts in Abkhazia and South Ossetia was mainly the consequence of US-Russian disputes in the international arena and the direct and indirect intervention of foreign powers in the conflicts" (Siddi *et al.* 2012: 7). Russia tries to transform the countries that host these conflicts into a federation or confederation, a political structure that would give the autonomous entities crucial influence over the foreign policies of the central governments. This would allow Russia to slow down, if not completely avert, the transatlantic ties of those countries with the help of the pro-Russian autonomous regions (Bugajski et al. 2016: 166).

To this end, the Russian policymakers invest a significant part of the country's GDP on military reinforcements. Russia is also pursuing a comprehensive military reforms program that is aimed at rearming Russian military. According to the initial plan which was unveiled during Dmitry Medvedev's presidency, i.e. when oil prices were on the rise, Russia was planning to spend 13 trillion roubles, or approximately $425 billion at the exchange rates of those years, on modernizing 70 percent of military equipment by 2020 (Gorenburg 2010: 1). In early 2016, the Russian Defence Ministry stated that the country was successfully implementing military reforms at twice the expected speed, despite the economic decline that Russia found itself in (TASS 2016a).

Since 2014 Russia has been continuously carrying out military build-up in the territories along its European borders, particularly in Kaliningrad, a Russian exclave sandwiched between Poland and Lithuania. NATO has warned that Moscow is deploying "thousands of troops, including mechanized and naval infantry brigades, military aircraft, modern long-range air defence units and hundreds of armoured vehicles in the territory" (Wesolowsky 2015). Particularly Russia's stationing of nuclear-capable Iskander-M missiles into the area is read as an "alarming threat" in the West. Moscow has also made a radical change in its commitments to the use of nuclear weapons. While the Soviet Union undertook not to use nuclear arms first, Putin's Russia does not single out this possibility. On the other hand, with military intervention in Georgia and Ukraine, Moscow, as NATO's secretary-general Jens Stoltenberg observes, "has shown it can deploy forces at very short notice…above all, it has shown a willingness to use force" (See NATO 2015).

However, along with developing its military power, Russia has also started to rethink the role of soft power in the aftermath of the first wave of the "colour revolutions". The geopolitical developments in the region since the collapse of the Soviet Union demonstrated that economic pressure, military force, energy, and other hard power elements failed to avert the growing influence of Western powers in the region which was based on non-hard power. Although Russia's military power succeeded in preventing the path of Georgia and Ukraine into the EU and NATO, it did not suffice to pull these countries fully back into Russia's orbit.

Notwithstanding Russia's military capabilities and its nuclear arsenal, three of the regional countries opted for alignment with Western powers signing the Association Agreements and free trade deals. The crucial role of the general public and non-governmental organizations in this process and the success of popular protests urged Russia to reconsider its foreign policy techniques in accordance with soft power principles. In 2008, a Russian political scientist, Gleb Pavlovsky, the then adviser to the Russian Presidential Administration, described the Orange Revolution as "a very useful catastrophe for Russia" and stated, "We learnt a lot" (quoted in Popescu *et al.* 2009b: 27). For Russian officials, it has become "impossible" to effectively defend national interests "without proper use of solid soft power resources" (See Official Website of Russia's Ministry of Foreign Affairs 2011). The remaining sections of this chapter will examine Russia's potential and its policies to develop power over popular opinion in the "common neighbourhood" countries.

Soft Power as Russia's Foreign Policy Tool

Russia's soft power has been one of the most debated political phenomena amongst scholars of international relations. In Western academic circles, a number of terms and expressions have been attributed to such policies of the Kremlin. Most Western experts argue that Russia's perception of soft power is rather different from that of Western countries (Saari 2014; Drent *et al.* 2015; Walker 2016). For example, the experts of the Netherlands Institute of International Relations point out that unlike the Western understanding of soft power "as a means to attract other countries to its own community", Russia perceives soft power as a tool "to influence or destabilise countries through non-military actions" (Drent et al. 2015: 10). For them, the Russian term *myagkaya sila* can be better translated as "soft force", rather than "soft power". Similarly, Andrew Monaghan (2013: 7) of the Chatham House claims that as Russia sees soft power "as a means of promoting Russian culture and language and countering 'soft' attacks on the country", a more appropriate term for Russia's understanding of this concept would be "soft strength". Another expert from the Chatham House proposed a new term to Russia's perception of soft power: "soft coercion" (Sherr 2013). Thus, there is a tendency amongst Western scholars to focus on the coercive elements of Russia's soft power while underestimating its potential to be loved and respected by people in the region.

Historically, co-optation, along with coercion, has been an integral part of Russia's strategy to expand its influence over foreign countries. Since the outset of imperial expansion, Russian leaders have paid significant attention to generate consent amongst the peoples of the lands where Russia was set to intervene. While during the Tsarist years these policies were guided largely by Christian ideals, which had a more local character, in the aftermath of the Bolshevik revolution Moscow adopted communist ideology with universal objectives and significant appeal amongst many peoples over the world. After the collapse of the USSR, Russia lost most of this soft power along with its military and economic power. Notwithstanding the fact that Moscow declared itself a liberal-market economy and remained largely committed to international cooperation in a number of international crises, for instance in the first Gulf war, its attractiveness dramatically plummeted in those years.

Throughout the 1990s, the Russian political elite mostly neglected policies of cultivating power over the public opinion abroad which once were one of the priorities of the Soviet government. Domestically, in those years Russia was experiencing political disorder, economic crises, internal wars, and the defeat of communist ideology which had been the cornerstone of Soviet soft power. The international conditions were not in favour of the former superpower, either. Moscow was withdrawing from international politics and recalling most of its personnel deployed to faraway countries. Under those circumstances, the soft power projects gradually faded in the foreign policies of the Kremlin. For example, Vladimir Shubin (2004: 110) writes that "in the 1990s approximately half of the Russian cultural centres in Africa were closed due to lack of funding". Thus, the primary reason for the apparent disinterest amongst Russian politicians in soft power was not due to lack of understanding of its importance, as some have argued (e.g. Van Herpen 2015: Kindle location 715 of 8957), but rather Russia's withdrawal from international politics and its enormous domestic socioeconomic and political problems.

After the political turmoil, economic crises and an unsuccessful war in Chechnya in the 1990s, Russia began an upward climb in the beginning of the new millennium. In the late 1990s, in response to the "unfriendly" geopolitical developments in its immediate neighbourhood Russia stepped into a more assertive foreign policy with overarching objectives. In 2003, the country managed to raise its GDP to the level it was in 1993 thanks to rising commodity prices. This propped up more assertive domestic and foreign policies of the new Russian President, Vladimir Putin. The growing military and economic capacity of the country allowed Russia to launch comprehensive policies to wield power over opinion beyond its borders. Moscow started to invest both in its military and non-military power to back up its international policies and counter the enlargement of the Euro-Atlantic military and political structures in the territories which it considered its "zone of privileged interests".

The 2000 Foreign Policy Concept stressed the importance of the promotion of "a positive perception of the Russian Federation in the world" and underlined the need "to popularize the Russian language and culture of the peoples of Russia in foreign states" and "to form a good-neighbour belt along the perimeter of Russia's borders" (Lankina *et al.* 2015: 103). This strategy gained momentum in the wake of the "colour revolutions" in Russia's backyard and the growth of the increasingly threatening Western soft power in the region. Russia claimed that since the end of the Cold War the USA had spent around 20 billion dollars in the former Soviet countries on non-governmental organizations, scholarly exchanges, civil society etc. for provoking pro-Western sentiments (Shilov 2014: 185). This urged both Russia's political elite to initiate more projects to wield influence on popular opinion in the "near abroad" and to steer the intervening influence of non-state actors in the region.

In 2007, the Russian Foreign Policy Review for the first time mentioned "soft power" as a new approach in Russia's foreign policy making (Kudors 2010: 2). The document stated that "A big role in modern diplomacy is played by factors, which are often described in terms of 'soft power'" (See Official Website of Russia's Ministry of Foreign Affairs 2007). The document made clear that the objective of Russia in using soft power was to build "the ability to influence the behaviour of other states". Both Russian officialdom and the expert community started speaking out about the importance of soft power as a tool to influence the domestic actors of other countries with the ultimate goal of affecting the policies of their respective governments. For example, a Russian expert, Gregory Filimonov (2010) argued that public diplomacy was "not just intervention in the minds, hearts and souls of people, but also an effective way of influencing the domestic affairs of a sovereign state".

Thus, amidst the geopolitical challenges in its neighbourhood Russia imported the Western concepts of soft power and public diplomacy and began to emulate the successful practices of Western powers. The import of these terms allowed the Russian authorities to avoid using old and pejorative terms, such as propaganda or psychological warfare about their own policies. The term "soft power" in Russia's latest Foreign Policy Concept (2013) was defined as "a comprehensive toolkit for achieving foreign policy objectives building on civil society potential, information, cultural and other methods and technologies alternative to traditional diplomacy" (See Official Website of Russia's Ministry of Foreign Affairs 2013). The concept mentions wielding soft power as a foreign policy goal of the state and underscores the importance of "improving the application of 'soft power' (ibid.).

Russia imported not only the concept of soft power but also emulated the instruments that the West had established to wield this power. The primary soft power tools of the Russian governments were a copy of the ones in the West. For example, RT emulated international news channels like BBC and CNN, the 'Russian World' foundation, and Rossotrudnichestvo was built on the basis of the model of USAID, Germany's Goethe Institute and the UK's British Council (Makarychev et al. 2015: 241).

The breakout of the Ukraine crisis in early 2014 brought about new elements into Russia's perception of soft power. The Kremlin reconsidered its soft power policies in general, its counter-revolutionary agenda in particular (Huseynov 2016). On the one hand, Russia's soft power policies with respect to the former Soviet Union, predominantly Ukraine, started to be more concentrated on one-way communication (i.e. propaganda) through media channels. Russian leaders began to put more emphasis on media and the dissemination of Russia-biased information. They described the media as "weapons" and the information war as "the main type of warfare" (Interfax 2015a; Yaffa 2014). Hence, the Kremlin also boosted the budget of its international media channels, for instance, there was a 41% hike in the 2015 budget of television channel RT compared to the previous year (Raybman 2014). Russia's state-directed projection also began to put more emphasis on programmes to discredit pro-Western governments in the "common neighbourhood" states and undermine their policies (Sherr 2015: 28; Drent et al. 2015: 10).

On the other hand, the Ukraine crisis made Russia become louder in declaring the possible use of military force to counter "colour revolutions" in the region (McDermott 2015). Russia's new Military Doctrine that was accepted in December 2014 and National Security Strategy that President Vladimir Putin approved at the end of 2015 characterize "colour revolutions" amongst the security threats that Russia is facing. These developments were widely interpreted as Russia's "[move] from securitizing the issue of anti-regime protests to militarizing it" (Bouchet 2016: 1). The presentation of those protests as a security threat would allow Moscow to intervene to protect pro-Russian political elite in the former Soviet countries.

However, although Russian leaders considered the possibility of responding to "colour revolutions" and hybrid warfare with conventional troops, they themselves were aware of the fact that this had little potential to be successful. That is why the Russian military was planning to develop its soft power concepts to fight against unconventional attacks (McDermott 2016). These concepts, which are not yet made public at the time of writing, are likely to include all the instruments that can be useful to influence popular opinion in and outside Russia. The statements of the Russian leaders demonstrate that the Kremlin is resolved to spare no effort to achieve this objective. For example, Russian Chief of General Staff Valery Gerasimov (2013), who believes that "responding to [hybrid warfare and "colour revolutions"] using conventional troops is impossible" (Sputniknews 2016b), had already written about these instruments in 2013:

> "The role of non-military means of achieving political and strategic goals has grown, and, in many cases, they have exceeded the power of force of weapons in their effectiveness. The focus of applied methods of conflict has altered in the direction of the broad use of political, economic, informational, humanitarian, and other non-military measures."

Thus, on the one hand Russia invests in soft power to influence the policies of the former Soviet states in the "common neighbourhood", to re-establish its control over them, and to get its foreign policies accepted as legitimate by local people, on the other hand it threatens with and prepares the legal ground for the use of military force if it fails in "softer" ways. The Ukraine crisis has evolved these two elements in Russia's foreign policy to an unprecedented level in the post-Soviet period.

Self-Projection

Russia is the largest country in the world with an area of approximately 17 mln. square kilometres. It is well endowed with natural resources. Russia is the second largest producer of fossil fuels, the third largest oil producer, the second largest natural gas producer and holds a significant share of all the world's available natural resources. The country also boasts the world's largest forest areas which account for approximately half of its territories. These natural resources have been historically a major enabling factor behind Russia's economic expansion and international standing. This has given the Russian people enormous potential to perform well in development of elements which this book regards as "human-constructed assets".

As a country that has a very old imperial past, Russia has been able to develop significantly attractive cultural properties over the centuries. The literature, music, theatre and other cultural elements produced in the Russian Empire and Soviet Union have made enormous contributions to global cultural heritage. Millions of people over the world, particularly in the countries that were previously a part of the USSR, still watch, listen, and read the works of Russia's cultural icons. Although its modern popular culture, arguably, fails to prevail over the attractiveness of that of America and Western Europe even in the former Soviet Union, Russia still has a strong cultural link with former Soviet countries. A public opinion poll conducted by the European Neighbourhood Barometer in 2014 found out that while just 11% and 40% of respondents feel a similarity with American and European cultures respectively, the number of people that feel closer to Russian culture was significantly higher—60% (See Figure 3; Enpi-info.eu 2014).

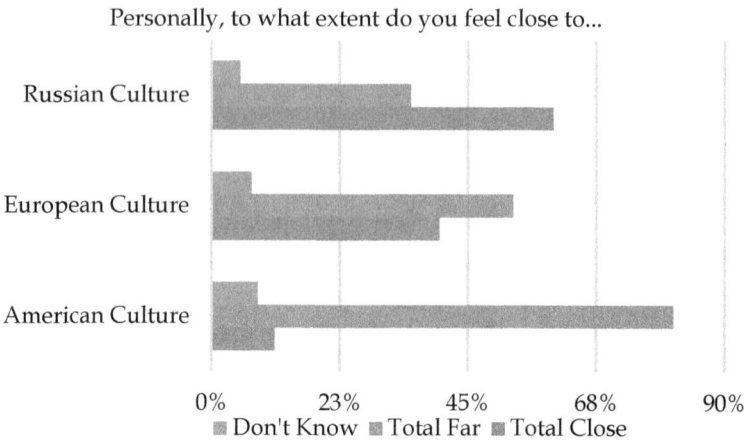

Figure 3. A public opinion poll in the EaP countries (conducted by the European Neighbourhood Barometer in 2014)

There are millions of people in the region who live with the nostalgia of Soviet times. A public survey in 2016 revealed that the majority of people between the age 35 and 64 think that their lives were better during the Soviet period than the present: Azerbaijan—69%, Armenia—71%, Belarus—53%, Georgia—51%, Moldova—60%, Ukraine—60% (Sputniknews 2016c). Similar results were reached by earlier polls (e.g. Esipova *et al.* 2013). Russia, being the successor of the Soviet Union, benefits from these sentiments and is able to wield power over the minds and feelings of the regional publics. It is partly due to the influence of shared history that a Gallup survey showed that 61 percent of those questioned said they approved of Russia's leadership (Ray 2011). This is a staggering number considering that the median percentage of approval for Russia across 104 countries over the world was only 27% in the same poll (ibid.).

The Russian language is one of the most important attributes of Russian soft power in the entire former Soviet Union. Although the number of Russian speakers over the globe has plummeted from 350 million (in the early 1990s) to 270-300 million (Panova 2015: 91-92), it is still widely spoken across the former Soviet Union. It is true that the English language is being taught more frequently than other languages at the schools of most of the regional countries

(Blauvelt 2013), but Russian is still more widespread than English. For example, in Georgia, one of the most Western-oriented countries of the region, while Russian is spoken by more than 70% of the overall population, the proficiency of English among Georgians is lower than 20% (Blauvelt 2013: 191). Not only in Georgia, but in the entire post-Soviet space, the Russian language is not considered by many as a "foreign" language in its real sense, "but rather a sort of second native language (regardless of how well they actually spoke it)" (Blauvelt 2013: 190). There is even growing interest in studying at Russian-language schools in some countries, particularly in Azerbaijan (See Azertag 2016).

Moscow supports this interest by establishing centres for learning the Russian language. For instance, in Armenia, since 2012, more than 100 such centres have been founded, where Russian-language courses are provided free of charge (Vardanyan 2015). This has been initiated by the Armenian Institute for Strategic Development, whose head Andranik Nikoghosyan in 2010 was awarded by the Russian President Dmitry Medvedev with the Friendship Order "for [his] great contribution to the development of cultural ties with Russia, for preserving and spreading the Russian language and culture abroad" (See Armenpress 2010).

However, although the Russian language is still popular in post-Soviet countries, the number of its speakers has faced a consistent decline in the region in recent years. Filimonov (2010) reports that "instead of the original 20,000 Russian-language schools in the former Soviet Union, now there are about 7,000." Besides, in this territory the number of children educated in the Russian language has fallen from 5 million to 3.1 million (ibid.). Although Russian is still spoken widely in Ukraine, Moldova and Belarus, it has ceased to be a language of everyday communication in the South Caucasus. On the other hand, a recent study by the Institute for Strategic Studies "Eurasia" has found that Russian speakers comprise a major part of emigrants from the former Soviet countries: Armenia—64%, Moldova—50%, Azerbaijan—35%-36%, Georgia—40%, Ukraine—32% (See Interfax 2015b). Tatiana Borzova, an expert of the Institute, called on the Russian leadership for more projects to support Russian speakers in those countries, stressing the fact that "Young people from Russian-speaking families are leaving the former Soviet Union, [if this remains so] in 10 years Russian influence in these countries will not exist (ibid.).

Narratives

Russian officials are most likely aware of the fact that "Soft power is effective only if its application generates and spreads positive social impulses and meanings" (Makarychev 2011: 2). During Soviet times, Russia used to have this potential. However, the disintegration of the USSR destroyed the ideological appeal of the communist utopia. This also debilitated the institutional basis which was necessary to continue the quite successful soft power policies of the Soviet Union (Maliukevičius 2013). Starting in the beginning of the new millennium, the soft power policies of the Kremlin started to be re-built and reinvigorated under the administration of President Putin. Particularly following the "colour revolutions", a wide range of fundamental measures were taken in this regard and the strategic narratives of the Kremlin began to be re-constructed. Russia began to develop its own normative agenda and put forward particular concepts for using its non-military arsenal (culture, language, media, etc.).

One of the most popular initiatives of the early 2000s was the concept of "sovereign democracy" that was prepared as a part of Moscow's efforts to counter Western soft power. In 2006, Vladislav Surkov, then deputy head of the presidential administration, pointed out that it was developed in response to the "colour revolutions" in the region (Surkov 2006). Although the concept was never coherently outlined, its two core ideas were clear from the beginning. Firstly, underlying the idea of sovereignty, the concept rejected any attempts of the Western states and institutions to meddle in the domestic affairs of Russia. Secondly, it stressed the fact that Russia has its own set of values, which are democratic but based on Russia's unique historical experience and its traditions (Popescu 2006). The concept, defending Russia's democracy, rejected the allegedly universal character of the Western standards of democracy. For the Russian leaders, "if there is western democracy, there should be an eastern democracy as well" (quoted in Popescu 2006: 1). However, Peter Shearman (2010: 23) correctly notes that Russia has not sought to export its model of democracy to other countries, or at least there is no evidence to argue otherwise.

In 2012, the Kremlin began publishing its own "Report on the Human Rights Situation in the European Union" to counter the negative assessments of the European powers on the conditions of human rights in Russia. The report, published in 2013, accused the EU of propagating of homosexuality and same-sex marriage. The Kremlin benefits from and inflames homophobic sentiments in the post-Soviet space to push the regional people against the EU. For example, it is reported that an NGO in Ukraine, financed by an oligarch close to Putin, distributed pamphlets saying that "association with the EU means same-sex marriage" (Tafuro 2014).

The national narratives that constitute important components of Russia's soft power policies are built on the combination of a set of diverse policies, primarily a state-promoted ideology of conservatism and the Russian World concept, manipulation of symbols and nostalgia for the glorious days of the Soviet past, the leveraging of socio-political, economic and cultural links with the post-Soviet states. These policies achieve greater success in Russia's "near abroad", compared to "far abroad".

The Russian World[10] (*Russkiy Mir*) concept is an element in Russia's soft power toolkit that puts emphasis on social, cultural,

---

10   Some of the ideas embedded in the Russian World concept associate also with those of Eurasianism, an ideology that has had various versions developed over its long history dating back to the late Middle Ages and in modern times is promoted largely by Alexandr Dugin. Its adherents, similarly, stress the differences between the West and Russia, presenting the latter as part of a distinct Eurasian civilization. In the aftermath of the announcement of Eurasian integration projects, the ideology gained momentum in academic and research circles. Although, Eurasianism as an ideological doctrine has some overlap with Putin's project of the Eurasian Union, this overlap is confined mostly to its geographical focus and is not taken as an ideological guide by Russian policymakers. Marlene Laruelle (2015) rightly argues that: "As we delve into the contents of the Eurasian project, in terms of political values and economic politics, critical dissonances soon emerge. The Eurasian Union takes nothing from (neo)Eurasianism in defining a political and economic strategy for the region. No official

and historical issues and projects a collective identity based on Russian roots. Following the dissolution of the Soviet Union, amidst an identity crisis, Russia began to recall the concepts of the Tsarist years. In those years, the Russian World appeared as a comeback of the Tsarist doctrine of *pravoslavie, samoderzhavstvo, narodnost* ("orthodoxy, autocracy and nationality") which the Russia of the Middle Ages had developed as a counterbalance of France's *Liberté, égalité, fraternité* ("liberty, equality, fraternity"). In the late 1990s, some architects of the concept, such as Efim Shchedrovitsky and Petr Ostrovsky (quoted in Laruelle 2015: 5), argued that the collapse of the Soviet Union divided the Russian World, and, hence, the existing borders of the Russian Federation did not constitute a complete area which historically had belonged to the Russian World. The concept allows Russia to claim responsibility for 300 million Russian-speakers, 30 million ethnic Russians outside Russia across the world and also embraces people who feel culturally close to Russia. 20 million of those ethnic Russians reside in the countries of the former Soviet Union (Sputniknews 2012).

In the early years of the post-Soviet period, the Kremlin tried to sign agreements on dual citizenship with the former Soviet countries. This plan failed largely due to the disinterest of the regional states, as these agreements would give Russia substantive leverage over those countries (Zevelev 2008). Following this failure, Moscow re-evaluated its relations with Russians outside of Russia by describing them as "compatriots living abroad" within the framework of the Russian World concept. Although the concept was initially widely discussed amongst academics and experts, it came into official usage only following Vladimir Putin's rise to power. Using this term for the first time at an official level during his speech at the October 2001 Congress of Compatriots, supported the view that the

---

text produced in Russia about the Eurasian Union mentions Eurasianism as an ideology. Dugin has not been given any official status since the coming into force of the Eurasian Economic Union; he is not a member of the Public Chamber and he even lost his position at Moscow State University since the onset of the Ukraine conflict." Therefore, in the analysis of Russia's soft power narratives, this book will remain focused on the Russian World concept.

Russian World comprises the territories where Russia's compatriots live: "The term 'compatriot' is definitely not a legal category. [...] For, since the very beginning, the concept 'Russian World' has gone far beyond the geographical boundaries of Russia and even beyond Russian ethnic boundaries" (See Putin 2001). During his presidency, the concept gradually "expanded from an internal search for Russian identity in the 2000s to a foreign policy imperative" (Lough *et al.* 2014: 2).

While all citizens of the former Soviet Union were considered "compatriots" in the early years of the post-Soviet period, afterwards the term was redefined and started to be based on "self-identification" of those people. The Foreign Policy Concept of 2013, like the previous two, particularly highlighted that "ensuring the comprehensive protection of rights and the legitimate interests of Russian citizens and compatriots residing abroad" was one of the goals of Russia's foreign policy (See Official Website of Russia's Ministry of Foreign Affairs 2013). These conceptual initiatives do not remain only in theory and are being pursued with practical consequences. As the existence of compatriots gives Russia a leverage to meddle in the domestic affairs of neighbouring countries, Moscow spares no effort in reinforcing its ties with these people. Most importantly, the distribution of Russian passports to these populations — a process known as "passportization" — has *de facto* generated a Russian contingent in the neighbourhood. The russification of these populations and promoting their linguistic and cultural attachment to Russia is of great strategic importance. This proved itself to be highly significant when the defence of their rights and physical security served as an excuse for a military intervention in Georgia (2008) and Ukraine (2014) and for exerting political pressure on the Baltic states and Kazakhstan.

The concept *Russkiy Mir* delineates Russia as a unique civilization and superior to the West that is allegedly in a moral crisis due to its deviation from traditional and Christian values (Speedie 2015). This civilizational approach is also reflected in the official narratives of the Kremlin. For example, the Russian Foreign Policy Concept of 2013 specifically noted that "for the first time in modern history, global competition takes on a civilization level," and that "the major states of the world...should be representative in geographical and civilizational terms" (See Official Website of Russia's Ministry of Foreign Affairs 2013). By presenting civilizations as a new type of factor in international relations, the Kremlin aims to defend the uniqueness of Russian civilization. The presentation of the West as the victim and promoter of "degeneration" and "moral degradation" takes a central line in this context (Igumnova 2014: 51).

This civilizational approach reinforces Russia's narratives to compete against rival narratives and to win over the hearts and minds of foreign publics, especially in its near abroad. The Kremlin calls upon others to respect the sovereignty of each civilization and thus the Russian civilization, as well. The Foreign Policy Concept (2013) presents it as "a priority for world politics to prevent civilizational fault line clashes and to intensify efforts to forge partnership of cultures, religions and civilizations" and highlights the threats (such as "a rise in xenophobia, intolerance and tensions in international relations") of "imposing one's own hierarchy of values". The Kremlin also employs this ideological stance to expand its ideals and values over other countries and to challenge the foundations of Western liberal democracy. In conservatism, the Kremlin sees the potential for filling the ideological vacuum created by the collapse of the Soviet communism (Whitmore 2013; Lewis 2016). Russia's enthusiastic promotion of conservativism and the establishment of strong ties with right-wing political parties and other groups in Europe are an example of this.

The elements of the Westphalian system and warnings against the erosion of this system constitute a central role in Russia's international narratives. "State sovereignty", "respect for international law", "non-interference", and similar Westphalian norms are largely employed by the Russian officials for the purposes for both soft power cultivation and self-defence. With this intent, Russia presents itself as a "norm enforcer" rather than challenging the existing international systemic norms (Sakwa 2011a: 970). The Kremlin strictly opposes the alleged attempt of the United States to preserve the unipolarity that the collapse of the USSR brought about and vows not to permit it.

Simultaneously, Moscow behaves like a revisionist power that seeks to challenge Western predominance in international relations. Complaints against the misdeeds of the West, its catastrophic consequences for many people across the world, and the need to avert this trend are likewise central in the international-level narratives of the Kremlin. However, as Richard Sakwa (2011b: 211) argues, "Russia is certainly not a fully-fledged revisionist power". Russia strives to enforce the normative basis of the existing world order and to get all other great powers, particularly the USA, to uphold these norms. As Moscow is largely unable to "pose a systemic alternative to the dominance of Western ideological and structural hegemony" (Wilson 2015: 297), the maintenance of the Westphalian system of international politics is considered as the most optimal choice for the Russian political elite. State-supported propaganda demonizes liberal and pro-Western political groups and instigates violence and aggression against them. The Kremlin has generated and supports a climate of hate against those groups which frequently leads to physical confrontations and bloodshed. The Russian propaganda vehicles broadcasting to the post-Soviet space maintains similar political tones. Russia's public diplomacy and propaganda institutions in those countries and pro-Russian political groups propagate anti-Western sentiments. Russian propaganda seeks to promote the harmony of interests between these people and Russians and creates an image of a devious external enemy which tries to destabilize these countries and ultimately to invade them.

International Broadcasting

Arguably, in recent years the Kremlin's most important broadcasting project was RT television channel (previously known as Russia Today) which was launched in 2005 with a $30 million initial budget and broadcasts to more than 100 countries (Evans 2005). The network already offers 24/7 programming in 6 languages (English, Arabic, Spanish, German, and French) and claims to be the most-watched YouTube channel (with more than 2 billion views) (See RT 2015). Russia's international broadcasting was further strengthened by the establishment of Sputnik News (an international multimedia news service launched on 10 November 2014), and Russia Beyond the Headlines (an international multimedia project which was launched by *Rossiyskaya Gazeta* in 2007). Russia's influential political scientist Igor Panarin (2010; 2014) distinguishes two waves of information warfare against Russia. He argues that the first one was launched in the late 1980s and ended with the collapse of the Soviet Union. According to him, Russia is presently under a second information aggression which the West initiated at the start of this millennium. Russian media channels disseminate this perception extensively in its neighbouring countries. Both Sputnik News and RT claim to fight against the informational hegemony of the West and deconstruct the "lies" propagated by Western politicians and media channels. The two news agencies with intriguing taglines like "Telling the untold" and "Question more" have been able to attract significant attention across the world. The rhetoric of these channels is obsessively centred on anti-Americanism.

The Kremlin also founds and/or supports pro-Russian local media channels in the neighbourhood countries. For example, in Georgia, Russia has connections with a number of local media outlets, such as information portals *Sakinformi, Iverioni, Geworld.ge,* and Internet television channel *Patriot TV*. These media outlets have been either founded by or are connected to Russia-oriented non-governmental institutions in Georgia (Eurasian Institute, Historical Legacy, etc.) (Bugajski *et al.* 2016: 343). In some of the regional countries, the audience of the Russian or Russia-supported local media channels even outnumbers that of the others. For instance, the local outlets of the Russian newspapers *Komsomolskaya Pravda v Belorussii* and *Argumenty i Fakty v Belorussii* are the most widely read newspapers in Belarus (Szostek 2015: 2).

Since Crimea's annexation, Russian media channels and other soft power outlets are particularly focused on denouncing the eastward expansion of the EU and NATO, "colour revolutions" and Ukraine's pro-Western geopolitical shift. They echo Putin's accusations that "the US instigated 'colour revolutions' in the former Soviet region, using grievances of people against their governments, in order to impose their values that contradict local traditions and culture. These efforts were directed against Ukraine, Russia and Eurasian integration."[11] These channels, when necessary, do not shy away from broadcasting disinformation and conspiracy theories to reach foreign policy goals. From this perspective, the policies of modern Russia are considered by many observers, including some Russians, more malevolent than those of the Soviet Union. In a similar vein, Gleb Pavlovsky points out that:

> "The main difference between propaganda in the USSR and the new Russia... is that in Soviet times the concept of truth was important. Even if they were lying, they took care to prove what they were doing was 'the truth.' Now no one even tries proving the 'truth.' You can just say anything. Create realities" (quoted in Pomerantsev *et al.* 2014: 9).

Russia also skillfully benefits from opportunities created by technological development in its information campaigns. It has given Moscow new instruments to project its narratives to millions of people in the "near abroad" at relatively low costs. The Kremlin's media outlets extensively use social media (Facebook, Twitter, *VKontakte*, etc.). Some studies on social media have disclosed that the Kremlin also makes use of social media bots, fake accounts (known as "trolls") for various purposes (See Stratcomcoe 2016). With this purpose, Russia is reported to have built a "troll" army whose task is commenting on articles on social media and other websites. In 2013, it was revealed by a Russian investigative journalist that a group of people in St. Petersburg have been hired on a permanent basis to comment on social media and to distribute the messages of the Kremlin on other online platforms (Garmazhapova 2013). Those people managing fake accounts are supposed to both defend Russian positions on various issues and create confusion through disseminating conspiracy theories (Kottasova 2015). The seriousness of this issue made Russia's opponents deploy similar tactics to fight (pro)Russian trolls. For example, in 2015 it was reported that Ukraine also started to build its internet army employing the same tactics as Russia used.

---

11   Translated by Lutsevych (2016: 6-7) from Vladimir Putin's Speech about Crimea: https://www.youtube.com/watch?v=ApP5sWCpjDY

Russia's propaganda outlets appear to be reaching some of their objectives in the former Soviet region. Peter Pomerantsev, an expert on the Russian propaganda, writes that, "Take Estonia, where viewers who followed rival Russian and Western stories about the downing of flight MH17 over Ukraine last year ended up disbelieving both sides" (Pomerantsev 2015). For the regional people, for most of whom Russian is a second language and for some of them a first language, there are not many alternative sources of information. In 2014, a public opinion poll conducted by Gallup in 12 countries that were formerly part of the Soviet Union (excluding the three Baltic States) concluded that many people in these countries considered Russian media a more reliable source than Western media (Bernstein 2016). The poll indicated that "majorities in most of the former Soviet states", particularly "who lived in urban areas and were better educated tended to be more supportive of Russia's policy in regard to Crimea" (ibid.). However, the "common neighbourhood" countries are not equally receptive to this rhetoric. Russian propaganda is less successful in countries that have territorial conflicts with Russia. The studies show that Russia's use of force in and occupation of some territories of Georgia and Ukraine has damaged its image in these countries. This year a Gallup poll found out that Russia is seen as the biggest threat by the residents of Georgia (48%) and Ukraine (52%) (Esipova *et al.* 2016).

Academic Exchange Programs

During the Soviet era, Russia was one of the most popular destinations for international students. In 1980, the Soviet Union (62,942) evolved to being the third most popular destination for international students after the United States (311,882) and France (110,763) (King *et al.* 2010: 10). Russian experts admit that "the USSR for a long time used higher education as a geopolitical tool and as an 'ideological weapon' at the time of confrontation and the Cold War (Torkunov 2013). However, the collapse of the Soviet Union relegated Russia's attractive power as an educational centre and decreased the country's share of the world's educational services market. In 2004, losing the position of the former USSR in the top list of most popular destinations for international students, Russia downgraded to the eighth place (75,786 foreign students) (King *et al.* 2010: 10). Presently Russia hosts a mere 2-3 percent of the global number of international students, most of whom come from developing countries and the former Soviet republics (Torkunov 2013).

Russia considers the growing influence of Western academic and cultural institutions in its neighbourhood as a threat to its influence over the regional countries. The official website of the Russian World Foundation makes clear that the exchange programmes and educational institutions of the United States, Europe, China, and Turkey pose "a serious threat to Russia's interests in this region" (Starchak 2009). In the wake of the first wave of "colour revolutions", the Russian political elite began to assess this threat seriously. The official documents started to feature public diplomacy and academic cooperation as a vital instrument of foreign policy. Public diplomacy was for the first time stressed in 2008's *Foreign Policy Concept of the Russian Federation* as a tool to promote "an objective image of the Russian Federation" and the "Russian language and the Russian peoples' culture" abroad (Fominykh 2016: 20). The Concept also underlined the importance of reintegrating the national education systems in the post-Soviet region to promote the common cultural and civilizational heritage.

These official statements were also reflected in the practice of the Russian government. In order to emerge as an attractive destination for the international students from its "near abroad" Russia invested more resources on its scholarship programmes for international students. If there were only 3,000 such students receiving financial help for their studies at Russian universities in 1995, in 2008 this number was raised to 10,000 (Fominykh 2016: 20). Following the breakout of the Ukraine crisis, this number increased further from 10,000 to 15,000 — a 50% increase in a year. Until 2014 those students were given the same amount of living allowances as Russian students, but travel expenses and health insurance were not covered. In 2014 Russia began to pay for travel allowances for some students: in that specific year 1,000 foreign students obtained this opportunity (Koshkin *et al.* 2014). Presently, most of the full-time international students studying in Russia are citizens of post-Soviet states — more than 50%. This share nears 70% in the number of students arriving in Russia for short time studies (one or two weeks) (Fominykh 2016: 28).

In its educational projects, the Kremlin also seeks to reverse the decline of the Russian language over the world and also in the post-soviet countries. In order to make progress in the expansion of the Russian language, the CIS Network University was created in 2008 on the initiative of the Peoples' Friendship University of Russia. This aimed to support education in Russian in the CIS countries (Filimonov 2010: 3). In 2011, the Federal Target Program "Russian Language" for 2011-2015 was adopted. The program operated under the control of Rossotrudnichestvo and the Ministry of Education of Russia.

The Kremlin also adopted a concept named "Russian schools abroad" in November 2015, which aimed at promoting the Russian language abroad. According to the concept, Russia would help with informational, methodological, logistical and professional support to Russian schools in foreign countries. The concept underlined the significance of the Russian language for the realization of Russia's foreign policy agenda and the formation of positive attitudes amongst these people toward Russia. Thus, not only does Moscow invest in projects to attract the students from the "common neighbourhood" states to its educational institutions in Russia, but also builds such opportunities in these countries themselves, by opening Russian-language courses, establishing branches of Russian universities, and financing or supporting education programmes in the Russian language or Russian studies. One of the most noteworthy elements of Russia's educational policies with regard to those countries is the establishment of the branches of Russian universities in the "shared neighbourhood". According to the Ministry of Education and Science of the Russian Federation, there are 30 such institutions in this region.

Russia's NGOs and Support to Civil Society

In the wake of the "colour revolutions", Russian politicians and political experts began to raise their voices for comprehensive counterrevolutionary policies both in Russia and in other CIS countries. In the immediate aftermath of these revolutions the Kremlin created the Presidential Directorate for Interregional and Cultural Relations with Foreign Countries which was entrusted with the task of conceptualizing Russia's new policy toward the "near abroad". Modest Kolerov, a political technologist and for whom "culture is a weapon that Russia is using to gain respect in the FSU" (cited in Jackson 2010: 110) was brought to the head of the Directorate. In an interview, shortly after his appointment, Kolerov admitted that his mission was to counter revolutions in the CIS countries, and, for this purpose, he underlined the importance of mobilization of "culture, "spirituality", and the Russian language (See Kommersant.ru 2005).

In a short period of time, a number of public diplomacy institutions were created, such as the *Russkiy Mir* (Russian World) Foundation (2007), Rossotrudnichestvo — the Federal Agency for the Commonwealth of Independent States, Compatriots Living Abroad, and International Humanitarian Cooperation (2008), the Gorchakov Foundation (2010), etc.). In late 2013, new plans to create a network of Russian-language-learning centres abroad named Pushkin Institutes (analogous to Germany's Goethe Institute and Spain's Instituto Cervantes) were made. Russia also began to support pro-Russian civil society, cultural and folklore clubs, youth movements, think thanks, and analytical centres in its "near abroad". These cultural organizations promote the Russian culture and language, youth movements recruit young people who stand for Russian values, and Russia-supported think tanks and research centres provide largely Russia-biased information. They are supposed to counter Western influence in their respective countries, defend ethnic Russians and Russian-speaking people, and promote conservative values and the Russian interpretation of the history. The Chatham House reports that in Moldova alone more than 100 pro-Russian organizations have been identified by Moldovan intelligence agencies (Lough *et al.* 2014: 4).

In 2012, in Russia, there were around 5,000 registered non-profit organizations—856 of which had the status of "international"—which were supposed to serve Russia's public diplomacy objectives (Kosachev 2012). These organizations were tasked with countering Western soft power and the promotion of the Russian language and culture with the ultimate goal of spurring positive sentiments towards Moscow's integration projects. Not only are they focused on countries that are on a pro-Western path but are also notably active in countries that are in the umbrella of the Eurasian Union (Bugajski *et al.* 2016: 308).

Having minimized the foreign funding of domestic non-governmental organizations to prevent any threat of colour revolution, the Kremlin launched its own funding programme for NGOs in 2005. Over the years, the major beneficiaries among the NGOs that are supported by this programme have been the Russian Orthodox Church (ROC) and organizations that promote Eurasian integration—both of which constitute primary elements of Russia's soft power projection into the neighbouring countries (See CEPR 2015). The study also found that since 2012, these non-commercial organizations have been receiving constantly growing government funding (from 1 billion roubles in 2012 to 4.2 billion roubles in 2015).

The existence of pro-Russian civil society in the neighboring countries is of great importance for the Kremlin. Russia supports pro-Russian cultural and folklore clubs, youth movements, think thanks, and analytical centres. These cultural organizations promote the Russian culture and language, youth movements recruit young people who stand for Russian values and Russia-led integration projects, and research centres provide largely Russia-biased information. As it was clearly mentioned above in the statements of Russian leaders, these groups are supposed to counter the interference of Western-backed non-governmental organizations and promote Eurasian integration. They, in line with the general foreign policy narrative of the Kremlin, defend the human rights of ethnic Russians and Russian-speaking peoples and promote conservative values as the core of Eurasian civilization and the Russian interpretation of history. These organizations provide access to works of authors who criticize US hegemony and NATO's expansion and praise the virtues of a multi-polar world. Likewise, the books of foreign writers who share these views are translated into Russian and used in the propaganda of these groups.

The rest of this section presents brief information about the key public diplomacy vehicles of Russian foreign policy which were operational in the "common neighbourhood" during the period under study (2004-2016).

The Russian Orthodox Church (ROC): The Russian Orthodox Church has been traditionally the largest and most influential Russian soft power tool. The adoption of the title "Third Rome" in 1517, a declaration of messianic ideals and supposedly unique merits of the church of Moscow, and the establishment of the Moscow patriarchate in 1589 were historically used "to justify the claim of the Muscovite ruler to lead a universal Christian Empire" (Duncan 2000: 11). The ROC was drawn under total state control during the reign of Peter the Great and "came to be seen as a pillar of the state" (Anderson 2007: 185). During Soviet times, it was the only Christian church allowed to act but remained under the total control of the government and most of the time worked for the KGB.

After the collapse of the predominant communist ideology, the emerging ideological vacuum made Moscow return to the ideological traditions of Tsarism. The percentage of Russians who identified as Russian Orthodox made a dramatic rise from 31% in 1991 to 70% in 2012 (See Levada Centre 2011). In post-Soviet Russia, the ROC became of principal importance both for governing the country and promoting its foreign policy goals. In 2007, President Vladimir Putin, likening the importance of the traditional relations to the nuclear shield of the country, estimated them "equally important for its security" (See Interfax-religion 2007).

Preserving the relations with the Russian and Russian-speaking communities abroad is a primary foreign policy task of the church. The ROC, in close cooperation with the Ministry of Foreign Affairs, strives to preserve and reinforce the spiritual bonds in

"Holy Russia", which denotes the canonical territory of the Patriarchate, i.e. Ukraine, Belarus, Moldova and Kazakhstan (Laruelle 2015: 15). With this purpose, the church also established an international organization named Day of Baptism of Rus (*Den Khreshchenia Rusi*) in 2007. It was aimed at promoting the integration of Russia, Belarus, and Ukraine as one *Holy Rus*. The organization was particularly active in 2013 prior to the Vilnius summit later that year. With slogans like "We Are One" and "Holy Rus is Indivisible" it tried to foment pro-Russian sentiments in Ukrainian society (Lutsevych 2016: 24).

The Russian Orthodox Church has branches in Belarus, Estonia, Latvia, Moldova, Kazakhstan and Ukraine, and claims exclusive jurisdiction over the Orthodox Christians in other post-soviet countries, except Armenia and Georgia. It is often considered one of the most respected institutions in the region. The church seeks to maintain an apolitical status and thus refrains from nationalistic and political statements that might damage its image. For example, after the break of diplomatic relations Georgia and Russia in the wake of the 2008 war, the ROC was the only national institution still maintaining formal ties with Georgians.

The Russian church firmly advocates traditional social values, demonizes "the cultural corruption of the West" and supports the Russian officials' view that western standards of human happiness are not applicable to all countries. The ROC and its conservative ideals attack at the very foundations of contemporary Western values and strive to consolidate a strong social basis against them. One of the flagmen of the new conservative Russian ideology, Metropolitan Kirill states that "The liberal idea does not call for a liberation from sin because the very concept of sin is absent in liberalism" (See Official Website of Russian Orthodox Church's Department for External Church Relations 2000). Henceforth, they call for a restriction of civil liberties, free competition, freedom of speech, which, for them, promote western style social and cultural degradation.

The Russian Orthodox Church, in the same vein with the Kremlin, criticizes Western perceptions of democracy and human rights. According to the church leaders, Western democracy, promoting individualism and competition, damages the foundations of a unified and consolidated society. Presenting competition and the clash of opinions as a threat to society, the church supports the Russian concept of "managed" or "sovereign" democracy and calls for a model of democracy in accord with national traditions (Anderson 2007: 191). According to the view of the church's main ideologue Patriarch Kirill of Moscow, Russia should respond to the criticism of western-backed international institutions by developing its own model and promote it internationally.

The Russkiy Mir Foundation: The *Russkiy Mir* (Russian World) Foundation institutionalizes the *Russkiy Mir* concept. The foundation, according to its director, is "a nongovernmental centre to support and popularize the Russian language and culture" (See Official Website of Russkiy Mir Foundation 2012). But, like many other Russian non-governmental organizations, it was established by the government (in June 2007). This is a joint project created by the Ministry of Foreign Affairs and the Ministry of Education and Science. The prime task of the foundation is to provide informational resources, educational programs, cultural events and the promotion of Russia's intercultural communication. The *Russkiy Mir* foundation maintains special relations with ethnic Russians and Russian-speaking publics living abroad. As of 1 November 2015, the foundation has opened more than 90 Russian centres in 45 countries across the world, of which 28 (around 30%) are in the territories of the former soviet countries: Azerbaijan (1), Armenia (1), Belarus (1) Kazakhstan (3), Kyrgyzstan (3), Moldova (4), Tajikistan (4) and Ukraine (11). The centres are aimed at popularizing Russian culture and language in the countries in which they are operational. Although the former Soviet countries and ethnic Russians living there are the main focus of the institution, its activities address also "those who speak Russian in their everyday life, also think Russian, and as a result- act Russian" over the world (Kudors 2010: 2-6).

Rossotrudnichestvo: The Federal Agency for the Commonwealth of Independent States, Compatriots Living Abroad, and International Humanitarian Cooperation (*Rossotrudnichestvo*) was established in 2008 and is focused on the countries of the former Soviet Union. The institution was built on the basis of *Roszarubezhtsentr* (Russian Foreign Centre), the roots of which date back to the early years of the Soviet Union. Unlike the *Russkiy Mir* Foundation, *Rossotrudnichestvo* is a government agency and more focused on the CIS region than the former.

Rossotrudnischestvo deals with the promotion of the Russian language, cultural, scientific and education exchanges, cooperation with compatriots abroad, and international development aid. Together with a number of institutions, such as the Governmental Commission on Compatriots Living Abroad (GCCLA), International Council of Russia's Compatriots, the Association "Homeland", the International Associations of Youth Compatriots, and the Moscow House of Compatriots, the organization aims at reinforcing ties with compatriots. Rossotrudnichestvo organizes regular events (such as forums, seminars, conferences) and scholarly exchange programs with neighbouring CIS states. The CIS countries are a priority for most of the programs of the agency.

<u>The Gorchakov Foundation</u>: The Gorchakov Foundation is a public diplomacy foundation named after Alexander Gorchakov, Russia's Foreign Minister from 1856 to 1882. The foundation was established with the decree of President Medvedev in February 2010. It serves the goals of supporting Russia's foreign policy strategy and to promote the participation of Russian non-governmental organizations in foreign countries. Leonid Drachevsky, Executive Director of the Foundation, proudly declares that the Gorchakov Foundation "is the first and unique mechanism of a state-society partnership in the field of foreign policy in modern Russia" (See Official Website of the Gorchakov Foundation 2015). Almost all the research, educational and cultural programs of the Foundation (such as "Dialogue in the name of the Future", "CSTO Academy", "School of Young Experts on Central Asia", "Caspian Youth School", and "Caucasus Dialogue") are directed at the CIS region. These programs, which focus on young experts and scientists from regional countries, have heavy political content and objectives. The

projects mostly cover issues of security, internal and external factors affecting the situation in the region and includes meetings and discussions with renowned Russian experts and politicians.

Economic Ties and Foreign Aid

An important link between Russia and the "common neighbourhood" states is the fact that the economies of the regional countries have been deeply integrated with Russia's economy through the long centuries of co-existence under common rule. For millions of people in the "near abroad", Russia has been the only source of income for years. After the collapse of the Soviet Union, Russia became the most popular destination for millions of labour migrants from the newly independent states. The existence of a visa-free regime between Russia and most other former Soviet countries has also facilitated the flow of people to Russian cities. Remittances are a very important source of income for the post-Soviet countries. For example, in 2013, 25% and 21% of the Moldovan and Armenian GDP, respectively, depended on remittances (See World Bank 2014). Around 70% and 80% of those remittances received by Moldova and Armenia, respectively, originated in Russia (See Teleradio Moldova 2014; Arka News Agency 2015). The inflow of remittances, which can be considered a form of foreign aid, help a lot of its recipients to survive in the difficult economic conditions of their own countries (Jackson 2010: 109). In 2006, Fiona Hill (2006: 341) noted that migration to Russia and remittances sent back to neighbouring countries had played an extremely crucial role in the life of millions of people during the turbulent years following the collapse of the Soviet Union: "Migration to Russia [had] become the region's safety valve."

Russia seeks also to benefit from its economic superiority over neighbouring former Soviet countries in its pursuit to develop soft power. An Oxfam analysis in 2013 reported that the post-Soviet region is the primary recipient of Russia's humanitarian aid, of which the annual budget was around 51 million dollars in 2012 (Brezhneva *et al.* 2013: 7). The analysts underline that Russia's allocation of aid in greater volumes and more frequently to the former Soviet countries is "often interpreted as a way of maintaining a degree of influence over these countries" (ibid.). The report concludes that the geographical distribution of Russia's aid must be viewed in the context of its long-term strategic ambitions which shows that "Russia regards former Soviet republics as its sphere of influence, and its willingness to maintain close ties with them explains why they receive such a large proportion of its aid" (Brezhneva *et al.* 2013: 13).

It is estimated that Russia's gas subsidies across the CIS region between 1992 and 2008 amounted to $75 billion (Bochkarev 2009). In this period, Russia sold natural gas to those countries at a lower price than that of the world market. This is a form of external aid which is not added to Russia's official data on foreign aid to the CIS countries (Sasse 2012: 557). Konstantin Kosachev, head of Rossotrudnichestvo, lamented this fact in 2014, stating that Russia helped Ukraine for many years by imposing lower gas tariffs and opened its market to Ukrainian products, but Ukrainian people did not see them. On the contrary, sums that were hundreds of times smaller from the USA and the EU "to support democracy" was seen as "bailout" to Ukraine. He emphasized that Ukraine was not the only such case (Khimshiashvili 2014).

Limitations of Russian Soft Power

Notwithstanding the above-mentioned potential and accomplishments, self-projection is the main soft power element that is mostly disregarded by Russia's political elite and is a largely underdeveloped aspect of its soft power. Many observers argue that "Russia lacks the attractiveness the EU has… [and] still needs to become sufficiently attractive in order to become the preferred partner for its neighbours" (Rostoks *et al.* 2015: 247). Russia's internal economic and socio-political structure, its authoritarian governance, economic backwardness, etc. destroy the image of the country and prevents it from developing itself as a worthy model to be followed or emulated. Despite having vast natural resources (e.g. 6% of global proven oil reserves and 17.3% of global proven gas reserves), Russia's gross domestic product (GDP) is far lower than that of the EU:

the EU's single market produced a GDP of $16.312 trillion in 2015, compared to Russia's total of $1.33 trillion (World Bank 2017a).

Russian leaders are mistakenly focused mostly on the elements of soft power that are controlled and managed by the state. For example, in his 2012 article "Russia in a Changing World", Putin defined soft power as "a complex of tools and methods for achieving foreign policy goals without deploying weapons, using information tools and other forms of intervention" (See Putin 2012). This incomplete understanding of soft power lays the foundation of future failures in Russia's soft power policies. The Kremlin continues its tight grip on the media and saturates the information landscape with nationalist propaganda while suppressing the most popular alternative voices (See Freedom House 2016). Despite the fact that some Russian leaders have acknowledged these problems and stress the importance of reforms, they have consistently failed to materialize them. For example, the former President Dmirty Medvedev, on many occasions, criticized the country's "humiliating dependence on raw materials", as well as its "inefficient economy, a semi-Soviet social sphere, a fragile democracy, negative demographic trends, unstable Caucasus" (See Medvedev 2009). Nonetheless, neither he nor his successor took effective measures to eradicate these problems.

Russia is widely seen as a force that supports authoritarian governments in its neighbourhood and as such promotes autocracy (Tolstrup 2009; Melnykovska *et al.* 2012; Furman *et al.* 2015). Although it might be inaccurate to argue that Russia exports autocracy to its neighbourhood (Tansey 2015), Russian leaders develop policies and practices aimed at blocking Western advance in its neighbourhood (Walker 2016). Despite disagreeing on some issues, Russia and some post-Soviet policy-makers in the region broadly share the objective of preventing "colour revolutions" — a mutual understanding which some depict as "Moscow Consensus" (Lewis 2016). This strategy of the Russian leadership to counter rival ideologies, particularly Western liberal democracy, through cooperation with post-Soviet leaders on narrow anti-Western rhetoric is strictly short-term unless the local leaders are able to advance socio-economic reforms which will address problems with corruption and the lack of good governance.

Russia's image suffers also from its controversial efforts to preserve its traditional influence over the neighbourhood countries and from its aggressive reactions to the pro-Western geopolitical drift of regional countries. All the countries in the "common neighbourhood", apart from Belarus, have been stuck in frozen conflicts in which Russia is a key player, directly or indirectly. Occupied by Armenia Nagorno-Karabakh region of Azerbaijan, Abkhazia and South Ossetia in Georgia, Transnistria in Moldova, Crimea, Donbas and Lugansk regions in Ukraine are the conflicts which Russia has been manipulating to have a word over the foreign policy manoeuvres of these countries. Unlike Western powers, who have never deployed military power *vis-à-vis* the "common neighbourhood" in the post-Soviet period, Russia does not shy away from using it when regional countries make decisive moves to join Euro-Atlantic political and military institutes. Thus, Russia's policies to fight against Western soft power have not been confined to soft power but also included hard power. This has been one of the most crucial problems in Russia's policies that have damaged its overall policies to wield power over popular opinion in the "common neighbourhood" and made it be seen as a threat by numerous people (Esipova *et al.* 2016).

Conclusion

This chapter analysed Russia's policies to retain the neighbouring post-Soviet states under its dominance. As opposed to the analyses which argue that Moscow sees military force as a means to re-establish its hegemony over regional states, this analysis concludes that the Russian leadership is aware that they could not establish an EU-like Union with military force. However, they tend to use military power as a last resort to prevent the loss of territories of existential importance. The Georgia war of 2008 and Russia's military intervention in Ukraine in 2014 are such cases that in which Russia became militarily involved and opposed the pro-Western drift of the two countries that it considers as part of Russia's sphere of influence. It was Russia's military force that succeeded in stopping the enlargement of NATO into the territories of the former Soviet Union. On this account, Karaganov rightfully writes that:

> "NATO's expansion was stopped, alas, not by persuasion or calls for common sense. The show of Russia's military muscle in Georgia did it" (Karaganov 2012).

This supported the hypothesis about the use of soft power as an expansive instrument in the rivalries between great powers and the use of hard power as a defensive tool to preserve the existing sphere of influence and to back up foreign policies.

The chapter built its analysis of Russia's soft power policies on the basis of the soft power model presented in Chapter 2. In accordance with the principles of this model, firstly, this chapter explored Russia's self-projection from the perspective of the "common neighbourhood" countries. It has found that Russia's natural endowments and human-constructed assets give it significant potential in its soft power policies *vis-à-vis* the regional people. The fact that these countries used to live together under Moscow's rule also affects their attitude to and perceptions of Russia. The public opinion polls cited in the chapter showed that most people in the region feel closer to Russian culture than to European or American cultures. The chapter has also analysed the role of the Russian language as a soft power asset. It concluded that although Russian is still of great importance for the regional people, many of whom speak this language, the number of its speakers is declining. This was mentioned as one of the problems of Russian soft power in general. However, Russia's self-projection has other, more serious problems as well. Its domestic socio-economic problems, relatively weak economic performance, authoritarian governance and economic backwardness damage the image of the country and prevent it from looking as the "shining city upon the hill" for the "common neighbourhood" countries. The image of the state is being damaged also by its foreign policies with respect to the regional countries. Russia's military interventions in the regional countries make it appear as a loser in the competition with the West whose policies *vis-*

à-vis this region have been always based on non-military power since the collapse of the Soviet Union.

The chapter focused also on Russia's state-managed soft power projection and explored Russia's strategic narratives, its international broadcasting, academic exchange programs, non-governmental organizations and foreign aid as dimensions of its state-managed projection with regard to the "common neighbourhood". This analysis showed that the existence of sufficient hard power resources (in particular, financial wealth) has allowed the Kremlin to establish a long series of propaganda and public diplomacy institutions to wield soft power in the region. The chapter concluded that the Russian political elite began to invest resources on this field in the aftermath of the "colour revolutions" in the beginning of this century. As expected by the soft power model of this book, Russia did not rely on only its hard power, but was forced to found numerous soft power instruments to fight the non-military power of the West.

The chapter concluded that Russia has been successful in these policies to some extent, despite its non-democratic structure and profound socio-economic and political problems. However, Russia's soft power cannot successfully compete against Western soft power unless the Kremlin resolves the above-mentioned problems that undermine the self-projection of the country. Probably this is why there is widespread pessimism about Russia's soft power potential in the Russian political expert community. Ruslan Pukhov, director of Moscow-based military think tank CAST, argues that "'Soft power' doesn't work for us. We need people to be afraid of us and we seem to be unable to find a proper substitute for military power" (Grove 2011).

5. States with Relatively Strong State Autonomy: The Case of Belarus

This chapter, along with the following chapter, complements the discussion provided in the previous two chapters which described the geopolitical nature of the Russia — West rivalries over the "common neighbourhood" countries and the use of soft power by the conflicting sides in the pursuit of their regional goals. Focusing on the case of Belarus, the chapter analyses the response of the regional countries to these rivalries. The chapter aims to test the hypothesis that if the leaders of a weak state, which is in between the rivalries of great powers who use soft power to expand their influence, are autonomous *vis-à-vis* the society and other internal non-state actors, they can control the inflow of the soft power projection of the foreign states, offset the intervening influence of the domestic non-state actors on foreign policy making, and augment their chances to more prudently and independently follow the imperatives of the international political system.

Belarus, a Slavic country situated in the geographically strategic location between Russia and the EU, gained its independence from the Soviet Union in 1991. Since 1994, the country has been led by Aleksander Lukashenko. He has amassed extensive control over the internal and external policies of the country. Since the early years of its independence, Belarus has remained Russia's closest ally in the region. However, according to its constitution, the state declares itself neutral in international relations and has invariably strived to preserve its sovereignty. The willingness and attempts of the surrounding great powers (i.e. Russia and the West) to pull Belarus into their orbit and the country's economic dependence on its northern neighbour (i.e. Russia) have complicated its international relations and restricted the possibilities it has to manoeuvre.

Belarus is of immeasurable geopolitical importance for Russia, *inter alia* due to its geographic proximity to Russia's important regions and its location between Russia and NATO countries. Over the years since the collapse of the Soviet Union, the Kremlin has spared no efforts to maintain warm relations with Belarus and preserve its control over Minsk's foreign policies. To this purpose, Moscow has invested a large sum of resources, including a huge amount of subsidies which, according to former Russian President Dmitry Medvedev, accounted for $50 billion between 1990-2009 (RT 2009).[12] Russia has also launched a number of projects to address the Belarusian people and wield soft power in the country. However, Russia has mostly worked with the Belarusian governing elite because of, on the one hand, the impediments the Lukashenko government builds before the external soft power projection and, on the other hand, the already widespread attachment of the Belarusians to Russia.

For many years, the European Union, in line with its broader neighbourhood policies, tried to extend its external governance to Belarus through democratic reforms in the country. The rapprochement of Belarus with the EU would boost the geopolitical leverage of the Union with respect to Russia. The detachment of the country from Russia's orbit would deal a crushing blow to Russia's geopolitical stance and preclude its integration plans. Likewise, the United States tried to build a relationship with Belarusian civil society and help the pro-Western political forces to come to power in the country. The fact that military power could not be deployed towards these goals, both the EU and the USA tried for many years to reach them via soft power policies. However, the strict domestic control of Lukashenko government left Western powers no room to affect its policies through influencing internal non-state actors.

This chapter will discuss the role of domestic non-state actors in shaping Belarus's foreign policy orientation and Minsk's interactions with the surrounding great powers. The geopolitical context Belarus has existed in since the early years of its independence is

---

[12] Some experts suggest higher figures about the amount of subsidies from Russia to Belarus. Alachnovič (2015), referring to the findings of the Economic Institute of the Belarusian National Academy of Sciences, pointed out that Russian subsidies had accounted for around 15% of Belarusian GDP annually. If Russia had imposed the prices gas exports to Belarus at the same level as the prices on gas exported to Poland, it would have costed $4.2 billion to Belarusian economy per a year (ibid.).

presented in the first section coming after this introductory part. The following section will analyse the autonomy Belarusian leaders have wielded with respect to the general public and other non-state actors since the country gained independence but particularly during the period between 2004 and 2016. This section will be followed by a wider discussion on the power of the West and Russia wielded over public opinion in Belarus. The section is divided into two parts providing a separate take on Western and Russian soft power. In its final section before the conclusion, the chapter will explore the attitude of the Belarusians towards the two geopolitical poles (i.e. Russia and West) and their role in the formation of the country's foreign policy orientation. The concluding part will summarize the major findings of the chapter in the light of the hypotheses presented in the beginning of the book.

Belarus Between the West and Russia

Belarus is the only Eastern Partnership (EaP) country whose Partnership and Cooperation Agreement (PCA) with the European Union (signed in 1995) never came into force. The decision to isolate Minsk in protest to President Aleksandr Lukashenko adopted by the EU and the USA in the early years of Lukashenko's tenure defined the framework of bilateral relations between the West and Belarus for the years to come. In 2004, the EU adopted sanctions on high-ranking representatives of the government (including President Lukashenko) and other persons who were blamed for undermining rule of law in Belarus. The sanctions consisted of travel bans and orders to freeze their assets at European banks. Similar sanctions were imposed by the United States, as well. In 2004, following the controversial referendum that lifted limits on presidential terms, the United States adopted the Belarus Democracy Act that prohibited, with limited exceptions, any form of assistance to Belarus. European and American leaders underscored the significance of cooperation with and support to the pro-democracy forces in Belarus (Shepherd 2006). The meeting between the US Secretary Condoleezza Rice and the Belarusian democracy activists in Vilnius in

2005 — amidst the popular uprisings in the wider region — was therefore remarkably symbolic.

President Lukashenko's unbending rejection of the criticism of the Western community strictly restricted the foreign policy options of the Belarusian leadership and pushed Minsk towards Russia economically and politically (Rontoyanni 2005: 47). Initially, Lukashenko attempted to establish a Union State with Russia and to take leadership of the new state. During the years of President Yeltsin, the sides made significant steps towards the Union, and the two states ratified the foundational treaty in early 2000, guaranteeing labour rights in both countries, removing border controls, and laying the foundation for the unification of legislation and the creation of a single economic space and single currency. Belarus has been a founding member in most integration projects initiated by Moscow, including the Customs Union, the Collective Security Treaty Organisation (CSTO) and the Eurasian Union.

Meanwhile, relations between Belarus and the West remained at a diplomatic impasse. The EU and the USA demonstrated an absolute aversion to Minsk's Russia-leaning policies. Although Lukashenko offered cooperation on many occasions, he never received a positive response. Western leaders drew explicit parallels between Lukashenko and Middle Eastern leaders who had been overthrown in the course of the "Arab spring". Some of them publicly spoke about the necessity of a government change in Minsk (Marples 2005: 895). Imposing financial sanctions and travel restrictions on Belarus, spending millions of dollars in aid to support the NGOs and independent media in the country, and thus basically seeking a regime change in and external governance over Belarus (Lynch 2005: 8; Myers 2006), the Western community has alienated Lukashenko in a way no other government in the "common neighbourhood" has ever experienced. Grigory Ioffe (2004; 2013) counts the frustration of the Western leaders in their expectations over the geopolitical reorientation of Belarus as a major reason for the rather critical attitude towards Lukashenko which remains unparalleled in the post-Soviet world.

In the aftermath of the failure of the Belarusian opposition in the 2006 elections, in which Western powers expended massive amount of resources on civil society and anti-Lukashenko forces, the approach of the West to President Lukashenko began to gradually change (Ioffe 2011; Vieira 2014a). This was also affected by growing disputes between Belarus and Russia over energy prices (Ioffe 2013) and Belarus's implicit support for Georgia following the 2008 war (Padhol *et al.* 2011: 3-4). Against this backdrop, relations between Belarus and Western powers improved: Belarus was invited to the EU's Eastern Partnership (2009) and visited by senior NATO officials after a long standstill (2008). This rapprochement persisted, in varying degrees, in the following years, as well. However, the Belarusian leadership never strictly changed its pro-Russian alignment in its external sphere.

Belarus, in return for its Russia-leaning geopolitical choice, insisted on discounts on the import of fuel and energy resources, demanding the prices found on the internal Russian market. On the one hand, it looked for alternative energy sources (from Venezuela and Azerbaijan) to decrease its energy dependence on Russia (Čajčyc 2010), on the other hand pressed Russia to keep the energy prices low and remove restrictions on trade. Lukashenko himself, on several occasions, reiterated that if Russia didn't meet these expectations, Minsk "[would] not be able to stay in the Customs Union, since we would not see any economic benefits from it" (Bohdan 2013). Siarhei Bohdan (2013) reported that:

> "Since 2011, Belarus has been importing duty-free Russian oil to reproduce at its own refineries. These petroleum products partly are sold to third countries. For these exports, Minsk pays duties directly to the Russian state budget: in 2012—$3.8bn, in 2011—$3.07bn. Meanwhile, Minsk believes that Moscow should not demand this money from them as Russia owes Belarus something for being its close ally."

Although Lukashenko fought to extract as many benefits as possible from Russia in return for being its geopolitical ally, he also dealt responsibly with the task of preserving the sovereignty and territorial integrity of his country. He never allowed Russia to transform Belarus into another autonomous republic of the Russian Federation. Belarus's approach to Russia and its integration projects was primarily driven by economic interests. Unlike the Kazakhstan leader Nazarbayev, Lukashenko did not demonstrate any affinity with the Eurasian ideology or the Russian World concept, either. The form of Belarus's approach to its relations with Russia is characterized by some observers as "sovereignty entrepreneurship", that means "the extraction of rents in the form of energy subsidies and credits in return for loyalty, or through the threat of a reorientation away from Russia" (Nice 2012: 7). Thus, it responds to Russia's attempts to reduce subsidies by threatening to make changes in its choice of partners in foreign sphere. Against this background, Nice (2012: 1) detects a continuity in Lukashenko's foreign policy: "the consolidation of Belarusian statehood and identity as an independent state".

The Lukashenko government sees the Russian and Western approach to Belarus in the same context in which each of them seeks to influence the internal structure of the country and establish external governance over it through coercion and incentives (Nice 2012). Ioffe (2015) has identified three reasons that have allowed Lukashenko to adroitly manoeuvre in this hostile international context: the absence of a strong cultural divide in the Belarusian population, the existence of a consolidated political elite, and the absence of oligarchic power centres. These factors played important roles for Lukashenko to strengthen his domestic autonomy. Unlike Ukraine, where these three elements were the opposite, Belarus attained the ability to play the external great powers against each other, follow the imperatives of the international political system and sustain a favourable foreign policy course. Belarus has on various occasions demonstrated that it does not trust the Kremlin in most security issues. For example, it is due to this fact that despite Moscow's offers and pressure, Belarus never recognized the independence of Georgia's breakaway territories. Minsk has gradually sought more diversification in foreign policy and more intense ties with the West in order to balance Russia's influence over the country, particularly in the wake of Crimea's annexation (Vieira 2014b). Belarus did not recognize the Russia-organized referendum's results in Crimea. Lukashenko criticized the annexation as a "dangerous precedent" in the post-Soviet space (Bogutsky 2015: 91). He, along with Nazarbayev, resisted Russia's attempts to adopt anti-Ukrainian restrictive measures within the Eurasian Economic Community.

Against this background, bilateral relations between Moscow and Minsk deteriorated and anti-Lukashenko statements swelled in Russia. The Russian media questioned the independence of Belarus, portrayed it as a natural part of Russia, began to discuss the possibility of a Western-orchestrated Euromaidan-style upheaval in Belarus and highlighted the importance of Russia's ability to intervene and prevent such a "colour revolution". Simultaneously, contacts between Minsk and Western capitals intensified and the sides embarked on negotiations to build cooperation in the field of technology, economy and security (Fedirka 2016). The visits of Pentagon officials and the EU Commissioner for the European Neighbourhood Policy and Enlargement Negotiations (2015) to Belarus for the first time after a long period signified a rapprochement between the sides. The EU, citing the release of some political prisoners as a sign of improvement and underscoring the need to encourage the Belarusian government for further democratic advancement, even permanently lifted the sanctions imposed on 170 individuals, including Lukashenko in early 2016 (Rankin 2016). Minsk's policies and Lukashenko's statements since the Ukraine crisis broke out indicate that Belarus was interested in the increasing involvement of Western powers in the post-Soviet region as a move to counterbalance Russia's influence and to ensure that Belarus would not become the next battleground between Russia and West. This intention was particularly clear in Lukashenko's interview with Bloomberg where he stated that:

> "The most worrying thing [about the Ukraine crisis] is that the United States hasn't been openly involved in this process. I believe that there would be no stability in Ukraine without the Americans" (See Bloomberg 2015).

However, despite this rapprochement with the West, Lukashenko's Belarus remains loyal to Russia. Although Belarusian leaders verbally criticize Russia's foreign policy, the transfer of this criticism into tangible deeds has been limited. For example, although they have, on several occasions, expressed their support for

Ukraine and its territorial integrity, Belarus never joined the countries recognizing Crimea's entry into the Russian Federation as "annexation" (Pankovski 2016).

State Autonomy *Vis-à-vis* Non-State Actors

The influence of non-state players on the domestic and foreign policies of the Belarusian government had been already strictly limited when the first wave of the "colour revolutions" set foot on the post-Soviet space. In 2004, the Lukashenko government, having nationalized around 80% of economy (Lawson 2003: 127), had also developed counter-revolutionary political instruments. Belarus had already built a "state ideology" devoting the country to the Eastern European Civilisation and rejecting Western liberal values. The Lukashenko government received assistance also from the Kremlin in developing resistance against those revolutions (Wilson 2011: 209). However, the unanticipated success of the popular uprisings across the region urged the Lukashenko government to take even more measures to further diminish the power of non-state domestic actors and prevent the import of a colour revolution into his country.

In the wake of the "colour revolutions" in neighbouring countries, in 2003-2004, Belarus shut down more than 50 NGOs and adopted new regulations to make it harder for NGOs with undesirable agendas to be registered (Silitski 2005: 31). In two years (2003-2004), 34 newspapers were forced to stop working (ibid.).

The fact that the Lukashenko government was remarkably successful in economic issues compared to other former Soviet states was often mentioned as one of the primary factors that created conditions for the silent acceptance of the tight control by the general public (Ioffe 2004; 2007). Unlike many other post-Soviet countries, under Lukashenko's leadership Belarus was able to sustain most of the achievements the country made during Soviet times. The Belarusian GDP in 1999 was 83.6% of its 1991 level with the second smallest decline among the CIS countries (Ioffe 2004: 91). The country recorded consistent economic growth for 15 years (1996-2010) at an average annual rate of around 7% (Yarashevich

2014: 1703-1704), which was also affected by the low cost of energy from Russia (Vanderhill 2014: 275-276; Alachnovič 2015). Belarus also stands out in the post-Soviet space for its low levels of poverty, unemployment, and inequality. Amidst the spread of the "colour revolutions" in the neighbourhood, the number of Belarusians who said in a poll that the economic provision of their families was very good, good, or middle amounted to 56%, while this figure was less than 30% in Ukraine at that time (Petuxov 2004: 5).

Very much like its external policies, the internal policies of the Lukashenko government also demonstrated a remarkable continuity in the period under study (2004—2016). In 2009, when the Belarusian economy was in decline in the wake of the global financial crisis, a survey concluded that the majority of respondents would vote for Lukashenko (39.2%) and not for opposition leaders (Alaksandar Milinkevich (former presidential candidate)—4.4%, Alyaksandr Kazulin (former presidential candidate and political prisoner)—2.3%, Sergei Sidorski (the Prime Minister)—1.6%) (Marples 2009: 761).

Non-State Actors under the Influence of External Powers

Non-State Actors under the Influence of Russian Soft Power

Russia and Belarus share a history that dates back to the middle ages. The formation of the cultural and societal characteristics of the latter have been continuously affected by the former. The transformation of Belarus from a weak agricultural region into the industrial hub of the entire Soviet Union under Moscow's rule further connected the Belarusian population to Russia. These bonds did not fade in the post-Soviet era, and, quite the contrary, were reinforced under the russification policies of the Lukashenko government. The deep, inter-societal links between Belarus on the one hand, Russia and other post-Soviet countries on the other hand is a major reason often mentioned for the perseverance of pro-Russian sentiments in Belarusian society (White *et al.* 2014). The two societies are so interconnected that a public polling concluded that for 80% of Belarusians Russia is not even viewed as a foreign country (Ioffe 2013: 1267). The visa-free travel between the two countries helps maintain the bonds between the two nations alive. More than 70% of the 34,801 Belarusian students abroad in 2014 studied in Russia (UNESCO 2017). Not surprisingly, during the period under study, the number of Belarusian migrant workers in Russia was approximately ten times higher than that of those who emigrated to the EU (Popescu *et al*. 2009b: 34). A public polling carried out in 2011 likewise proves the remarkable strength of this bond between Belarus and Russia:

> "More than half (54%) of our Belarusian respondents, in 2011, had at least one close relative living in Russia, and 42% had at least one close relative living in one of the other post-Soviet republics. Twenty years after independence, this was also where most of our respondents had travelled. More than three-quarters (76%) had visited Russia, and nearly as many (72%) had visited Ukraine; substantial numbers had also visited Poland (37%) or one of the Baltic republics, such as Lithuania (36%). But fewer than 5% had visited Hungary, and only 3% had ever visited the USA" (White *et al*. 2014: 3).

The Belarusian language was severely marginalized under the Soviet regime. The number of Belarusians speaking and studying in their native language continuously decreased during those years. In early 1989, the Belarusian Soviet Socialist Republic had the highest number of people who spoke only Russian (29,9%) or spoke fluently in Russian (over 50%) within the Soviet Union (Ryder 2002: 137). In that year, no major Belarusian cities had Belarusian-language schools (Ryder 2002: 137)—a stark decline in less than 40 years: 95% of Belarussian schools operated in the native language in 1955 (Astapenia 2016). At the time of Soviet collapse, only 20% of Belarusian pupils were studying in Belarusian. The proportion of these pupils declined to 13,7% towards the end of 2016, when only 0,1% of university students studied in Belarusian (Astapenia 2016). More than 80% of the published books are in the Russian language in Belarus (Astapenia 2014). The Belarusian constitution recognizes the Russian language as an official language along with the Belarusian language. But Belarusian is rarely used at the official level.[13]

Over the years of co-existence and thanks to ethnic, religious, and linguistic proximity Russia has acquired various channels to build soft power in Belarus and to transfer this power into tangible state policies. Its soft power outlets are distinguishably stronger in Belarus than those of Western powers. The approach of the state towards Russian soft power projection was also significantly friendlier than it was towards that of the West. For Lukashenko, who opted for Soviet ideology as the ideological foundation of his government from the very beginning of his power, the Russian cultural influence was more acceptable than the Western or even national ones. This was why while allowing the Russian soft power instruments to more freely operate in Belarus, he strictly restricted the activities of the groups and organizations who promoted national or Western culture. For example, Belarusian (Civil Society Platform) National Platform complained that:

> "The Russian propaganda mass media are being broadcast without restrictions, while the values connected with the Belarusian people's identity, i.e. the Belarusian language, culture, and historical memory, still have no state institutional support and remain marginalized" (See Centre for European Transformation 2015).

Nevertheless, the Kremlin have not built or was unwilling to build a strong pro-Russian political movement in Belarus. According to some, it has been so due to the lesser incentives of the Russian leaders to develop pro-Russian civil society organizations in Belarus (Vanderhill 2014: 270; Astapenia 2014). As the Kremlin enjoys closer links to the Belarusian government, they are more successful in imposing more direct influence on the Lukashenko government

---

13 Despite the lamentable situation of the Belarusian language, in recent years there are signs that its usage is expanding amongst both the population and at official meetings, religious ceremonies, schools, art galleries, etc. (Vasilevich 2016: 177). The government has also started to show more support for the revival of the nation's language (Ioffe 2014). However, observers note that increasing government support might be simply aimed at preventing the extinction of the Belarusian language, rather than reviving it and overtaking the Russian language (Astapenia 2016).

than in reaching out to and developing pro-Russian civil society institutions (Vanderhill 2014: 270). The fact that there is only one cultural centre (in the city of Brest) of the *Ruskiy Mir* Foundation in Belarus, which was established in 2014 — much later than many other such centres in other former Soviet countries — also indicates the unwillingness of the Russian officials to invest substantial resources in soft power policies concerning Belarus. This has been equally, if not more, affected by the limited political environment for the activities of the non-state actors in Belarus. Russia probably would have liked to develop strong pro-Russian movements in Belarus considering the long-term perspectives and possible internal shake-up in the post-Lukashenko period.

One of the assets the Russian government used to wield power over popular opinion in Belarus is religion. The Belarusian Orthodox Church (BOC) is a branch of the Russian Orthodox Church (ROC). The two churches are administratively connected. The former is under the jurisdiction of the latter and thus depends on its cultural and ecclesiological settings (Vasilevich 2014). Although other churches face continuous legal and bureaucratic impediments, the Orthodox Church, under the tutelage of the government, operates on a larger scale and disseminates pro-Russian sentiments (Vasilevich 2016). However, in line with other non-governmental institutions, the activities of the BOC are also required to be registered by governmental agencies. The unauthorized activities of the BOC are usually persecuted (Vasilevich 2014: 9). The BOC is a substantial influencing tool in Belarus, considering that 63.5% of the Belarusian population define themselves as believers, 83% as supporters of the Orthodox religion (Vasilevich 2016: 172).

Despite tight control over the media, the Belarus government has not banned the Russian media from domestic media space — quite the contrary, it was "allowed and facilitated" to realize the cross-border flow of news from Russia to the Belarusian audience (Szostek 2015: 2). Belarus and Russia came to terms on the establishment of a "single information space" (*yedinoye or obshcheye informatsionnoye prostranstvo*) and thus provided unrestricted access to the same news providers. Szostek (2015: 2) has found that the two most widely read newspapers by Belarusians are *Komsomolskaya*

Pravda v Belorussii and *Argumenty i Fakty v Belorussii* which are subsidiaries of the Moscow-based tabloids *Komsomolskaya Pravda* and *Argumenty i Fakty*. He reports that a similar situation exists in the television sector as well: "In the period under study [i.e. during the second half of 2010], three of Belarus's major state-owned TV channels [ONT (Obshchenatsionalnoye televideniye), RTR-Belarus, NTV-Belarus] had line-ups based wholly or substantially on Russian made content" (ibid.). Besides, as Russian TV channels produce programmes with higher standards than Belarusian local TV channels, they are widely watched across the country. The online media is also dominated by Russian internet outlets so that Russian internet pages are more popular in Belarus than local ones. Alas, Russian dominates Belarus's information space.

Usually the narratives of the Russian broadcasters have been in line with the official narratives of the Lukashenko government. That is the reason why the Russian media has not been driven out of the country. However, from time to time, especially when there were disputes between the governments of the two countries, Russian media broadcasted programmes critical of Lukashenko's policies. Thus, media was not always used by Russia as a tool to garner attraction amongst Belarusians for Russia, but it also aimed to "elicit aggravation" occasionally (Szostek 2015). In order to minimize the hostile influence of the Russian media, Lukashenko reduced the number of Russian newspapers available in Belarus. Local transmitters of Russian TV channels (ONT, NTVBelarus and RTR-Belarus) dropped unwanted content from their broadcasting and introduced increasingly more domestically produced content along with programmes produced in Russia (ibid.). The transmission of Russian channels via cable network has been also complicated by local producers. As a result, Szostek (2015: 3) reports that for most of the population the three local re-broadcasting channels "are now the only platforms where Russian TV news can be watched."

Non-State Actors under the Influence of Western Soft Power

The internal policies of the Lukashenko government have been, to some extent, successful in countering the self-projection of Western countries. The massive use of official narrative has managed to blur the perception of the Belarusian population about the neighbouring Western countries (Raik 2006b: 173). The surveys indicate that over the years under the current government, the number of Belarusian people who considered the life standards of the neighbouring EU countries as lower than in Belarus gradually rose. For example, between 2004 and 2006 the percentage of people who considered the living standards of Latvia, Lithuania and Poland as higher than in Belarus plummeted from 24% to 12% (Manaev 2006: 41).

The state-managed soft power projection of Western powers also encountered interruptions posed by the Belarusian authorities (Kowalski 2008: 189). In 2009, Giselle Bosse (2009: 215) observed that, although the neighbourhood policies of the EU impacted the local perceptions in Ukraine and Moldova, they did not produce similar results in Belarus. Referring to the United States as a "dark force" that seeks to destabilize Belarus, Lukashenko resisted American pressure which he called "stupid", "immoral", and "unfair" (Kudrytski et al. 2004). Belarusian authorities prevented the financial assistance of Western powers from going to anti-government forces in Belarus. This paralyzed the agenda of Western non-governmental organizations. For example, Balazs Jarabik (2006: 86) notes that the European Initiative for Democracy and Human Rights (EIDHR) was not allowed to provide effective support to local groups and was forced by governmental structures to deal with non-political issues (e.g. children's rights). This was one of the most important factors that distinguished Belarus from Ukraine and Moldova, where reforms were being conducted by the government and thus supported by the EU (Raik 2006b: 170).

US government assistance to Belarus is formed in the frame of "selective engagement", which confines assistance almost exceptionally to humanitarian assistance, educational exchange programmes, independent civil society and media institutions. From 1997, the International Republican Institute (IRI) was involved in programmes addressing political parties in Belarus. The Institute, with the financial backing of USAID, offered training for political parties in 2001-2002 (Vanderhill 2014: 273). Afterwards it began to provide trainings to pro-democracy forces in developing campaign messages and strategies. Similarly, the National Endowment for Democracy (NED) provided support to political groups in mobilizing voters and building pro-democracy political party coalitions (ibid.). In the wake of the regional "colour revolutions", prior to the 2006 presidential elections, which proved to be the last chance for regime change in Belarus for a long time, this assistance gained momentum. Many Western agencies (e.g. the National Endowment for Democracy, its British counterpart called the Westminster Foundation for Democracy, the Foreign Ministry of Germany, and the US Department of State) and a large amount of financial resources were involved in this process. The US Secretary Condoleezza Rice met with some Belarusian NGO leaders in 2005. In the same year, a supplementary assistance bill gave a democracy assistance allotment worth $5 million earmarked for Belarusian political parties, civil society, independent media, radio and TV channels (Jarabik 2006: 89). For 2006 and 2007, the amount of this assistance sharply rose to $24 million (ibid.). The amount of EU assistance to Belarus was raised from $10 million annually to an annual $12 million for 2005 and 2006 (Jarabik 2006: 90). The EU member states supported the Belarusian democratic forces separately as well. For example, Swedish assistance to Belarus amounted to $3 million in 2005 and $4 million in 2006, of which around half was earmarked to civil society (Raik 2006b: 176).

The information space, since the early years of the Lukashenko tenure, has been also an important part of the Western soft power projection to Belarus. The New York Times reported that a German organization, Media Consulta, signed a $2.4 million contract with the EU "to break an information blockade that has left most Belarussians isolated from, and ignorant about, even neighboring countries" (Myers 2006). Besides, Belarusian civil society leaders visited their Ukrainian and Serbian counterparts in their respective countries to learn about their experiences. They were also visited by members of Ukrainian and Georgian civil society organizations.

In those years, there were several movements in Belarus that were heavily supported by the West. For example, *Zubr*, one of the three Belarusian youth movements in the early 2000s, whose manners and rationale were analogous to the other youth movements in Serbia (*Otpor*), Ukraine (*Pora*), and Georgia (*Kmara*), was reported by various sources as having received financial backing from the West. Andrew Wilson (2011: 2015) cites an interview with a former NGO leader who argues that: "Zubr was always more 'externally inspired. Its activities were mainly based on money from US foundations.' But 'US money was destructive in the long term. When the flow of money ended, they [Zubr] disappeared.'" The other two youth movements—*Khopits*! ('Enough!') and the Youth Front—were less organized but still supported by the Western agencies (Myers 2006; Wilson 2011: 215-216).

However, following the failure of the opposition in the 2006 presidential elections, according to the observation of some Western experts, "There… [was] no longer the slightest possibility of some form of 'colour' revolution in Belarus: the cases of Georgia and Ukraine, in different ways, hardly foster enthusiasm for such a cause, and the Europeans… [had] evidently abandoned such an idea… as failed plans" (Marples 2009: 774). The failure of pro-Western forces in spite of massive external support made Western powers understand that regime change in Belarus through popular upheaval was improbable for the time being. They began to make changes in their approach to Lukashenko and reduced their assistance to anti-governmental non-state actors in Belarus (Ioffe 2011). Prior to the 2010 elections, some Western Foreign Ministers visited Minsk. Lukashenko himself paid a visit to Lithuania whose president Dalia Grybauskaite "endorsed him as the most suitable candidate for the presidency of Belarus" (Padhol *et al.* 2011: 3). The diminishing Western intervention allowed Lukashenko to hold the 2010 and 2015 presidential elections without problems. In early 2016, the EU lifted sanctions that had been imposed in 2004 and began to normalize relations with Minsk.

Non-State Actors and External Alignment

The previous sections indicated that the Lukashenko government has effectively minimized the influence of civil society organizations on the formation of not only internal but also external policies. However, public opinion polls show that the external orientation of the state is in line with the preferences of the general public. Certainly, the elements of Russia's self-projection, the domestic policies of the Belarusian government and Russia's state-managed projection have played an enormous role in the formation of these preferences. The entrenched cultural attachment of the Belarusians to Russia, shared history, linguistic and economic bonds in combination with the pro-Russian cultural and political stance of the Lukashenko government have minimized the chances of pro-Western groups to realize their agenda in the country.

The results of the public opinion polls carried out between 2004 and 2016 by the Independent Institute of Socio-Economic and Political Studies (IISEPS), a public institution based in Lithuania (indicated in Figure 4) demonstrate that when Russia is in an intense confrontation with the West, supporters for closer relations with Russia (i.e. unification) tend to outnumber those who support European integration. Between 2004 and 2008, when pro-Western groups were marching "colour revolutions" across the post-Soviet world and later Russia was engaged in a war with Georgia, Belarusians appeared more Russia-leaning. In this period, the majority reported they would choose integration with Russia rather than joining the EU in a hypothetical referendum on the either/or question between Russia and the European Union (See Figure 4). The difference was notable in a 2008 survey as well: 46% of respondents preferred integration with Russia to the EU integration (30%) in response to the question "If you had to choose between Belarusian reunification with Russia and integration with the EU, which would you go for?" (Ioffe 2013: 1269). Over the period between 2000 and 2010, the number of Belarusians who self-identified as "European" declined as well (White *et al.* 2010).

A similar tendency was noticed in the wake of the Ukraine crisis. While in the 2013 polling, the ratio between accession to the EU and integration with Russia in a hypothetical referendum on the either/or question was 45% vs. 37%, this ratio changed to the opposite in the following year (34% vs. 45%). The trend continued in the next two years as well: 2015 — 25% vs. 53%; 2016 — 34% vs. 42% (See Figure 4). The upward changes in public support for an alignment with Russia during the confrontational periods can be interpreted as evidence for the strength of anti-Western propaganda in Russian media which, as the previous sections showed, gets intensified when Russia is in a face-off with the West. However, the outcomes of the public opinion polls show that when Russia — West relations were at ease (2009-2013), Belarusians tended to be more supportive of European integration (See Figure 4). For example, in the 2011 poll, half of the respondents said that they would vote for accession to the EU in a hypothetical referendum posing the either/or question between Russia and the European Union, while only 31% chose unification with Russia.

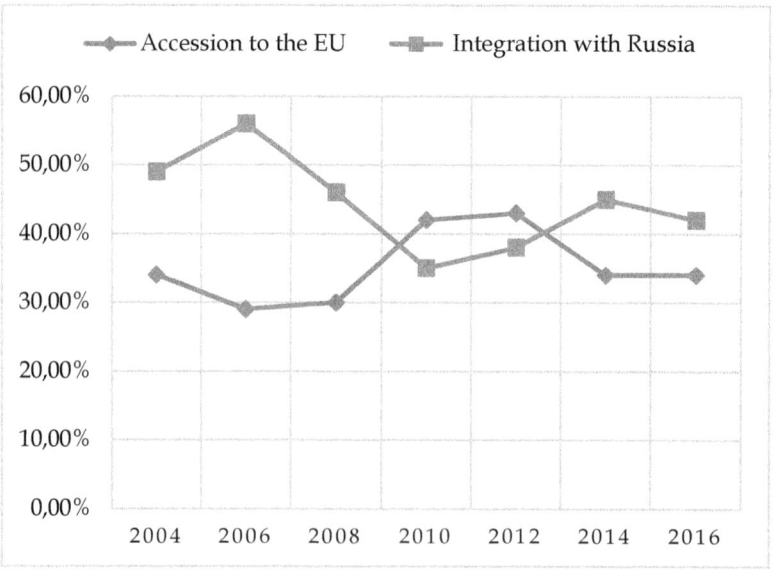

Figure 4.   Belarussian Public opinion on foreign policy (The question in the surveys: "If you had to choose between integration with Russia and joining the European Union, what choice would you make (For details, see the internet page of Independent Institute of Socio-Economic and Political Studies: http://www.iiseps.org/?lang=en ?)

However, the public support to Belarus's admission into the Transatlantic bloc has been always low amongst Belarusians. A survey in early the 2000s identified that NATO was considered "a significant threat" by most of the Belarusian population. 47% of the respondents defined NATO as either "a platform for Western expansion" or "a relic of the Cold War", while for 22% its objective was the "strengthening of international security" and for 30% it was "hard" to portray NATO's aims (White *et al.* 2006: 179). The same survey found that for just a minority in Belarus, the country's admission into NATO would be "very good" (6% in 2000; 5% in 2004) or "quite good" (23% in 2000; 17% in 2004). A similar antipathy towards the transatlantic bloc was also seen in a survey by Gallup which indicated that 44% of respondents considered closer relations with Russia as important even if this entails harming relations with the United States (Esipova *et al.* 2008).

This attitude towards NATO is still prevalent amongst Belarusians. 54% of Belarusians considered NATO a threat in a Gallup poll in 2016 (a mere 3% associated the alliance with protection) (Smith 2017). This was the second highest such result in the former Soviet countries after Russia, where 67% thought NATO was a threat (ibid.). In June 2016, a public opinion poll in Belarus found that 26,1% of respondents supported Russia's actions in its confrontation with the West over Ukraine and believed that Russia would protect Belarus "from possible NATO aggression" (IISEPS 2016). The proportion of those who supported the West and trusted it as a potential ally in the case of possible Russian aggression was significantly lower: 10,6%. However, another major finding of this poll was that for most Belarusians (58%), it is more important to maintain neutrality between the two geopolitical centres.

The growing preference for neutrality and for policies aimed at maintaining national sovereignty rather than making a clear-cut choice about the geopolitical poles amongst Belarusians has been noticed also in IISEPS surveys. The 2015 survey concluded that more people would vote "against" joining an external power in a hypothetical referendum (IISEPS 2015). 19.8% of respondents would vote "for" and 56.1% would vote "against" in a referendum on joining the European Union. The survey identified that a negative outcome would be produced also in a referendum on the unification of Belarus and Russia: 29.7% of respondents would vote "for" and 51.5% of respondents would vote "against". This signified a steady decline from back in 2002, when the ratio was 53,8% to 26,3% in favour of unification with Russia (Ioffe 2013: 1268).

Thus, for most of the time during the period under study, particularly when Russia found itself in a face-off with the West, the public support for pro-Russian alignment in the international sphere prevailed in Belarus. This has forced even Western-supported oppositional candidates to refrain from publicly favouring integration into Western blocs (Manaev 2006: 43). However, it does not give sufficient evidence to designate pro-Russian sentiments as the decisive factor in the foreign policy orientation of the country (Clem 2011). Apparently, President Lukashenko can disregard public opinion when he thinks it necessary. For example, during the Georgia war and the Ukraine crisis, when public support for unification with Russia outweighed public support for European integration (See Figure 4), Belarusian leaders in fact tried to counterbalance Russia's pressure and looked into opportunities to approach the West. However, Belarusians' pro-Russian sentiments and the disinterest of the public towards pro-Western foreign policy changes contributed to the failure of Western-supported political groups' attempts to topple the incumbent government. It is one of the major factors that secures the persistence of a pro-Russian geopolitical alignment. A Belarusian political analyst argues that "Belarusians' addiction to Russian culture and media is in large part responsible for the nation's political dependence on Russia and the geopolitical situation in Belarus" (Astapenia 2014).

Conclusion

This chapter tested the hypothesis that if states that are subject to a geopolitical confrontation between external great powers, enjoy autonomy from domestic non-state actors, they can control foreign attempts to influence these non-state actors and augment their chances to follow the imperatives of the international political system more independently and potentially more prudently. The analysis of the chapter supported this hypothesis. During the period under study (2004-2016), Belarus's foreign policy was formed under a vigilant consideration of the distribution of capabilities between the two geopolitical poles (i.e. the West and Russia). In this period, the imperatives derived from the distribution of capabilities between the two poles could easily transfer into certain state actions. The internal dynamics of the state did not pose a serious challenge for the government in foreign policy. The fact that the Russia-leaning external orientation of the state corresponded to stronger, pro-Russian sentiments amongst the Belarusian people minimized the countervailing influence of the public as an intervening variable between the international political system and foreign policy. The relatively homogenous internal cultural environment, the absence of antagonist ethnic divides within society, and weak non-governmental groups are the major factors that removed internal non-state actors as the intervening variable between the international political system and foreign policy.

6. States with Relatively Weak State Autonomy: The Case of Ukraine

This chapter, along with the preceding chapter, complements the discussion provided in Chapters 3 and 4 which described the geopolitical nature of the Russia—West rivalries over the "common neighbourhood" countries and the use of soft power by the conflicting sides in the pursuit of their regional goals. The chapter, focusing on the case of Ukraine, aims to portray the response of regional countries to these rivalries and analyse the impact of the lack of strong state autonomy on foreign policy. The chapter's purpose is to defend the argument that when leaders of states are not autonomous *vis-à-vis* domestic non-state actors, the latter become politically more influential with the potential of affecting foreign policies, mostly in a negative way. The non-existence of strong state autonomy in such states allows the external powers to more effectively pursue policies to wield soft power there. This gives external powers the chance to impact the foreign policies of these states through influencing their domestic non-state actors and push a favourable reconfiguration in their geopolitical orientation which might be at odds with the national interests of the regional states.

In the wake of the disintegration of the USSR, Ukraine emerged as a geopolitical actor that had never existed before. For the first time in history, Ukrainian leaders gained control over both the Western and Eastern parts of the country, including the Crimean Peninsula that had been part of Russia until recently (1954). However, the leaders of the newly independent Ukraine soon found themselves in the middle of an intense geopolitical competition between Russia and West. A large number of internal problems—*inter alia* the country's political instability, the incapability of the Ukrainian governments to properly deal with economic challenges, the uncontrollable influence of oligarchic groups on the political establishment and their influence in internal and external policies, the entrenched economic ties with and dependence on Russia, and against this background an enormous cultural divide within society — dramatically complicated the political landscape of the country.

From the Russian perspective, the geopolitical importance of Ukraine is immeasurable. The "encroachment" of rival powers into Ukraine has been always considered by the Kremlin as an existential threat. This is why, from the very beginning of the post-Soviet era, Russia tried everything possible to keep Kiev in its orbit and prevent its pro-Western aspirations. For this purpose, Moscow applied various strategies including sticks, carrots and soft power. Along with pressuring Ukrainian leaders into staying away from Euro-Atlantic organizations, the Kremlin maintained a compromising stance in bilateral deals. For example, Moscow put low prices on energy exports to Ukraine: it has been estimated that between 1992 and 2008 Russia's gas subsidies to Ukraine alone amounted to $47 billion — out of the total $75 billion across the CIS countries (Bochkarev 2009). Currently half of Ukrainians working abroad are in Russia and the remittances sent by them back home is close to $4 billion — around half of the total remittances that Ukraine receives annually (See IFAD 2015: 20; 31). For a country of which around 4% of GDP is formed on the basis of money transfers by its citizens working abroad, this is an important factor (Sakwa 2015: 77). The economic interconnectedness between Ukraine and Russia and the former's energy dependence on the latter used to be a potential source of practical leverage for the Kremlin to influence Ukrainian leaders.

Ukraine is an important, if not the most important, country in the coverage of the EU's eastern neighbourhood policies. It is the largest country whose territories are entirely located in Europe and is one of the top European countries in terms of population size. Hence, any serious turmoil in this country or its submission to Russian control has been considered as a potential threat to the EU's security. To counter this threat and promote the European integration of Ukraine has been a priority in Europe's eastern neighbourhood policies for decades. Likewise, Ukraine is of a great geopolitical importance for the United States. For American geopolitical thinkers, Ukraine's subordination to Russian control would lead to Russia's re-emergence as a Eurasian empire (Brzezinski 1994).

Therefore, Ukraine has also been in the focus of American efforts to prevent Russia's alleged policies to "re-Sovietize" the region.

Under these circumstances, the multivectorial stance between the West and Russia appeared as the most prudent option for Ukrainian foreign policy. As presented in the theoretical framework, neutrality (nonalignment) is seen in the realist school as the most optimal strategy for weak states that are in between great power rivalries (Labs 1992: 385). For example, Kissinger (2014), in the beginning of the Ukraine crisis, rightfully argued that "Far too often the Ukrainian issue is posed as a showdown: whether Ukraine joins the East or the West. But if Ukraine is to survive and thrive, it must not be either side's outpost against the other — it should function as a bridge between them." However, the growing tensions between the West and Russia did not allow Ukrainian leaders to maintain neutrality.

The relatively more democratic environment in Ukraine and the restricted autonomy of Ukrainian leaders allowed Western powers to reach out to sizeable, non-state groups in the country and to affect the country's foreign policies through influencing these groups. Russia also invested largely in its counter-revolutionary policies *vis-à-vis* Ukraine and sought to create politically active, strong pro-Russian, non-state groups. The competition between the two geopolitical centres (i.e. the West and Russia) over Ukraine over the period under study (2004-2016) was largely of a soft power nature and never evolved to a direct military confrontation though it entailed economic warfare to some extent. This chapter is going to pursue an in-depth analysis of the soft power confrontation between the West and Russia, the role of Ukrainian non-state groups in this confrontation and their impact on the formulation of the country's geopolitical orientation.

This chapter replicates the structure of the previous chapter on Belarus. It will discuss the role of domestic non-state actors in shaping Ukraine's foreign policy orientation and its interactions with surrounding great powers. The geopolitical context in which Ukraine has existed since the early years of its independence is to be presented in the first section coming after this introductory part. The following section will analyse the autonomy Ukrainian leaders have had with respect to the general public and other non-state actors since the country gained independence but particularly over the years between 2004–2016. This section will be followed by a wider discussion on the power the West and Russia have wielded over popular opinion in Ukraine. The section is divided into two parts, providing a separate take on Western and Russian soft power. In the final section before the conclusion, the chapter will explore the attitude of the Ukrainian people towards the two geopolitical poles (i.e. Russia and West) and the role they have played in the formation of the country's foreign policy orientation. The concluding part will summarize the major findings of the chapter in the light of the hypotheses presented in the beginning of the book.

Ukraine Between the West and Russia

Ukraine, under the presidencies of Leonid Kravchuk (1991-1994) and Leonid Kuchma (1994–2004), balanced between the West and Russia (Szeptycki 2014: 37, Fesenko 2015: 134-135; Wolczuk 2002). For Ukrainian politicians in the 1990s, cooperation was more favourable than integration in relations with NATO, since integration into the Alliance would have risked economic relations with Russia and other CIS countries (White *et al.* 2006: 170). During the tenure of President Kuchma, Ukraine–NATO relations gradually evolved through Ukraine's active participation in Partnership of Peace, the establishment of the NATO–Ukraine Commission, the formation of a Polish–Ukrainian peacekeeping battalion and its dispatch to Kosovo, Ukraine's support to the USA in the wake of 11 September terror attacks, etc. In 2002, Kuchma even expressed Ukraine's desire to enter NATO. However, his administration did little to actually join the alliance. Integration was considered a more permissible option in the case of non-military organizations, such as the European Union and the World Trade Organization (ibid.). Membership into the European community had remained a priority in foreign policy ever since 1993, when the document "On the Key Directions of the Foreign Policy of Ukraine" declared it as a priority (Domaradzki 2014: 278).

After the presidential elections of 2004, the Western-supported popular uprising—known as the Orange Revolution—defeated political groups led by Viktor Yanukovych who was supported by Leonid Kuchma and Russia. The uprising led by young movements and non-governmental organizations brought pro-Western political elite led by Viktor Yushchenko to power. It was a turning point in the history of the country. For the new government, EU and NATO membership was a primary objective in foreign policy. Yushchenko launched formal governmental preparation for Ukraine's entry into NATO and accelerated reforms with the hope of receiving the Membership Action Plan (MAP) from the alliance. Despite the fact that societal support to NATO membership was rather low (less than 20%), in January 2008, the Orange elite asked NATO to give the MAP to Ukraine at the Bucharest summit later that year (Samokhvalov 2015: 1383).

However, Yushchenko's pro-Western course failed to realize the expectations of the Orange Revolution in domestic politics (Kuzio 2011). The new government did not end the influence of the oligarchic groups on Ukrainian politics and against this background the popularity of President Yushchenko plummeted to 4% towards the end of his term (Wapinski 2014: 59). The disillusionment of the Ukrainian people with the Orange government resulted in an electoral loss for Yushchenko in the 2010 presidential elections which was won by Viktor Yanukovych (Åslund 2015: 80). During the presidency of Yanukovych, the country returned to a multi-vector foreign policy. In 2010, Ukraine's new Law on Foreign and Domestic Policy adopted a non-aligned status in the international sphere, prohibited the country's participation in military blocs, and thus ruled out accession into the transatlantic alliance. This was a fundamental change to the 2003 Law on Fundamentals of National Security which had declared NATO membership as the country's foreign policy goal. The new law named both Russia and the European Union as Ukraine's strategic partners and underscored cooperation with each of them as the country's foreign policy priority. In his article for the Wall Street Journal, Yanukovych (2010), just after his victory in the 2010 presidential elections, highlighted the importance of the "non-bloc" status:

"Ukraine should make use of its geopolitical advantages and become a bridge between Russia and the West. Developing a good relationship with the West and bridging the gap to Russia will help Ukraine. We should not be forced to make [a] false choice between the benefits of the East and those of the West" (See Yanukovych 2010).

However, EU membership remained a main foreign policy goal in the new law as well. The law also recognized the necessity for reforms in the Ukrainian legislation to bring it into accord with the EU's *acquis communautaire*.

During Yanukovych's presidency, relations with Russia returned to a friendlier path. One of the most contentious issues in the bilateral relations — the extension of the deployment of the Black Sea Fleet — was resolved. In exchange for a $100 discount on the import of Russian gas, Kiev extended the lease on the naval facilities in Crimea and Sevastopol to Russia's Black Sea Fleet beyond 2017 until 2042 (Shapovalova 2014: 252). This extension was another move that was to complicate Ukraine's NATO admission, as this *de facto* limited Ukraine's sovereignty over some parts of its internationally recognized territories (Shapovalova 2014: 252).

Although many critics used to portray Yanukovych as a Russian puppet, there is little evidence to defend this speculation (Götz 2015: 4). Yanukovych's foreign policy strategy was in fact similar to Lukashenko's: like his Belarusian counterpart, in pursuing a pragmatic foreign policy, Yanukovych tried to play the West and Russia against each other and to extract economic benefits from the geopolitical importance of Ukraine's location (Samokhvalov 2015: 1379-1380). The attitude of the Russian leaders to him was not different from their attitude to Lukashenko. For the Kremlin, Yanukovych was the lesser of two evils. US embassy cables released by Wikileaks revealed that Putin, as a matter of fact, "hated" him (Götz 2015: 5). However, compared with Lukashenko, Yanukovych and his cabinet members were more suspicious of Russia's Customs Union project. Yanukovych sought alternative sources of energy to reduce Ukraine's gas dependence on Russia, thus hoping to offset Russian pressure and to bypass its integration projects (Fesenko 2015: 137; Samokhvalov 2015: 1379-1380; Åslund 2015: 92-95).

On the other hand, he continued cooperation with the EU, elevated the status of the Ukrainian Ambassador to the EU to the level of a State Representative, and seriously approached the adoption of EU technical norms (Samokhvalov 2015: 1380). Under his presidency, Ukraine finalized the negotiations on the Association Agreement and DCFTA with the European Union and initialled them. For several months before the Vilnius summit, his government "carried out an information and propaganda campaign for a closer association with the EU in Ukraine" (Savin 2014: 7). Although no immediate considerable economic benefits were expected from these agreements, it was widely believed that the agreements would allow Ukraine to gradually evolve in political, legal and socio-economic standards to the European level (Åslund 2013; 2015: 46-47). Ukraine's entry into the Customs Union with Russia, Belarus and Kazakhstan, on the contrary, promised no comparable development in the situation of the rule of law and human rights.

In terms of the economic benefits of the two integration options, pro-Western groups had estimated that the AA and DCFTA would help the Ukraine economy grow more than 10% in the long run, while joining the Customs Union would reduce Ukraine's welfare by almost 4% in the long run (Movchan et al. 2011: 11). The pro-Russian groups, on the contrary, argued that the DCFTA with the European Union would cause a 1.5% reduction in Ukraine's baseline GDP" (Ivanter et al. 2012: 40). According to them, "Over the period of 2011-2030, the total cumulative effect of the creation of the SES [Single Economic Space] and Ukraine joining it on the four countries can reach $1.1 trillion in 2010 prices...." (Ivanter et al. 2012: 41). However, the methodology of the analysis of the pro-Russian groups is highly disputed (Åslund 2015: 48).

Yanukovych's Ukraine made a number of offers to Russia (e.g. exclusive rights to Russian Gazprom and an alternative 3+1 formula in cooperation with the Customs Union, which meant maintaining special status, but not membership, within the organization of Kazakhstan, Russia, and Belarus) to assuage Moscow's concerns about the Association Agreement and DFCTA with the EU. This attempt did not suffice to assuage Moscow's geopolitical fears. Russia was pressing hard to prevent Yanukovych from signing the Association Agreement with the EU. Moscow both threatened Kiev with damaging consequences for Ukraine's economic and political future (e.g. abolition of preferential trade agreements and imposing stringent customs and sanitary controls on imports from Ukraine) and offered huge amounts of loans, subsidies, and discounts on energy imports in return for its retreat from the deal. This pressure, along with deteriorating internal economic and financial situation, forced the Ukrainian president to withdraw from the EU agreements before the EaP Vilnius summit (Fesenko 2015: 137-138). Instead, he signed the so-called Moscow agreements with Russia, according to which the Kremlin agreed to provide Ukraine with $15 billion in financial aid and a 30% discount in natural gas supplies (Fesenko 2015: 138). However, although the agreement was likely to increase Russia's influence on Ukrainian politics, it was not an accession agreement to the Customs Union and the Yanukovych government did not take on such an obligation for the future.

The internal non-state actors, however, did not allow Yanukovych to implement his decision. Protesting the *volte-face* of the Yanukovych administration, pro-Western political groups and ordinary citizens marched to the *Maidan Nezalezhnosti* (Independence Square) in central Kiev—or Euromaidan, as it later came to be known because of the pro-EU protests. US and European leaders rejected Yanukovych's offer to hold trilateral negotiations between the EU, Russia and Ukraine on integration issues (RFE/RL 2017a). Seizing the opportunity created by anti-governmental upheaval, they decided to finally pull Ukraine into West's orbit. US Senator John McCain, the Assistant Secretary of State for European and Eurasian Affairs at the United States Department of State Victoria Nuland and many other European and American officials met the demonstrators and encouraged them to stand firmly for their ideals. McCain's address to the protesters declaring "We are here to support your just cause" (Guardian 2013) and Nuland's meeting with them at Maidan are a few examples that demonstrated the extremely concentrated engagement of the United States in the process. These Western politicians could never have had this chance to support anti-governmental demonstrations so overtly in Lukashenko's Belarus. From the very beginning of Euromaidan, these politicians openly stood with protestors and encouraged them to fight for their cause despite the Ukrainian authorities. For example, the address of one of the first EU politicians who travelled to Ukraine to speak to protestors at the beginning of Euromaidan in late November 2013, Polish MEP Pawel Kowal, the head of Parliamentary Delegation on Co-operation with Ukraine, deserves to be quoted here:

> "I could not just sit there, in Brussels, and watch you freeze on this square. I came so that the whole of Europe could see and pay attention to what is happening here. They will ask me why you are here. I think it is because you want to be able, just like every Polish, German or French person, to decide about your future. I would like them in Brussels to know that you, young people, are here for the sake of your country [...]. Standing here, you are opening the European gates for Ukraine!" (cited in Przelomiec 2014: 300).

These actions of the Western politicians have been characterized by some experts as a crude violation of international law and a form of interference in Ukraine's domestic affairs. For example, Rein Müllerson (2014: 135), President of Tallinn Law School, at Estonia's Tallinn University, in his article titled *Ukraine: Victim of Geopolitics*, fleshed out that:

> "...[I]t was the representatives of Western states who completely ignored one of the cornerstone principles of international law—the non-interference in the internal affairs of other states. Such unconditional support of the opposition not only constituted a flagrant interference in the internal affairs of Ukraine but it also raised expectations and made uncompromising revolutionaries even more intransigent."

Truly, the Euromaidan protestors were seriously emboldened by and became more determined thanks to the clear support of the European Union and United States. In February 2014, they finally toppled President Yanukovych through an unconstitutional[14] overthrow; and Western-supported[15] politicians came to power in Ukraine. Following Yanukovych's fall, the Kremlin realized that it would lose Ukraine to NATO unless it intervened immediately and unwaveringly. Therefore, regardless of all the risks, Moscow adopted the decision to occupy Crimea and instigate separatism in Eastern Ukraine. Only an intervention on this scale would suffice to deal a crushing blow to Ukraine's Euro-Atlantic prospects.

Thus, Ukraine became a victim of geopolitical rivalries (Müllerson 2014). Its democratically elected leader Yanukovych fell prey to these rivalries that pushed him to the either/or choice between Russia and the West. On one side, the Western fear of and distrust in the resurgence of Russia as a strong regional power had generated in the Western capitals a desire to tear away Ukraine from Russia's sphere of influence and thus to undermine its projects to reintegrate the post-Soviet countries. Russia's determination to push back against such expansion of Western military and political structures and reinstate control over its immediate neighbourhood brought it into a stand-off with the West over Ukraine. On the other side, as expected by neoclassical realism, the internal factors (i.e. the general public and non-governmental organizations) played a crucial role in the formation of the state's external alignment along with international pressure. The intervening influence of domestic

---

14   As a matter of fact, Euromaidan supporters argue that the removal of President Yanukovych from his office was consistent with the norms of the Ukrainian constitution, particularly because, in their opinion, "the change took place in an extraordinary situation" (Musiyaka 2014). However, the four circumstances in which, according to the constitution, the president may cease to exercise his power were not present before Yanukovych's removal from the presidency: (1) resignation, (2) inability to exercise his or her powers for reasons of health, (3) removal from office by the procedure of impeachment, (4) death (Morrison 2014).
15   The role of the United States in the formation of the post-Yanukovych government "became embarrassingly clear" in a leaked telephone conversation between Assistant Secretary Victoria Nuland and US ambassador to Ukraine, Geoffrey Pyatt (Sparrow 2014: 328). On the phone, the two American politicians assessed the skills of the Ukrainian opposition leaders to lead the government (See BBC 2014),

non-state players empowered by Western forces made Yanukovych's decision to retain neutrality a political suicide for him. Thus, the pressure derived from confrontation between the great powers and intensified by the intervening influence of domestic non-state groups did not allow Kiev to maintain its geopolitical neutrality which leading geopolitical minds considered the best option for Ukraine (Kissinger 2014; Mearsheimer 2014).

The Euromaidan revolution and its aftermath costed Ukrainians a dramatic economic breakdown, political turmoil and territorial losses. Ukrainian sources evaluated the economic damages incurred due to the occupation of Crimea to be $40 billion in the losses of oil and gas reserves in the Black Sea and $90 billion in other losses (Shapovalova 2014: 264). Donetsk and Lugansk — the two Ukrainian regions that have been under the control of Russia-supported separatists since 2014 — had contributed to well-nigh 16% of the Ukrainian GDP until the secessionist war broke out (Poluneev 2014). These losses are still growing. For example, government estimates show that Russia's move to deviate the route of its gas exports from the pipelines going through the territories of Ukraine will cost Ukraine a 10% loss in its annual budget (Rapoza 2017). On the other hand, contrary to the optimistic prognoses of observers back in early 2014, Yanukovych's departure did not change Ukraine substantially and did not trigger tangible economic progress and democratic political reforms.

However, in the wake of Yanukovych's overthrow, Ukraine massively intensified its relations with Western powers. An Association Agreement and DCFTA were signed shortly after Yanukovych's departure. The country has already launched the implementation of these agreements. The volume of trade with the EU currently accounts for 40% of Ukraine's foreign trade, while the share of Russia has dropped from 27.3% to 11.5% over the last three years since early 2014 (See lb.ua 2017). Ukraine obtained a visa-free regime with the EU which would certainly increase the integration of Ukrainian society into the European community. The range of integration with the West expands beyond the borders of the Europe: in 2016, Kiev signed a free trade agreement with Canada

(CUFTA). In the same year of Yanukovych's fall, the Ukrainian parliament revoked the law on neutrality and declared the country's goal to be NATO membership. A state programme for the adoption of NATO standards by the Armed Forces of Ukraine by 2020 has been accepted and is being implemented (See Interfax-Ukraine 2017). On the other hand, the gap between Russia and Ukraine is increasingly widening. The post-Euromaidan government took a series of actions in order to accelerate this process and minimize Russian cultural influence on Ukraine. Towards this end, the government-imposed restrictions on Russian language textbooks, Russian media, Russian language, Russian symbols and the promotion of Soviet heritage.

State Autonomy *Vis-à-vis* Non-State Actors

The autonomy of the state *vis-à-vis* society in Ukraine has never been as strong as it has been in Belarus. The economic challenges that independence brought about, the existence of influential and politically active oligarchic groups and the ethnic composition and social characteristics of the state have played a decisive role in the failure of Ukrainian state leaders to consolidate power entirely in their own hands. The revolutionary or anarchist attitude of many Ukrainians towards state authorities has also been an influential factor in curbing the power of their leaders and preventing them from using force to protect their regimes (Chernega 2015). The annual approval ratings of Ukrainian leaders since the Orange Revolution indicate that, although the leaders are usually elected with some expectations and hope, they fail to live up to those expectations and the people withdraw their support *en masse* and rapidly (Table 3). Despite the fact that there have been consistent attempts by the state to limit the influence of non-state actors, neither have these attempts evolved to massive repression campaigns against independent voices nor were they sufficient to totally counterbalance them. This section will briefly discuss the form of interaction between the Ukrainian state and non-state actors and the scope of the latter to influence the policies of the former.

The collapse of the Soviet Union unleashed the ambitions of Ukrainian businessmen to accumulate their wealth and expand their influence. The post-Soviet political history of the country is inherently related to the internal conflicts between these businessmen who are known as oligarchs, due to their involvement in politics. Most of the influential non-state actors, particularly non-governmental organizations and media channels, have been founded or are supported by oligarchic groups as part of their strategy to exert pressure on the internal and external policies of the state. Although President Kuchma was rather repressive towards non-state actors, he failed to entirely eradicate their influence on government. The crackdown on media during his presidency included attacks on or the murder of journalists, imposing censorship and specifying what could be covered, reducing access to Radio Liberty's Ukrainian service and other Western radio broadcasts, etc. (Bunce et al. 2011: 120). However, Kuchma was not able to silence opposing voices across the country. His power was structurally constrained by the relatively influential authority of the parliament and the oppositional forces that had, though limited, still some access to the media (ibid.).

There were around 40,000 registered non-governmental institutions in the country in early 2003 (Puglisi 2015: 4). Almost one tenth of them were active and functional (ibid.). Despite these high figures, prior to the Orange Revolution Ukrainian civil society had a long range of problems, particularly a lack of sufficient funding and a low level of public participation (Stepanenko 2006). In those years, state funding of civil society organizations was insufficient, complicated and non-transparent. Consequently, only a few organizations could receive it. For example, around half of the direct budget funding of CSOs was allotted only to eight organizations (Ghosh 2014: 7). Therefore, most of the CSOs were dependent on external funding (ibid.: 7-10). However, thanks to the existence of a relatively more liberal environment many civic organizations were still in operation. They cooperated within small coalitions, such as the Freedom of Choice Coalition, "Ukraine without Kuchma", "Rise, Ukraine", the Committee of Voters of Ukraine, etc.

	2008	2009	2010	2011	2012	2013	2014	2015	2016
President V. Yushchenko	17	7							
President V. Yanukovych			46	29	28	28			
President P. Poroshenko							47	17	6.4

Table 3. Job Approval of Ukrainian presidents (percentage) [16]

Thus, the relatively larger scope of the media and a stronger civil society were one of the most important factors that facilitated the emergence of a social upheaval protesting election fraud in 2004 which went down in history as "Orange Revolution". Assessing the political opportunities for a social movement prior to these events, Abel Polese (2009: 257) points out that:

> "[There] were many [political opportunities] ranged from a united and growing opposition to the pressure of international attention towards the country, through the organization of a protest network that was close to perfection, to the existence of an increasingly divided regime."

The Orange Revolution took place in such a political environment. The revolution, led by non-governmental organizations, particularly a civic campaign called PORA (in Ukrainian: It's Time) that included hundreds of NGOs, empowered the potential of civil society in Ukraine and generated a favourable environment for non-state actors to directly influence the policies of their leaders. There were also consistent legislative improvements on the Law on Civic Associations in this period: each year throughout 2005-2009, progressive amendments were adopted on the Law (Ghosh 2014:

---

[16] The figures for the period between 2008-2015 have been retrieved from Gallup's official website (See Ray 2015). 2016's figures are from the official website of Rating Group Ukraine — Ratinggroup.ua.

3). Some ministries founded public councils dealing with civil society organizations and holding policy dialogues (ibid.). A 2014 study supported by the Friedrich Ebert Stiftung notes that:

> "The number and variety, levels of registration and scope of activities in civil society and the free media in Ukraine made them among the most vibrant and diverse in the former Soviet Union countries (Ghosh 2014: 3).

In the wake of these developments, the democratic environment of the country experienced some progress which was reflected in the assessment of Freedom House that upgraded the status of Ukraine to "free" in 2006, for the first time (See Freedom House 2006). However, the advent of Yanukovych's presidency negatively affected this process. President Yanukovych did in fact consolidate power largely in the hands of his family and close associates to an extent previously unaccomplished by any other Ukrainian president (Åslund 2015: 82). He initiated a constitutional amendment, expanded the presidential powers, and consequently got the de-facto chance to rule over all the executive, legislative and judicial institutions of the country (ibid.). Due to his undemocratic policies, crackdown on opposition, non-governmental institutions and media, Freedom House downgraded the score of Ukraine to "partly free" in 2011 (See Freedom House 2011). The country's press freedom was also downgraded by various international organizations, such as Human Rights Watch, Freedom House, Reporters without Borders, etc. (Bachmann *et al.* 2014: 352-353; Åslund 2015: 82).

The circumscription of political liberties and the growing authoritarian tendencies of the political leadership generated popular discontent with the Yanukovych administration (Solonenko 2014: 224-228). Deteriorating economic conditions in the country, on the other hand, further decreased the popularity of his government. Similar to the situation before the Orange Revolution — when, although the state had managed some economic growth (5.2% in 2002 and by 9.6% in 2003), it failed to generate noteworthy improvement in the living standards of the majority (Bunce *et al.* 2011: 118) — Ukrainians under the rule of Yanukovych struggled with substantial economic challenges. The economic situation was one of the most important factors that increased the vulnerability of the governments prior to both revolutions. Klaus Bachmann (2014: 424) has rightfully counted the economic challenges as a cause of the anti-governmental upheaval in the wake of Yanukovych's decision not to sign the Association Agreement with the EU:

> "[Yanukovych's *volte-face* prior to the Vilnius summit of the EaP] was a trigger, but not the only cause of the protests. During the last years of Yanukovych's rule, Ukrainians had observed a steady decline of their economy, with rising unemployment, shrinking foreign currency reserves, high inflation and decreasing foreign direct investment..."

Yanukovych, although had attempted on many occasions, failed to establish complete control over non-state actors and media (Szostek 2014: 467). The public effect of the independent news outlets (e.g. *Ukrainskaya pravda*, Weekly Mirror), television channels (e.g. Channel 5, 1+1 and ICTV owned by businessmen Petro Proshenko, Ihor Kolomoisky, and Victor Pinchuk, respectively), online media services, internet-based TV channels (e.g. Hromadske.TV and Espreso.TV) and social media (e.g. Facebook, Twitter, etc.) cannot be underestimated (Åslund 2015: 103-104). A public opinion poll revealed that the "vast majority" of the people who watched non-partisan television channels were more likely to support the Euromaidan (Bachmann *et al.* 2014: 360). The growing access to the internet amongst the Ukrainian population affected the wider dissemination of information: 46% of the whole adult population aged over 16 had internet access in 2013 while only 15% had it in 2008 (Bachmann *et al.* 2014: 353). The existence of independent television channels was, however, much more crucial, as for around 90% of the population local TV was the main source of political information (Szostek 2014: 467; Bachmann *et al.* 2014: 352) (Table 4).

	Whole Population
Ukrainian TV	90,5
Russian TV	22,7
Western (American, European TV)	2,9
Radio	28,9
National newspapers	20,1
Local newspapers	36,7
Magazines	2,5
Websites (news, political analysis)	21,0
Social networking sites	5,7
Internet TV & Internet radio	3,4
Other	2,0
Hard to say	0,6

Table 4. The main sources of political information for Ukrainians in 2013 (percentage) (The table is retrieved from Bachmann et al. 2014: 352).

This environment was also favourable for the solid growth of civil society between 2004-2014. Freedom House recorded an improvement in the rating of Ukrainian civil society's performance from 3.00 in 2005 to 2.50 in 2014 (See Freedom House 2014). Tellingly, the crackdown on anti-governmental forces in Ukraine under Yanukovych never evolved to the scale it was observed in the fully authoritarian states. Solonenko (2014: 220-221) reports that:

> "Since the Orange Revolution, there has been a steady increase in officially registered civil society organizations (CSOs) in Ukraine. By 2014 there were already 75,414[17] non-governmental organizations (NGOs), known officially as 'civic organizations', as well as 28,851 trade unions, 15,904 associations of co-owners of multiple-family dwellings, 15,708 'charitable foundations or organizations', 1,369 self-organized territorial communities, and 276 professional organizations."

On 16 January 2014, during the Euromaidan protests, Yanukovych forced the parliament to adopt a list of laws to restrict the influence of anti-government protestors. These laws required externally funded non-governmental organizations to be registered as "foreign agents", put massive restrictions on the internet and anti-government protests, etc. (Wilson 2014: 81-82). However, by the end of January, Yanukovych had to repeal most of these laws. Thus, his power to fight back against the forces who opposed him was structurally limited. Although the sniper shootings against the protestors were attributed to him, a wide range of sources and revelations disputed this claim (Sakwa 2015: 81-100). Later Yanukovych counted his restrained reaction as "the most important" mistake he made prior to his ouster: "I made a number of mistakes, and the most important one was that I wasn't able to force myself to bring troops and impose martial law in Ukraine, this being the only way to stop the radicals. I didn't opt for bloodshed." Retrospectively, some analysts consider the "inadequate response" of the Yanukovych administration to the Euromaidan upheaval as a more determining reason for the eventual fall of his government rather than "support for European integration, continued police brutality, or the size of the protest movement" (Peisakhin 2014).

Non-State Actors under the Influence of External Powers

Ukraine, as the "biggest prize" (Gershman 2013) in Russia—West rivalries over the "common neighbourhood", has attracted a vast

---

17 Solonenko (2014: 220-221) later notes that not all of the officially registered non-governmental organizations were active. She, referring to Ukrainian experts, points out that only some 3,000-4,000 of them were operating, the rest existed only nominally.

amount of soft power investment from the two geopolitical foes since the very beginning of the post-Soviet period. The two great powers have strived to influence the political processes in Ukraine through influencing the minds and feelings of the Ukrainians via media, non-governmental organizations, exchange programs, etc. The following two sub-sections will briefly explore the soft power of the West and Russia over Ukrainian society and their policies to wield this power.

Non-State Actors under the Influence of Russian Soft Power

Ukraine is inherently connected to Russia through linguistic, religious, historical, cultural, ethnic and economic bonds. The long years of common existence within the same country have made these bonds distinctively strong and enduring. It has provided Russia with various assets to be used to affect the internal affairs of Ukraine through influencing the minds and feelings of the Ukrainian people. According to the only census carried out in the independence period (2001), 17,3% of the Ukrainian population were ethnic Russians and 80% had fluency in Russian (Marples 2015: 9) (See State Statistics Committee of Ukraine 2001). Russian is the first language for more than a quarter of the Ukrainian people (See Lenta.ru 2007).

Most of the ethnic Russians living in the Eastern part of the country have demonstrated a strong tendency to support pro-Russian candidates in nationwide elections (Marples 2015: 9). On the contrary, the Western territories, which had been under Poland or Austria-Hungary dominance up until World War II, have an equally strong tendency to support Euro-Atlantic integration of the country and politicians who are on a pro-Western track. Beissinger (2014) has found that "Orange revolutionaries were more than eight times more likely to be from Western Ukraine… [and] 92 percent of… [them] claimed Ukrainian as their native language." The Westerners, of which 80% supported the anti-Yanukovych protests while only 30% of Easterners did so, constituted also the majority both in the Orange and Euromaidan revolutions (Andreyev 2014;

Petro 2014). Eastern regions differed from the Western part also in their judgement of the post-Yanukovych bloodshed in eastern Ukraine: in a survey asking respondents who they found responsible for the bloodshed in the east of the country, only 19,1% of Easterners found Russia responsible, while for 81,6% of Westerners Russia was the aggressor to be blamed (Petro 2015: 28).

From the disintegration of the Soviet Union up until the Orange Revolution, Russia did not have a substantial pro-Russian NGO network in Ukraine, and instead built ties with Ukrainian elites. As its governmental support to Viktor Yanukovych failed to reach its goals in the 2004 presidential elections and Western-supported non-governmental institutions played a decisive role in this process, the Russian leaders realized the importance of these institutions and interactions with ordinary people. The Russian political elite and expert community widely related Russia's failure to its negligence of civil society as an influential tool. Gleb Pavlovsky, a Kremlin political consultant, who had been dispatched to Kiev to assist Yanukovych in electoral processes, regretted the fact that: "during the electoral campaign in Ukraine there was an underestimation [by Russia] and a low level of cooperation between Russian society and Ukrainian NGOs. We will try to avoid such an underestimation in the future" (Socor 2005).

Soon after the Orange Revolution, the number of such organizations founded and supported by Russia started to rise. In the years before the Euromaidan, the Kremlin had already formed connections with a large number of NGOs in Ukraine. For example, the "Russian-speaking Ukraine" organization, under whose umbrella 120 civic organizations and 10,000 members come together, had been supported by Russian foundations such as Russkiy Mir, the Gorchakov Foundation and the Moscow House of Compatriots World Foundation (Lutsevych 2016: 15). "Ukrainian Choice" (in Ukrainian: "Ukrayins'kyy vybir") was another popular pro-Russian civil society organization which opposed European integration and advocated for closer relations between Ukraine and Russia. The organization was established in 2012 by business tycoon and former lawmaker Viktor Medvedchuk who has close personal ties to the Russian political elite and President Putin. It organised regular demonstrations and posted billboards protesting the Association Agreement. In parallel with the mainstream Kremlin narrative, they equate closer relations with the EU to the adoption of same-sex marriage and warn against dramatic economic repercussions of signing trade deals with Europe.

Russia-supported non-governmental organizations and political parties were more active in Crimea. **Political parties** (e.g. "Russkiy Blok" (Russian Block), "Russkoe Edinstvo" (Russian Unity), "Soyuz" (Union), and Rus' Edinaya" (Russia United)), **NGOs** (e.g. Russkaya Obschina Kryma" (Russian Community of Crimea), "Russkaya Obschina Sevastopolya" (Russ Community of Sevastopol), Narodny Front "Sevastopol'-Krym-Rossiya" (Popular Front "Sevastopol-Crimea-Russia")), **Cossack organizations** (e.g. Ob'edineniye Kozakov Kryma (Crimea Cossack Union) and Chernomorskaya Kazachya Sotnya (Black Sea Cossack Sotnia)), and **Coalitions of pro-Russian organizations** (e.g. Sevastopol "Front protiv NATO" (Front against NATO)) helped Russia to sustain and reinforce pro-Russian sentiments amongst Crimeans and eventually to annex the region without shooting a single bullet (Bjorn 2014).

However, arguably the most active and influential non-governmental organization in Russia's soft power arsenal concerning Ukraine has been the Russian Orthodox Church. The fact that the majority of the people in both countries believe in Orthodox Christianity and that Ukrainians trust churches (60-70%) more than any other institution (Kochan 2016: 105) have helped post-Soviet Russia to deploy religion as a tool in its foreign policy *vis-à-vis* Ukraine. Before the annexation of Crimea, the Ukrainian branch of the Russian Orthodox Church (ROC) — the largest religious confession in Ukraine — has had more or less equal popular support amongst the Orthodox believers in Western (19.8%) and Eastern (24,2%) parts of Ukraine (Suslov 2016: 135). The ROC has invariably considered Ukraine a major part of the *Russkii Mir* and generously invested to wield influence on Ukraine's religious discourse and to maintain a "special relationship" with Ukraine (Suslov 2016: 133). Although the Ukrainian Orthodox Church of the Moscow Patriarchate (UOC-

MP) has financial and administrative independence from the Moscow Patriarchate, the latter has not granted autocephaly to the former. The Moscow Patriarchate maintains symbolic superiority over the UOC-MP: according to the UOC-MP Statute, "the patriarch blesses every new head of the UOC-MP, the patriarch's name is mentioned first in all church services, and the UOC-MP maintains contacts with other Orthodox Churches through the ROC" (Suslov 2016: 134). The UOC-MP also has stronger institutional capacity than its main rival, the anti-Russian Ukrainian Orthodox Church Kiev Patriarchate (UOC-KP): approximately 40% of the 34,000 religious institutions in the country belong to UOC-MP, while the UOC-KP holds only about 15% of them (Suslov 2016: 136).

Even during the times when the relationship between the two countries was at its worst, the ROC avoided politicizing its role and tried to maintain "spiritual unity" of the Russian World (See TASS 2014). The ROC often addressed the Ukrainian people, defended the importance of the brotherly ties on the religious grounds and prayed for the peaceful resolution of the disputes between the governments of the two nations. Likewise, the UOC-MP used to advocate closer relations between Ukraine and Russia and supported pro-Russian politicians and presidential candidates. For instance, prior to the 2004 presidential elections, Volodymyr Sabodan, Metropolitan of Kyiv took part in Russia-supported candidate Yanukovych's electoral campaigns and gave his blessings to him in the elections (Gretskiy 2007: 8).

However, this religious affinity did not inhibit numerous members of the UOC-MP from taking part in Euromaidan (Krawchuk 2016: 175). Most of the UOC-MP synod and church members condemned the "the criminal actions of the government" for committing bloodshed during the protests, refused to take a pro-Russian position, and declared their support for European values and Ukraine's territorial integrity (Krawchuk 2016: 182). Although there were many priests in Donbass and some Eastern regions who supported the separatists, none of the bishops of the Church "dared to openly support Russian aggression on Ukraine" (Olszański 2014).

As a matter of fact, there are substantial groups within the UOC-MP, particularly amongst the younger hierarchs, who support gaining full canonical independence from Moscow and European integration (Olszański 2014).

In general, Crimea's annexation and Russia's support to separatist groups in Eastern Ukraine weakened the popular support for the ROC and its Ukrainian branch (Olszański 2014; Suslov 2016). Olszański (2014) mentions that growing anti-Russian sentiments amongst the members and parish clergy and the fact that some of them have left the UOC-MP to join the Kiev Patriarchate and many others want to do so "will force the UOC to identify itself increasingly strongly with the Ukrainian state and nation."

Russia is one of the most popular destinations for Ukrainian students who go abroad to study. In 2015, approximately 16 thousand students from Ukraine were enrolled in Russian universities (Semonov 2016). The Russian authorities claim that more than 75% of these students choose to remain in Russia following their graduation (ibid.). Apart from that, millions of students used to study in Russian at Ukrainian schools: In Ukraine at the time of the collapse of the Soviet Union, there were 4633 Russian schools where more than 3 million pupils were studying (ibid.). Over the years since then there has been a drastic decline in these numbers. In 2011, only 1149 of these schools remained in operation (ibid.). The number of pupils also dramatically decreased to below 700,000 (ibid.). In 20 years following the disintegration of the Soviet Union, the proportion of pupils studying in Ukrainian increased from less than 50% to 83% (See Polit.ru 2010). The Russian government could not take any effective counter measures to prevent or reverse this trend.

As it happened in the case of non-governmental organizations, Russia came to understand the importance of educational programmes in the aftermath of the Orange Revolution. In 2007, Russia started an exchange programme for international students, including Ukrainian students. The program covered the costs of study for a certain number of Ukrainians (less than 100 students per a year)[18] at Russian higher education institutions (Semonov 2016). In the same year, it also opened the first cultural centre of Rossotrudnichestvo in Kiev. However, compared to scholarly exchange programmes of Western countries in Ukraine, Russia's programmes were rather belated and provided limited opportunities. For example, the United States had already started an exchange programme addressing post-Soviet countries in 1993 and thousands of Ukrainians have obtained the support to study in the USA since then. Likewise, the educational channels of Western countries had been operating in Ukraine long years before Russia opened the first Rossotrudnichestvo centre in Kiev: the Ukrainian offices of the British Council (1992), the Goethe Institute (1993), and the French Institute (1994) had been in Ukraine since the first years of Ukraine's independence (ibid.).

In the post-Soviet period, the Russian media has experienced a steady decline in its reputation amongst Ukrainians. Several surveys conducted by Razumkov institute between 1999-2013 concluded that the majority of the population in Ukraine found Russian media untrustworthy and biased (Petro 2015: 38). Nevertheless, both Russian TV channels and newspapers are amongst the most watched and read in Ukraine. For example, in 2011, the three biggest Russian state-controlled TV channels, *Pervyy Kanal*, *RTR Planeta* and *NTV Mir* weekly reached out to 32.8%, 24.9% and 19.8% of the Ukrainian population, respectively (Szostek 2014: 468). Similarly, *Komsomolskaya Pravda v Ukraine* and *Argumenty i Fakty v Ukraine*—Ukrainian editions of Moscow-based publications—are one of the few publications in Ukraine that have readerships to compete with the viewership of the TV news bulletins that dominate Ukraine's media space (Szostek 2014: 467-8). Besides, the Russian language had a predominant position in the cultural and information sphere of the country: Nicolai Petro (2014: 5) cites a 2012

---

18 In the aftermath of the Ukrainian crisis, Russia increased the quota for international students, including Ukrainians. For the period 2016-2017, 455 places were allocated for Ukrainian students (Semonov 2016). However, Semonov (2016) accurately argues that this is a rather small figure for a nation of 40 million. For example, the places (494) allocated for Moldovans (less than 4 million population) was even higher than that for Ukrainians.

study which has found that "over 60 percent of newspapers, 83 percent of journals, 87 percent of books and 72 percent of television programs in Ukraine are in Russian." He (ibid.) points out that the predominance of Russian has been further reinforced in the wake of the massive use of the Internet by Ukrainians whose most preferred language on websites is Russian (80%).

Crimea's annexation and separatist escalation in Eastern Ukraine strictly worsened the conditions for Russian soft power projection in Ukraine. On the one hand, the aversion to everything Russian grew rapidly amongst the Ukrainian people which was reflected in various spheres of their daily life. This was wide-ranging as the Russian people also supported the Kremlin's policies regarding Crimea and Eastern Ukraine (See UNIAN 2016a). Tellingly, while just 4% of the respondents rated Russia unfavourably in Ukraine in 2010 (See ICPS 2010), the percentage of these people went up to around 60% in 2014 (See Pew Research Centre 2014). The majority (68% of the Ukrainian people) found Russia's Crimean policies as "an attempt to break Ukraine into several parts and threaten its independence" (See IRI 2014). These sentiments affected also the use of the Russian language by Ukrainians. Ievgen Vorobiov, a Ukrainian expert, points out that:

> "Now many Russian speakers in Ukraine — who live primarily in the country's east and in large cities — are demonstratively turning to Ukrainian as a badge of self-identification... Patriotic Russian-speakers in Kiev and big eastern cities are pledging on social networks to speak Ukrainian to their children, hoping to make the next generation more fluent and natural speakers of their native tongue. For the first time in decades, speaking Ukrainian is seen as fashionable rather than backward" (Vorobiov 2015a).

On the other hand, the government adopted a series of measures against Russia's soft power projection. The post-Yanukovych Ukrainian leaders imposed a range of restrictions on Russian media outlets, non-governmental organizations, and other soft power instruments that addressed the Ukrainian public. Immediately after Yanukovych's fall, in March 2014, Kiev restricted the broadcasting of a number of Russian TV Channels (e.g. *Vesti, Rossia 24, ORT, RTR Planeta* and *NTV-Mir*) in Ukraine (UNIAN 2014a).

Several media agencies had to cease operation in Ukraine. For example, *Kommersant-Ukraina* — the Ukrainian branch of Russian business daily *Kommersant* founded in 2005 and owned by Russian tycoon Alisher Usmanov — terminated its activities in 2014 (Szostek 2014: 469). These restrictions covered even films produced by Russians: in March 2016, the "films of the aggressor state" produced or released for the first time after January 1, 2014 were banned from broadcasting (See RT 2016).

In December 2014, in a controversial manner, the Poroshenko government established the Ministry of Information Policy with the declared purpose of counteracting Russian propaganda (Interfax-Ukraine 2014). More importantly, the Poroshenko government adopted a law on de-communization in 2015 (Ukraynskaya Pravda 2015a). The law prohibited the propagation of Soviet-style communism in Ukraine and ordered the removal of its symbols. In the course of this process, the remnants of the Soviet past were targeted by the Ukrainian authorities. In less than two years after Yanukovych's fall, over 800 of the remaining 1400 Lenin monuments were dismantled across the country. The names of dozens of cities and villages which had been associated with the Russian past were changed (Ukraynskaya Pravda 2015b).

In some regions, even the use of the word "Russia" in signs at enterprises, offices and advertising spaces was banned (TASS 2016b). The communist parties were outlawed and prohibited from taking part in the political processes and elections. In line with the previous policies countering Russian soft power projection, in May 2017, the Poroshenko government ordered the leading Russian social networks and search engines to be completely blocked or restricted in Ukraine (RFE/RL 2017b). The list of websites that were affected by this order included VKontakte, Odnolkassniki, Yandex and the Mail.ru Group that had been widely used by the Ukrainian people.

Non-State Actors under the Influence of Western Soft Power Projection

From the early years of the post-Soviet era, the relatively more favorable political environment in Ukraine made it possible for Western countries to wield soft power in Ukraine through various channels. The existence of independent media outlets and a large number of non-governmental organizations helped the West to easily deliver its narratives to the Ukrainian people and to successfully compete against Russia's soft power. Unlike Russia, that tried to capitalize on the historical past and cultural bonds, Western powers have been projecting a future-oriented soft power armed with the attractiveness of European values, democratic ideals and the relative prosperity of Western countries. The relatively stronger desire of many Ukrainians for rapprochement with Western powers and their support for pro-Western political developments in the country have laid favourable ground for Western soft power projection.

For numerous people in Ukraine, integration into the club of the European Union and NATO promised a chance to establish the rule of law in the country which for over 70% of Ukrainians was "the most important human need of which they felt deprived" (Ryabchuk 2014; Kochan 2016: 106). Although Ukrainians find the "cultural" values of Europe different from those of Ukraine and feel culturally closer to Russia (Stegniy 2011: 64), it is not reflected in their geopolitical vision. Considering Russia as a backward country with no progressive development model, many of them—particularly those who live in the Western part of the country—have seen geopolitical divorce from their northern neighbour as an imperative to pursue the Europeanization of Ukraine (Ryabchuk 2014; Chernega 2015).

Due to the fact that Western Ukraine was historically under either the rule of Poland or the Austro-Hungarian Empire and had never been under Russian control up until World War II, the people currently living in this region feel a special attachment to the West. Hence, the Western power over popular opinion in Western Ukraine is especially stronger than in other parts of the country.

These people are also politically more active than their fellow countrymen both in other regions of Ukraine and abroad. Western Ukrainians, comprising the major part of the Ukrainian diaspora in Europe and America, have advocated Ukraine's integration into the Western community at the expense of its ties with Russia. Those Ukrainians, abroad and at home, promote the image of Russia as a historically aggressive neighbour that has committed a series of crimes against Ukraine, including the Holodomor. They also distinguish their ethnic identity from that of Russia, claiming that the latter is more of a mixed identity containing Slavic, Finnish and Tatar heritage (Rywkin 2014: 125). Since the collapse of the Soviet Union, this attitude towards Russia has been propagated at Ukrainian schools as well (Chernega 2015).

The "European dream", associated with the rule of law, social justice, and freedom, was a key motive for Ukrainians in pro-Western social upheavals (Portnov 2014: 13; Ostrovs'kyj 2014: 21; Onuch 2014: 48). There has been an unrealistic expectation amongst many Ukrainians, particularly amongst younger people, that their country would progressively reform itself and establish high living standards in a short period of time if it were to succeed in integrating itself into the West. Ukrainian leaders, themselves advocating European integration, have never substantially opposed this discourse. Vladimir Chernega (2015), the Russian advisor to the Council of Europe, in his analysis on Russia's failure in the Ukraine crisis, writes that:

> "[In Ukraine] many sincerely believe that the rapprochement with the EU will not only quickly stop the impoverishment of the majority [of the public], that has never stopped since the country gained independence, but also will evolve Ukrainian welfare standards to the European level. It should be noted that this hope was strengthened by Ukrainian governments, including during Yanukovych's period. In 2012, I took part in a conference in Kiev where the Minister of Labour and Social Policy declared that the average pension in the country would reach 1,000 euros in a few years after the signing of the Association Agreement. In Ukraine, the average pension did not exceed 100 euros at that time." (my translation)

The desire of Ukrainians to integrate into the European community has been augmented by the wide-ranging public diplomacy and propaganda campaigns of the Western countries which cover all the dimensions of soft power making including scholarly exchanges, mass media, non-governmental organizations, etc. On the contrary to Russia's strategy aimed at reinforcing ties primarily with Ukrainian elites or pro-Russian political groups, Western powers have, since the beginning of the post-Soviet period, sought to promote their connection with the ordinary people and oppositional forces (Chernega 2015).

European countries and the United States launched educational exchange programmes for Ukrainians in the immediate aftermath of the Soviet collapse. The programmes provided by the United States (e.g. the Fulbright Program, Humphrey Fellowships, the Future Leaders Exchange (FLEX) Program, Global Undergraduate Exchange Program (UGRAD), Benjamin Franklin Program) and the European countries (e.g. German Academic Exchange Service (DAAD), Erasmus Mundus), and Open Society Institution (OSI) have brought thousands of Ukrainians to study at Western universities. According to UNESCO statistics, the number of Ukrainian students studying in European countries (EU members plus non-EU Western European countries), in the USA and Canada (more than 31,000) far outweighed that of those studying in Russia (12,043) in 2014 (See UNESCO 2016). The ratio of Ukrainian students studying at Russian universities to those studying at Western universities has further increased in favour of the latter over the period between 2004 and 2014 (See Table 5).

Host country or region	2004	2014
Russian Federation	6841	12,043
Western countries	12,333	31,000

Table 5. The number of Ukrainian students studying at the universities of Russia and West (See UNESCO 2017).

Over the years since the 1990s, the West has supported emergence of an army of non-governmental organizations in Ukraine. These organizations played a key role in the anti-governmental protests and the pro-Western drift of their country. The Western NGOs operational in Ukraine have supported the local NGOs on a large scale and played a crucial role in their empowerment (Beissinger 2007: 261; Wilson 2005: 183–189). Without the financial and technical support of those Western agencies, it would have been hardly possible for Ukrainian NGOs to evolve to the current significantly influential level in the civil and political life of the country (Ghosh 2014: 7-10). By the virtue of the non-governmental institutions, Western powers succeeded in influencing political developments in Ukraine without direct involvement. Cooperation with those non-state actors also helped Western agencies in their rhetoric to downplay their own role in the anti-governmental upheavals that changed the tide of history for Ukraine. Ann Marie Yastishock, the deputy regional USAID director, refused claims that USAID had supported revolutions and protestors in Ukraine and pointed out that "We don't finance revolutions, we support civil society and NGOs. We financed neither the Orange Revolution nor the Maidan protests in 2014. Those were citizens out there at the Maidan, rising up against their corrupt government" (Bota *et al.* 2015).

The United States, as the "top bilateral donor" to Ukraine since the very beginning of the latter's independent statehood (Shapovalova 2010: 2), played a crucial role in the Westernization of Ukraine. In December 2013, a couple of weeks after the Vilnius summit, Victoria Nuland, the US assistant Secretary of State for European and Eurasian affairs, declared that the United States had invested more than $5 billion since 1991 "on supporting the aspirations of the Ukrainian people to have a strong, democratic government that represents their interests" (UNIAN 2014b). The carriers of American aid to Ukrainian non-state actors—USAID, the National Endowment for Democracy (NED), the Public Affairs Section of the US Embassy, the National Democratic Institute (NDI), the International Republican Institute (IRI), the American Bar Association, and others—significantly empowered the Ukrainian pro-Western forces. Not only were the American non-governmental organizations actively involved in political life in Ukraine and contributed to its pro-Western developments, European agencies participated in this process as well. One of the most prominent EU civil society initiatives in Ukraine was the establishment of the Ukrainian National Platform (UNP) of the Eastern Partnership Civil Society Forum in January 2011. Uniting Ukrainian NGOs and in close cooperation with other National Platforms in EaP countries, the UNP coordinates public support for the implementation of the EaP programme in the country.

Apart from the soft power projection of the European Union, member states also considerably contributed to the promotion of Western values in Ukraine. In 2007, Matthias Brucker (2007: 308) identified three German political foundations operational in Ukraine: the Hanns-Seidel-Stiftung (HSS), the Friedrich-Ebert-Stiftung (FES) and the Konrad-Adenauer-Stiftung (KAS). Involved in different sectors, they in general cooperated with the government in reforming the administrative apparatus, police and security forces and supported the emerging civil society, non-governmental organizations and trade unions (ibid.; Shapovalova 2010: 4). Coordinating the cooperation between German and Ukrainian NGOs, organizing conferences for Ukrainian non-governmental organizations, organizing trainings for political parties on efficient party management, election campaigns and professional public relations, German foundations were an influential supportive force for Ukrainian democratization. Brucker (2007: 311) makes an important observation about the function of those foundations:

> "...the foundations are more than norm entrepreneurs and agents of socialization—they actively interfere in domestic processes. Thus, the HSS educated police forces, which later refrained from the use of force against civilian protestors; FES fosters an emergent civil society; KAS has good contacts with all leading members of Nasha Ukraina and trains youth organizations, a social stratum that later represented the major part of the protesters in Kyiv's central square. Hence, the work of the foundations is not simply about norm dissemination, but also about moulding domestic processes."

The other European countries, particularly Poland, have also taken part in this process individually. The promotion of European values in the European countries bordering Russia is a key part of Poland's security strategy (Petrova 2014: 1). Thus, it is unsurprising that these countries, particularly Belarus and Ukraine, are the top recipients of Poland's foreign democracy assistance

(Kaźmierkiewicz 2008: 107). A 2008 assessment of European democracy aid calculated that Poland's democratization aid to Ukraine outweighed the combined assistance of the UK and Sweden (Kucharczyk *et al.* 2008: 21). Poland's support was more visible in the Euromaidan protests where Polish politicians and civic activists physically appeared and supported the cause of the revolution (ibid.). For most of the other Central European and Baltic members of the EU, the democratization and Westernization of Ukraine is of similar geostrategic importance and attracts a significant part of their foreign aid.

These countries have sought to affect the domestic political process in Ukraine also through international broadcasting and supporting "independent" (pro-Western) media outlets in Ukraine. Most of the above-mentioned Western non-governmental organizations that have been active in Ukraine have also supported the development of independent media in the country. USAID/Ukraine's flagship media support program, Strengthening Independent Media in Ukraine (U-Media), launched in 2003 and has been one of the most prominent amongst these projects. In less than ten years, it supported 12 non-governmental institutions (e.g. *Telekritika* and Internews Ukraine) that deal with the problems of independent media in Ukraine. The NGOs supported by U-Media have become leaders in media monitoring, journalist training, legal support and awareness and investigative journalism (ibid.). Stopfake.org is another media project that is supported by Western donors (the international Renaissance Foundation, the Foreign Ministry of the Czech Republic, the British Embassy in Ukraine and the Sigrid Rausing Trust). According to the website, its primary goal is "to verify information, raise media literacy in Ukraine and establish a clear red line between journalism and propaganda" (See Stopfake.org 2017).

In addition to these projects, the government supported international broadcasters of Western powers have also addressed the Ukrainian people in broadcasting programmes in local languages. The Ukrainian service of Radio Liberty has been in operation since 1954 in three languages (Russian, Ukrainian, and Crimean Tatar).

RFE/RL expanded its Ukrainian service in the aftermath of the outbreak of Crimea's annexation. In September 2015, the Ukrainian Service began broadcasting to Crimea on AM and in July 2016 it began broadcasting to parts of separatist-controlled Donbass on FM (RFE/RL 2017c). The agency has also launched a website to broadcast news about events in Crimea in Russian, Ukrainian, and Crimean Tatar, which in short time became one of the most quoted news sources on the peninsula (ibid.). The BBG reports that the audience of the Ukrainian services of American international media significantly increased following the outbreak of the Ukraine crisis. While before the crisis (in 2012) only 9,8% of adults turned to Ukrainian or Russian-language American media platforms for news, the percentage of those people reached 20,8% in 2014 (See BBG 2014). However, the audience of the US media channels varies considerably across Ukraine: while more than 40% of Western Ukrainians choose these channels for news, only around 10% of Ukrainians in the East and South regions chose these channels as sources of news in 2014 (ibid.).

Non-State Actors and External Alignment

The discussion on the autonomy of Ukrainian leaders *vis-à-vis* non-state actors and the application of Western and Russian soft power in the country indicated that Ukrainian non-state actors have had relatively more opportunities to be politically influential and been subject to stronger soft power projection of the external powers. On several occasions over the last decade, Ukrainian society played decisive roles in shaping not only domestic politics but also foreign policy. To say the least, the Orange and Euromaidan revolutions, which were movements of the ordinary people, civil society and other non-state actors, had more revolutionary implications for the foreign policy orientation of the country than its internal structure. This characterization of the Ukrainian public differs dramatically from observations by experts in the late 1990s and early 2000s. For example, in 2003, some argued that "Ukrainian society is passive, atomized and its power is 'submerged' relative to that of the state" and thus "public opinion [in Ukraine] is of minimal importance in the area of foreign policy" (Chudowsky *et al.* 2003: 273). A year later, the Ukrainian public proved these estimations wrong by exerting substantial influence on the foreign policy orientation of the country. This demonstrated that in Ukraine "public opinion can force elites to rethink foreign policy and/or bring to power counter-elites whose preferences are different" (Munro 2007: 44).

The internal socio-economic and political problems were often noted as the underlying reason behind the anti-governmental upheavals of the Ukrainians both during the Orange Revolution (Stepanenko 2006) and Euromaidan (Bachmann 2014; Surzhko-Harned *et al.* 2017). This was the dissatisfaction of the Ukrainian public with the performance of the government that fomented massive protests across the country. However, the geopolitical dimensions of these upheavals, particularly the Euromaidan revolution, should not be underestimated. For example, Surzhko-Harned and Zahuranec (2017: 760) argue that "Euromaidan's unique frame centres on opposition to the Yanukovych regime" rather than on the "choice between Europe and Russia". They underrate the significance of the fact that Euromaidan protests started in the immediate aftermath of Yanukovych's refusal to further move on the path of integration to Europe which was seen by the protestors as a progressive alternative to the country's traditional geopolitical master (i.e. Russia) (Ryabchuk 2014). The involvement of Western powers in the Euromaidan protests and their support to the anti-governmental forces further reinforced the external dimension of the protests and its character as a choice between the West and Russia.

In the period under study (2004–2016), the attitude of the Ukrainian people towards Russia and the West did not remain stable. In the beginning of this period, integration with one or the other of these two powers was not widely supported: public opinion polls showed that the Ukrainian public was ambivalent towards rapprochement with either of the two geopolitical poles (White *et al.* 2010: 359-362). For example, in 2008, supporters (42%) of integration into Russia-initiated projects outnumbered those supporting

European integration (34%) (Popescu *et al.* 2009b: 28). However, as seen from Figure 5, this ambivalence remained up until September 2013. The surveys prior to the Euromaidan uprising concluded that there were more supporters of EU integration and the Association Agreement was supported by almost two-thirds of the Ukrainian people (Savin 2014: 7).

Ukrainians used to be more suspicious of the transatlantic alliance: more than 40% of the respondents found the alliance a "threat" in the 2008 and 2009 Gallup polls, while only less than 18% perceived it as "protection" (Esipova *et al.* 2010). A 2009 poll concluded that 60% of Ukrainians said they were against NATO membership, while only 21% supported it (Vorobiov 2015b; See Figure 6). Therefore, it is not surprising that Yanukovych's push to adopt the law on non-bloc status in 2010 did not face any substantial opposition. These foreign policy perceptions were noticed also in reaction to the Georgia war (2008). During the war, although the Orange government took sides with Georgia, 23.5% of the Ukrainian people found Russia's use of force in the conflict justified and for 60.5% use of force by Georgia was illegal (Bogomolov *et al.* 2012: 10). However, the regional West−East difference was evident in the polls on Ukraine's possibility of joining NATO: the 2010 polls indicated that while the majority in the East (72%) and South (60%) were more likely to oppose accession, most people in western Ukraine said they supported it (Sprehe 2010).

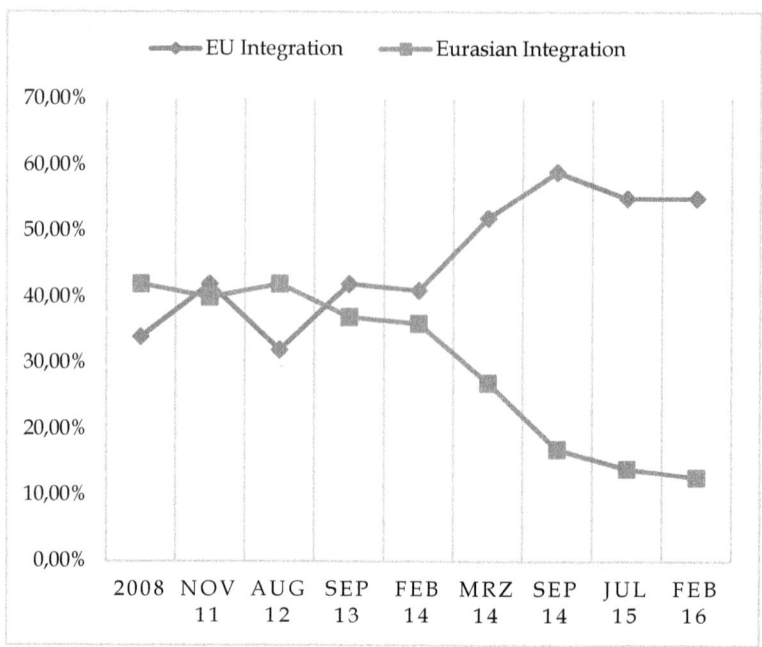

Figure 5. Ukrainian Public opinion on foreign policy (Support for the EU integration vs. the Eurasia integration[19] in the Ukrainian society.[20])

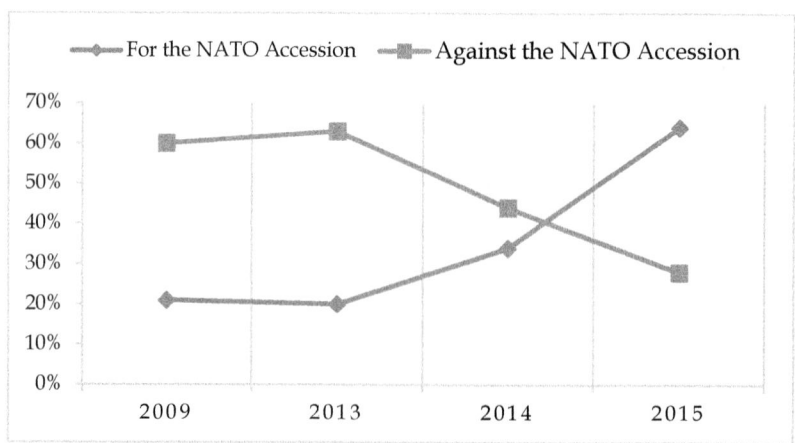

Figure 6. Ukrainian Public Opinion on Accession to NATO

The Euromaidan revolution and its aftermath caused drastic changes in the perception of the Ukrainian public about the foreign policy orientation of the country. The supporters of Eurasian integration dropped to 12% in two years after the revolution, while the percentage of EU integration supporters neared 60% of the Ukrainian nation. Before these events, many Ukrainians supported EU integration, but they were more reserved on NATO accession. After Euromaidan the Ukrainian public became increasingly more supportive of the membership to the transatlantic club as well.

In 2013, just before the start of the Euromaidan revolution, Ukrainian public opinion about NATO was the same as it had been several few years ago: only 20% supported accession into the Alliance, while the majority remained against it (See Radio Svoboda 2013). What happened after the Euromaidan revolution was remarkable: In 2014, 44% of those polled said they would vote against joining NATO in a hypothetical referendum, whereas 34% said they would vote for accession. In 2015, however, in the course of the persistence of the Ukraine—Russia conflict in the East and the continuation of Crimea's occupation by Russia, all of a sudden 64% said that their vote in a hypothetical referendum on NATO accession would be in favour of it (Vorobiov 2015b). The percentage of the people who were against accession decreased dramatically to 28% (ibid.; See Figure 6).

The pro-Western dramatic shift in public opinion was reflected also in the parliamentary elections of October 2014. Compared to the previous elections (2012), the voters of the pro-Russian parties decreased from 28.3% to 16,4% and the pro-Western parties won a stunning 81%, which happened so partly due to the non-participation of the citizens lived in the annexed Crimea and parts of Donbas (Kochan 2016: 108). Late 2016 surveys showed that 73% of

---

[19] Eurasian integration in this chart implies joining the integration projects offered by Russia, primarily the Customs Union while the EU integration implies accession into the EU as a member.
[20] For the source of data from 2008, see: Popescu & Wilson 2009b: 28; For the source of the data for the period November 2011—March 2014, see: IRI 2014; For the September 2014 and July 2015 surveys, see: IRI 2015; For the results of the March 2016 polls which were conducted by Gorshenin Institute, see: UNIAN 2016b.

Ukrainians did not support Poroshenko's presidency, 79% — his cabinet, and 87% — the parliament (Kyivpost 2016). As the public support to him and his cabinet dramatically decreased and support to NATO membership conversely shot up, Poroshenko began to try to be seen as an increasingly stauncher supporter of the country's pro-Western course. In early 2017, Poroshenko announced that he would hold a referendum on the accession to the Alliance. In an interview to the German media, he pointed out that:

> "Four years ago, only 16 percent favoured Ukraine's entry into NATO. Now it's 54 percent… As president, I am guided by the views of my people, and I will hold a referendum on the issue of NATO membership" (Reuters 2017).

The widespread anti-Russian mood in the country — which, as the previous sections demonstrated, was supported and intensified by the Ukrainian government — affects the foreign policy making of the state. The geopolitical situation over Ukraine, Russia's seemingly irreversible decision not to return Crimea and its continuous support to the separatists in Eastern Ukraine, and against this backdrop, the West's reluctance to counter Russia with heftier sanctions or military force might generate an international imperative for the Ukrainian authorities to sit down at the negotiation table with Russia and look for a solution. However, neither the public in Ukraine nor the Poroshenko government seems willing to launch such negotiations with the Kremlin which eventually could reverse the country's pro-Western moves that have been made since the Euromaidan revolution. In August 2015, commenting on growing pro-NATO support amongst the Ukrainian people in the aftermath of the failure of negotiations on the settlement of the conflict in Eastern Ukraine, Ievgen Vorobiov, a Ukrainian analyst, pointed out that:

> "Even if the Ukrainian political leadership were ready to make a behind-the-curtain 'anti-NATO' deal with Russia, it would attract little support from the citizenry and would certainly backfire politically" (Vorobiov 2015b).

Conclusion

This chapter aimed to explore Ukraine's foreign policy amidst the rivalries of the West and Russia and the influence of domestic non-state groups on its formulation. The chapter was guided by the hypothesis that when state leaders are not autonomous *vis-à-vis* domestic non-state actors, the latter become politically more influential with the potential to affect foreign policy and run the risk of undermining independent and potentially more prudent foreign policy making. The non-existence of strong state autonomy in such states allows external powers to pursue more effective soft power policies there. This gives the external powers the chance to impact the foreign policies of these states through influencing their domestic non-state actors and push for a favourable reconfiguration in their geopolitical orientation.

The chapter has found that the location of Ukraine in the geopolitically sensitive position between Russia and the West has shaped the country's external policies since the early years of the post-Soviet period. The geostrategic and geo-economic environment of its location between two geopolitical centres necessitated neutrality as the most prudent option for Ukrainian foreign policy. Such a position would have allowed Ukraine to maintain its economic and political relations with both centres and extract benefits from each of them. The first leaders of the newly independent Ukraine of the 1990s were relatively more successful in pursuing a multivectorial foreign policy maintaining ties with Russia and the West but keeping both of them at bay. From the beginning of the new millennium it became increasingly more difficult to maintain a multivector approach. The intensifying rivalries between the two geopolitical poles forced Ukraine to make a choice in its external orientation. In the aftermath of the inception of the integration projects by the EU and Russia, Ukrainian leaders found themselves in a serious dilemma between the two great powers. The internal non-state groups played a crucial intervening role in this process and reinforced the pressure to make a choice on the country's external alignment. The Ukrainian leaders' unconsolidated control over these groups opened room for their influential activities. The external great powers, making use of different public diplomacy and propaganda channels, were able to reach out to these non-state groups seeking to mould their feelings and opinions.

The Orange and Euromaidan revolutions, being decisive events in the formation of the geopolitical destiny of Ukraine, demonstrated the superiority of Western soft power *vis-à-vis* Russian soft power. The combination of successful self-projection and state-managed projection allowed Western powers to realize their goals in Ukraine. Notwithstanding the existence of strong cultural, linguistic, ethnic, historical bonds between Ukraine and Russia, Western soft power won over Russia's soft power. The latter's corrupted political system, backward economy and stagnating living standards marred its state-managed soft power projection and reduced its potential to succeed in its mission. The West's association with higher living standards and a liberal democracy model and its support for the pro-democracy politicians and civil society put itself in stark contrast with Russia's authoritarian governing structure and its closer ties with Ukraine's corrupted political elites. This situation affected the policy vision of the Ukrainian people and was ultimately reflected in their anti-governmental protests.

The Euromaidan revolution, which erupted immediately after President Yanukovych refused to sign the Association Agreement with the EU, was thus also the triumph of Western soft power. The public intervention resulted in the overthrow of Yanukovych in February 2014, Crimea's annexation by Russia next month and Russia-supported separatist upheaval in Eastern Ukraine. The post-Yanukovych Ukrainian leaders signed the Association Agreement and a free trade deal with the European Union, revoked the law on non-bloc status which opened the path to NATO membership, dramatically restricted Russia's soft power channels in Ukraine, boosted trade relations with the West and minimized those with Russia, etc. Although Russia was able to secure its control over Crimea which was of supreme geostrategic importance and put obstacles on Ukraine's Euro-Atlantic path by supporting separatism in Eastern Ukraine, it failed at large. It lost Ukraine as a potential member in its integration projects which are of lesser meaning without Ukraine. As Vladimir Chernega (2015), the Russian advisor to the Council of Europe, admits, Russia underwent its "worst geopolitical defeat" in the post-Soviet period in Ukraine.

7. Conclusions

This section will summarize the findings of the research on the Russia—West confrontation over the "common neighbourhood" states (i.e. Armenia, Azerbaijan, Belarus, Georgia, Moldova, and Ukraine) from the perspective of the nexus of neoclassical realism and soft power. This concluding section proceeds as follow. The first sub-section will present the puzzle and theoretical arguments that formed the basis of this study. The next sub-section will summarize the empirical findings of the research in the light of the research hypotheses. The final sub-section will present the implications of the research for international relations theories.

The Puzzle and Theoretical Arguments

This study began with a puzzle identified in the external alignment of states that are in between great power rivalries. It questioned the rationale behind the fact that the post-Soviet states located in Eastern Europe and South Caucasus—a region which is known as the "common (or shared) neighbourhood"—have pursued dissimilar foreign policy strategies (i.e. pro-Western or pro-Russian) notwithstanding their similar geopolitical situations. The book presented the rivalries between Russia and the West (i.e. the EU and the United States) over the post-Soviet region as the independent variable, while the foreign policies of the regional states and the formation of their dissimilar geopolitical strategies served as the dependent variable of the research. Both of the conflicting great powers have made use of a diverse set of instruments to distance the regional states from the orbit of the rival geopolitical centre and draw them towards their own orbit. The book analysed the policies of the great powers to interact with and influence non-state actors (i.e. general public, non-governmental organizations, religious groups, etc.) in target states with the eventual aim of affecting the external alignment strategies of their respective states. This impact of the domestic non-state actors on foreign policy has been treated as the intervening variable in the study.

Herein the book subscribed to realist assumptions about the intervention of the general public in foreign policy making and the conditions in which their intervention could be impactful. It was argued that this intervention could push the state to opt for a foreign policy strategy which is not expected by realist theories such as Kenneth Waltz's (1979) "balance of power", Stephan Walt's (1987) "balance of threat", or Randall Schweller's (1994) "balance of interests" in the given circumstances. The book drew on the realist conviction that public pressure on foreign policy is likely to bring about detrimental consequences for the whole country as public perceptions of international threats and the subtleties of balance of power politics mostly are inaccurate because of a lack of proper expertise and complete knowledge (Christensen 1996: 17; Lobell 2009: 61). The book stressed the level of state autonomy as an important variable that defines the degree of the influence the non-state actors can exert on foreign policy. It argued that when state leaders have strong autonomy *vis-à-vis* the domestic non-state actors, they can control the soft power projection of external great powers and offset the intervening influence of domestic non-state actors on foreign policy.

The preliminary literature review found that neoclassical realists recognize domestic non-state actors as a potentially influential intervening variable between the pressure of the international political system and foreign policy. However, the analysis of the school has not incorporated the policies of the great powers to reach out to these actors in the target states and mould their perceptions and attitudes with the ultimate objective of affecting the external alignment of their respective state. The book argued that these policies could gain momentum when the conflicting sides are nuclear armed great powers and the object of their conflict is a region that hosts smaller states. The policies that great powers pursue and the instruments that they deploy to deliver their narratives to the publics of target states have been analysed in this study under the notion of "soft power".

On this basis, the book built two major guiding hypotheses for this study: (1) if nuclear armed great powers compete against the same type of powers to expand or sustain their sphere of influence over a populated region, they use soft power as a major expansive instrument while military power remains a tool to defend themselves and back up their foreign policies; (2) If the leaders of a weak state, which is in between the rivalries of great powers who use soft power to expand their influence, are autonomous *vis-à-vis* society and other internal non-state actors, they can control the inflow of soft power projection of foreign states, offset the intervening influence of the domestic non-state actors on foreign policy making and augment their chances to more prudently and independently follow the imperatives of the international political system. Conversely, if such autonomy does not exist, then the external powers find a favourable environment in which to wield soft power, the domestic non-state actors can influence the external orientation of the state, the state fails to offset their influence, and this may bring about suboptimal foreign policy decisions.

The book also presented its model on the soft power policies great powers pursue in order to reach out to and influence public opinion in target states. This model differentiates two sources of soft power: attractiveness (self-projection) and state-managed projection (propaganda and public diplomacy). It argues that the attractiveness of a state is built on the basis of its natural endowments and human-constructed assets (policies, political values, economic standards, foreign aid, military power, technological and scientific advances, music, movies, TV channels, popular culture, ideas and customs, etc.). The book regarded international broadcasting as a one-way communication channel which was conceptualized in the model as propaganda. Two-way communication with foreign publics through non-governmental organizations, scholarly exchange programs, etc. were considered as instruments of public diplomacy. It also presented its conceptualization of the hard power—soft power nexus based on four principles: (1) The possession of hard power (i.e. economic and military power) is a precondition to develop strong soft power; (2) The diminishing utility of military power in international politics compels great powers to develop their soft power capacity in the pursuit of their foreign policy goals; (3) Soft power is not a substitute for hard power, and, therefore, states need and must pay adequate attention to the development of their hard power; (4) The possession of strong, hard power elements (i.e. economy) does not automatically produce soft power; states need to take appropriate measures to wield soft power.

Empirical Findings

The book opted for the Russia—West (i.e. the EU and the United States) rivalries over the states located between the EU and Russia—a region which is known as "common (or shared) neighbourhood" in political and academic circles—as the case study. It particularly focused on the cases of Belarus and Ukraine representing regional states with relatively strong state autonomy and states with relatively weak state autonomy, respectively.

Chapters 3 and 4, supporting the hypothesis on the use of hard power as a defensive instrument and soft power as an expansive instrument by nuclear-armed great powers in their rivalries, concluded that although both the West and Russia maximize their military power to ensure their security, it has been non-military power that they make use of to expand their influence over states in the "common neighbourhood". The recent decades of Russia—West relations have shown that military power primarily serves the purpose of ensuring security, backing up foreign policy and maintaining international standing. Although both sides invest heavily in their military power, they cannot deploy it to completely kick the rival powers out of the areas of conflicts, as great powers used to do in the past. The possibly catastrophic costs of military confrontation, the relatively greater role of international organizations, conventions and laws in the management of international relations, and probably also Russia's awareness of the far superior military capabilities of NATO countries strengthen the status of military power as *ultimo ratio*. Although Russia is militarily far superior to its post-Soviet neighbours and is the second strongest military power after the United States, this does not suffice for Moscow to establish its unchallenged hegemony over its entire immediate neighbourhood.

The analysis of Russian and Western policies concluded that as expected by the theoretical foundation of this study, the diminishing utility of military power in international politics compels great powers to develop their soft power capacity in the pursuit of their foreign policy goals. The circumstances portrayed in the West—Russia competition over the "common neighbourhood" require both sides to develop strong, non-military means to realize their goals with regards to the post-Soviet region. This increases the importance of soft power. However, this analysis concluded that soft power is not seen by Russia and the West as a substitute for hard power. Therefore, they do not downplay their policies to produce more hard power resources. This is where some Russians mistakenly argue that strong military power may offset Russia's relative weakness in non-military spheres—economy, ideology, culture, technology, etc. (Karaganov 2012). On the contrary to these views, the weakness in soft power cannot be effectively counterbalanced by relative strength in hard power. Russia's strong military has demonstrated impotence against the growing influence of the West in the post-Soviet region. Georgia, Moldova and Ukraine, countries that are of the utmost geostrategic importance for Russia, have signed agreements with the EU that have prevented their integration into the Russia-promoted Eurasian Union. The driving force that led these countries to making pro-Western geopolitical moves was primarily the superiority of Western soft power.

Analysing the self-projection (attractiveness) of Western powers (i.e. the EU and the USA) and Russia, the book found that each side has its own strength and weakness in terms of self-projection. However, it concluded that the problems concerning Russia's self-projection are more serious and damage its potential to successfully compete against Western soft power. Unlike the EU and the USA that produce more than 45% of the global gross domestic product (US$73,502 trillion), Russia's economy is heavily dependent on natural resources and remains inferior to Western economies (See World Bank 2017b). The success of the Western model is one of the major factors that attracts the attention and admiration of the post-Soviet people. On the other hand, while the Western model of liberal democracy based on freedom of speech, human rights, the rule of law, and accountability has been able to build power over public opinion in post-Soviet countries, Russia has failed to develop an attractive ideology. Moscow's aggressive reactions to the pro-Western drift of the "common neighbourhood" states have further worsened its image in the region.

Chapters 5 and 6 explored the cases of Belarus and Ukraine to test the hypothesis on the external alignment choices of smaller states caught between great power rivalries, the potentially strong influence of the intervening variables (in this case: domestic non-state actors (i.e. general public)) on the formation of their foreign policy decisions, and the role of the (non)existence of strong state autonomy in this context. This choice was especially important as one of these cases (i.e. Belarus) represents the "common neighbourhood" states (Azerbaijan and Armenia) in which state leaders possess relatively strong autonomy with respect to internal non-state players, while the other case (i.e. Ukraine) represents those with relatively weak state autonomy (Georgia and Moldova). The book concluded that in each case the external great powers (i.e. the West and Russia) have strived to wield power over public opinion in these countries.

However, Belarusian leader Alexander Lukashenko's consolidation of power in his own hands and thus his build-up of strong autonomy *vis-à-vis* the society has allowed him to prevent the inflow of external soft power projection which his government deems hostile. He has also circumscribed the influence of the general public, civil society and media on the governance of domestic and external politics. Consequently, Belarus, as expected by the hypotheses of this study, has been able to adroitly manoeuvre amidst the confrontation of the two surrounding great powers and economically benefit from its alignment with Russia. Although Belarus officially aligned with Russia and joined its regional integration projects, it sought to maintain warm relations with Western powers and prevented the Kremlin from violating its sovereignty. The analysis concluded that in the case of Belarus the soft power projection of the West and Russia was largely ineffective, and the intervening influence of internal non-state players was mostly minimal.

The analysis on Ukraine produced results opposite to the Belarusian case. The relatively more democratic political structure of Ukraine and the stronger influence of media, civil society and the general public on the government considerably impacted the foreign policy of the state since the collapse of the Soviet Union. Although the first leaders of the country in the 1990s managed to maintain neutrality between the West and Russia, which was in fact more beneficial for the country both in terms of economic and political benefits, this gradually became impossible due to the intensifying rivalries between the two conflicting great powers and the growing pressure of internal non-state actors on foreign policy. The book concluded that internal non-state actors played a crucial role in the decision the state eventually made between these two powers in its external alignment.

The superior self-projection and profound state-managed projection of Western powers succeeded in neutralizing Russian soft power and wielding influence over popular opinion in Ukraine. The limited internal autonomy of Ukrainian leaders circumscribed their chances to offset the pressure of the domestic non-state actors and follow the imperatives of the international political system. The systemic factors pushed the state to abandon neutrality which would have been more advantageous for Ukraine (Kissinger 2014), and the domestic non-state groups affected its choice in external alignment through massive anti-government protests (e.g. the Orange and Euromaidan revolutions). Thus, as expected by the hypotheses of this research, limited state autonomy created a favourable environment for the external powers to wield soft power over Ukrainians, the domestic non-state actors of the state were able to influence the external orientation of the state, the state failed to offset their influence, and this brought about suboptimal foreign policy decisions which *inter alia* led to the loss of state control over some parts of the country (i.e. Crimea and Eastern Ukraine).

Implications for Theory

This study has a number of theoretical implications. Firstly, the analysis it carried out supported the hypothesis that soft power is deployed as an expansive instrument amidst the territorial rivalries between nuclear-armed great powers while military power remains a tool for defence and backing up of foreign policies. The book exhibited that this is caused by several factors — primarily by the nuclear dimension of the conflict which significantly discourages the use of military power, but also by the growing role of numerous international organizations, non-governmental organizations, conventions, international courts, etc. in the management of international relations. The great powers cannot easily intervene in smaller states and invade them anymore. Instead they make use of soft power to win over public opinion in the target state and eventually push it to an alignment through influencing its internal non-state players (i.e. general public and non-governmental organizations).

Although Russia and the West neared the verge of an all-out war over the "common neighbourhood" states twice (2008 and 2014) during the period under study (2004-2016), none of them dared to launch such a war. Russia proved itself much more determined than Western powers to do "everything possible" to prevent the admission of regional post-Soviet states into Western military and political structures. The Kremlin demonstrated this determination by deploying military force against Georgia and Ukraine in response to the possibility of their admission to NATO. Russia occupied some of the territories of these two states and as such rolled out insurmountable obstacles on their pro-Western path. The case shows that military power remains relevant as the *ultimo ratio* in international relations, and therefore, states (must) invest in developing their military capabilities. However, the case also indicates that Russia tried to prevent the pro-Western integration of Georgia and Ukraine through soft power and invested sizeable resources in these policies since the first wave of colour revolutions (2003-2005) in the region. However, its soft power failed in the competition with that of Western powers who also deployed soft power to prevent the integration of the regional countries into Russia's re-integration projects.

This result is particularly relevant for neoclassical realism, the mission of which is defined as "building theories of foreign policy, rather than theories of the system within which states interact" (Taliaferro *et al.* 2009: 19). The incorporation of soft power as a foreign policy tool for the great powers to expand their influence enriches the theory and allows it to develop its analysis of situations akin to the Russia—West confrontation over the "common neighbourhood" (e.g. USSR—West rivalries over the Third World countries). Although some scholars, such as Felix Berenskoetter and Adam Quinn, have discussed the integration of the soft power concept into the analytical framework of neoclassical realism, their emphasis has been different. They have stressed the importance of ideas to preserve the hegemony achieved through the use of military and economic superiority (Berenskoetter *et al.* 2012). Thus, this research presented a different perspective and allowed for an examination of great power policies to encourage smaller states to bandwagon through the use of non-military power.

Secondly, the research supported the hypothesis that lower autonomy from internal non-state actors restricts the ability of state leaders to offset the intervening influence of these groups in foreign policy. This opens up the possibility for great powers to effectively pursue soft power policies *vis-à-vis* that state and affect its external alignment through influencing its general public and civil society. This hypothesis was tested in the case of Ukraine. The pro-Western choice Kiev made in its external alignment in the aftermath of the Euromaidan uprisings can be explained by neither "balance of power" nor "balance of threat" theories. In the given geopolitical context, Russia was the more powerful and more threatening power. The Kremlin was more resolved to deploy military power and even nuclear weapons if necessary to defend its interests in the post-Soviet region. The West, on the contrary, held a reserved position and was unable to employ military force in the region against Russia. These two theories would predict Ukraine's bandwagoning with Russia, since it was more powerful, geographically close and more threatening; on the other hand, no real ally was available to fight against Russia. Nor can the "balance of interests" theory convincingly explain Ukraine's pro-Western alignment in the aftermath of the colour revolutions. The consequences of the Ukraine crisis (2014) indicated that the abandonment of neutrality between the West and Russia and the disruption of economic relations with Russia could not be quickly offset by the benefits Ukraine gained in its pro-Western alignment.

This study provided another analytical tool to predict the choices made by small states amidst great power rivalries in their external alignment when the maintenance of neutrality becomes impossible. It implies that domestic non-state actors could play a crucial role in this process. Even a small state would opt for an alignment which is at odds with the imperatives of the international political system and potentially dangerous when its non-state actors, under the soft power projection of external powers, intervenes in foreign policy making. The popular uprisings in Ukraine and the state's dramatic changes in its foreign policy direction under the pressure of the public support this argument. While the geopolitical location of the country, the distribution of power between the West and Russia, the threats posed by the Kremlin and the state's economic relations with these powers necessitated non-alignment in foreign policy or predicted bandwagoning with Russia should non-alignment have not worked out, the country opted for balancing against Russia. This turned out catastrophic for Ukraine: Russia occupied Crimea and territories in Eastern Ukraine. More than 10,000 people died in the clashes with Russia-supported separatist groups, the country encountered a severe economic crisis and lost important sources of revenue.

Third, the book reconsidered the principles of the soft power concept. The analysis of Western and Russian soft power showed that soft power is not a given power; it must be garnered and wielded through appropriate policies and strategies. The soft power model presented in this book distinguished two sources of soft power as self-projection (attractiveness) and state-managed projection (propaganda and public diplomacy). The comparison of Western and Russian soft power in the "common neighbourhood" demonstrated that self-projection is a necessity for effective soft power making abroad. When a state fails to build attractive human-constructed qualities (political values, high living standards, good quality of education, culture, etc.), its chances to be seen as a role model by foreign publics considerably decrease.

However, attractiveness does not suffice to vanquish contending narratives in the target regions. To this purpose, states also need to develop a comprehensive network of state-managed projection. The case of Belarus was a relevant example to defend this assumption. The comparative perspectives presented in the study identified that the self-projection of Western powers (i.e. the liberal democracy model, higher living standards, political values, etc.) performed more successfully in the "common neighbourhood" than Russia's self-projection does. However, the superiority of Western self-projection failed to defeat Russian soft power in Belarus. The blockage of the entrance of Western soft power outlets into the country by the Lukashenko government has succeeded in isolating people from Western narratives. Compared to the West, Russia had more channels to interact with the Belarusian public and dominated Belarus's information space during the period under study (2004-2016). Nevertheless, in spite of the non-existence of significant state-managed projection and weaker societal and cultural links with Belarus than Russia has, the EU succeeded to become a challenge for Russia in the fight to win approval amongst Belarusians. The public opinion polls by the IISEPS (See Figure 4) show that if Belarus opens its doors to soft power outlets of West, in a short period of time Western soft power has the potential to further grow and provoke the emergence of powerful pro-Western movements in the country.

Bibliography

Alachnovič, A., 2015: "How Russia's Subsidies Save the Belarusian Economy", *Belarus Digest*, available at: http://belarusdigest.com/story/how-russias-subsidies-save-belarusian-economy-23118 (accessed: 10 February 2017).

Anderson, J., 2007: "Putin and the Russian Orthodox Church: Asymmetric Symphonia?" *Journal of International Affairs*, Vol. 61, No. 1, pp. 185-201.

Andreyev, O., 2014: "Power and Money in Ukraine", *OpenDemocracy*, available at: https://www.opendemocracy.net/en/odr/power-and-money-in-ukraine/ (accessed: 27 March 2014).

Arka News Agency, 2015: "Private remittances to Armenia slash by 31 percent in 2014 November- central bank", available at: http://arka.am/en/news/economy/private_remittances_to_armenia_slash_by_31_percent_in_2014_november_central_bank/ (accessed: 11 May 2017).

Armenpress, 2010: "Ukazom prezidenta RF sopredsedatel' Rossiyskoy-armyanskoy blagotvoritel'noy organizasii "Delo chesti" Andranik Nikogos'yan nagrazhden ordenom Druzhby", available at: https://armenpress.am/rus/news/624900/.html (accessed: 1 June 2017).

Astapenia, R., 2014: "How Russian Culture and Media Shape Belarusian Politics", *Belarus Digest*, available at: http://belarusdigest.com/story/how-russian-culture-and-media-shape-belarusian-politics-16833 (accessed: 12 February 2017).

Astapenia, R., 2016: "The Belarusian Language in Education: a Reluctant Revival?", *Belarus Digest*, available at: http://udf.by/english/featured-stories/146871-the-belarusian-language-in-education-a-reluctant-revival.html (accessed: 5 February 2017).

Åslund, A., 2013: "Ukraine's Choice: European Association Agreement or Eurasian Union?", *Peterson Institute for International Economics*, Number PB 13-22, available at: https://piie.com/publications/pb/pb13-22.pdf (accessed: 18 March 2017).

Åslund, A., 2015: *Ukraine: What Went Wrong and How to Fix it*, Peterson Institute for International Economics, Washington, DC.

Asmus, R., 2010: *A Little War That Shook the World: Georgia, Russia, and the Future of the West*, Palgrave Macmillan, New York.

Azertag, 2016: "Minister: '90,000 Pupils Study in the Russian Language in Azerbaijan'", available at: https://azertag.az/xeber/Azerbaycanda_90_min_sagird_rus_dilinde_tehsil_alir-1014364 (accessed: 28 November 2016).

Bachmann, K., 2014: "The Challenges: Political and Economic Transition", in Bachmann, K. & Lyubashenko, I., (eds.) *The Maidan Uprising, Separatism and Foreign Intervention: Ukraine's Complex Transition*, Peter Lang, Frankfurt am Main, pp. 405-442.

Bachmann, K. & Lybashenko, I., 2014: "The Role of Digital Communication Tools in Mass Mobilization, Information and Propaganda", in Bachmann, K. & Lyubashenko, I., (eds.) *The Maidan Uprising, Separatism and Foreign Intervention: Ukraine's Complex Transition*, Peter Lang, Frankfurt am Main, pp. 349-378.

Bachrach, P. & Baratz M., S., 1962: "Two Faces of Power", *The American Political Science Review*, Vol. 56, No. 4, pp. 947-952.

Bachrach, P. & Baratz, M., S., 1963: "Decisions and non-decisions: an analytical framework", *American Political Science Review*, Vol. 57, No. 3, pp. 632-642.

Bader, M., 2010: Against All Odds: *Aiding Political Parties in Georgia and Ukraine*, Amsterdam University Press, Amsterdam.

Baldwin, D., 2013: "Power and International Relations", in Carlsnaes, W., Risse, T. & Simmons, B., A., (eds.) *Handbook of International Relations*, SAGE Publications Ltd, London, pp. 273-297.

BBC, 2014: "Ukraine crisis: Transcript of leaked Nuland-Pyatt call", available at: http://www.bbc.com/news/world-europe-26079957 (accessed: 26 February 2017).

BBG, 2014: "BBG audience reach doubles in Ukraine", available at: https://www.bbg.gov/2014/06/05/bbg-audience-reach-doubles-in-ukraine-2/ (accessed: 13 May 2017).

BBG, 2015: "BBG 2016 Budget Request Calls for Expansion in Key Markets and Technologies", available at: https://www.bbg.gov/2015/03/10/bbg-2016-budget-request-calls-for-expansion-in-key-markets-and-technologies/ (accessed: 16 June 2017).

BBG, 2017: "Budget Submissions", available at: https://www.bbg.gov/strategy-and-performance/budget-submissions/ (accessed: 16 June 2017).

Beissinger, R., M., 2006: "Promoting Democracy: Is Exporting Revolution a Constructive Strategy?", *Dissent*, Vol. 53, No. 1, pp. 18-24.

Beissinger, R., M., 2007: "Structure and Example in Modular Political Phenomena: The Diffusion of Bulldozer/Rose/Orange/Tulip Revolutions", *Perspectives on Politics*, Vol. 5, No. 2, pp. 259-276.

Beissinger, R., M., 2014: "Why We Should Be Sober about the Long-Term Prospects of Stable Democracy in Ukraine", *The Washington Post*, available at: https://www.washingtonpost.com/news/monkey-cage/wp/2014/03/11/why-we-should-be-sober-about-the-long-term-prospects-of-stable-democracy-in-ukraine/?utm_term=.00427af422a1 (accessed: 27 March 2017).

Berenskoetter, F. & Quinn, A., 2012: "Hegemony by Invitation: Neoclassical Realism, Soft Power and US-European Relations", in Asle, T. & Barbara, K., (eds.) *Neoclassical Realism in European Politics: Bringing Power Back In*, Manchester University Press, Manchester, pp. 214-233.

Bernstein, J., 2016: "Pollster: Russia Winning 'Information War' in Former Soviet States", *Voice of America*, available at: http://www.voanews.com/a/pollsters-russia-winning-information-battle-former-soviet-states/3177888.html (accessed:25 September 2016).

Berridge, G., R. & James, A., 2001: *A Dictionary of Diplomacy*, Palgrave Macmillan, Basingstoke.

Bjorn, F., 2014: "Pro-Russian Organizations and Key Figures Carrying Out Subversive Actions in Crimea", *Inform Napalm*, available at: https://informnapalm.org/en/pro-russian-organizations-and-key-figures-carrying-out-subversive-actions-in-crimea/ (accessed: 5 May 2017).

Blauvelt, K., T., 2013: "Endurance of the Soviet Imperial Tongue: the Russian Language in Contemporary Georgia", *Central Asian Survey*, Vol. 32, No. 2, pp. 189-209.

Bloomberg, 2015: "We Are a Long Way from Peace in Ukraine: Lukashenko", available at: https://www.bloomberg.com/news/videos/2015-04-02/we-are-a-long-way-from-peace-in-ukraine-lukashenko (accessed: 10 February 2017).

Bochkarev, D., 2009: "European Gas Prices: Implications of Gazprom's Strategic Engagement with Central Asia", *Pipeline and Gas Journal 236*, No. 6, available at: https://pgjonline.com/2009/06/08/european-gas-prices-implications-of-gazproms-strategic-engagement-with-central-asia/ (accessed: 6 December 2016).

Bogomolov, A. & Lytvynenko, A., 2012: "A Ghost in the Mirror: Russian Soft Power in Ukraine", *Chatham House Briefing Paper*, available at: https://www.chathamhouse.org/publications/papers/view/181667 (accessed: 14 May 2017).

Bohdan, S., 2013: "Belarusian Officials Criticise Eurasian Integration", *Belarus Digest*, available at: http://belarusdigest.com/story/belarusian-officials-criticise-eurasian-integration-16121 (accessed: 10 February 2017).

Bogutsky, O., 2015: "Belarus—Ukraine: Strategically Important Neighbourhood", in Pankovsky, A. & Kostyugova, V., (eds.) *Belarusian Yearbook*, Lohvinaŭ, Vilnius, pp. 90-96.

Bosse, G., 2009: "Challenges for EU Governance through Neighbourhood Policy and Eastern Partnership: The Values/Security Nexus in EU-Belarus Relations", *Contemporary Politics*, Vol. 15, No. 2, pp. 215-24.

Bota, A. & Kohlenberg, K., 2015: "Did Uncle Sam buy off the Maidan?", *Zeit*, available at: http://www.zeit.de/politik/ausland/2015-05/ukraine-usa-maidan-finance/seite-2 (accessed: 29 March 2017).

Bouchet, N., 2016: "Russia's 'Militarization' of Colour Revolutions", *Policy Perspectives*, Vol. 4, No. 2, pp. 1-4.

Brown, M., E., 1995: "The Flawed Logic of NATO Expansion", *Survival: Global Politics and Strategy*, Vol. 37, No. 1, pp. 34-52.

Bremmer, I., Gvosdev, N. & International Herald Tribune, 2004: "NATO Looks East: Why not Really Make Russia a Partner?", *The New York Times*, available at: http://www.nytimes.com/2004/06/22/opinion/nato-looks-east-why-not-really-make-russia-a-partner.html (accessed: 24 June 2017).

Brewster, M. 2016: "Canada Considers European Troop Commitment as CSIS Warns Russia is 'Mobilizing for War'", *CBC*, available at: https://www.cbc.ca/news/politics/canada-baltics-troops-russia-1.3635139 (accessed: 22 June 2016).

Brezhneva, A. & Ukhova, D., 2013: "Russia as a Humanitarian Aid Donor", *OXFAM Discussion Paper*, available at: https://www.oxfam.org/sites/www.oxfam.org/files/dp-russia-humanitarian-donor-150713-en.pdf (accessed: 11 May 2017).

Brucker, M., 2007: "Trans-national Actors in Democratizing States: The Case of German Political Foundations in Ukraine", *Journal of Communist Studies and Transition Politics*, Vol. 23, No. 2, pp. 296-319.

Brzezinski, Z., 1994: "The Premature Partnership", *Foreign Affairs*, Vol. 73, No. 2. Pp. 67-82.

Bugajski, J. & Assenova, M., 2016: *Eurasian Disunion: Russia's Vulnerable Flanks*, Jamestown Foundation, Washington DC.

Bunce, V. & Wolchik, S., 2011: *Defeating Authoritarian Leaders in Postcommunist Countries*, Cambridge University Press, New York.

Burnell, P., 2007: "Does International Democracy Promotion Work?", *German Development Institute*, Discussion Paper 17, available at: http://edoc.vifapol.de/opus/volltexte/2011/3094/pdf/BurnellPromotionWork.pdf (accessed: 4 June 2017).

Burrows, S., 1997: "The struggle for European Opinion in the Napoleonic Wars: British Francophone Propaganda 1803-1814", *French History*, Vol. 11, No. 1, pp. 29-53.

Čajčyc, A., 2010: "Belarus To Diversify Away from Russian Oil Supplies", *Belarus Digest*, available at: http://belarusdigest.com/story/belarus-diversify-away-russian-oil-supplies-1891 (accessed: 10 February 2017).

Carothers, T., 2006a: "The Backlash against Democracy Promotion", *Foreign Affairs*, available at: https://www.foreignaffairs.com/articles/2006-03-01/backlash-against-democracy-promotion (accessed: 26 June 2016).

Carothers, T., 2006b: *Confronting the Weakest Link: Aiding Political Parties in New Democracies*, Carnegie Endowment for International Peace, Washington, D.C.

Carr, E., H., 1951: The Twenty Years' Crisis 1919-1939: An Introduction to the Study of *International Relations*, Macmillan, London.

Cecire, M., 2015: "The Kremlin Pulls on Georgia", *Foreign Policy Magazine*, available at: http://foreignpolicy.com/2015/03/09/the-kremlin-pulls-on-georgia/ (accessed: 23 June 2017).

Central Bank of the Russian Federation, 2017: Statistical data has been retrieved from the official website of the organization, available at: http://www.cbr.ru/ (accessed: 16 June 2017).

Centre for European Transformation, 2015: "The statement of the Belarusian National Platform on the eve of the EaP Summit in Riga", available at: https://cet.eurobelarus.info/en/news/2015/05/19/the-statement-of-the-belarusan-national-platform-on-the-eve-of.html (accessed: 10 February 2017).

CEPR, 2015: "Prezidentskiye Granty NKO: Pooshchreniye Loyal'nosti Vmesto Razvitiya Grazhdanskogo Obshchestva", available at: http://cepr.su/wp-content/uploads/2015/12/Президентские-гранты-НКО_Поощрение-лояльности-вместо-развития-гражданского-общества.pdf (accessed: 2 October 2016).

Chatham House, 2011: "Soft Power? The Means and Ends of Russian Influence", available at: https://www.chathamhouse.org/publications/papers/view/109675 (accessed: 11 May 2017).

Chernega, V., 2015: "Ukrainskiy urok", *Russia in Global Affairs*, No. 4, available at: http://www.globalaffairs.ru/number/Ukrainskii-urok-17645 (accessed: 7 May 2017).

Christensen, T., J., 1996: *Useful Adversaries: Grand Strategy, Domestic Mobilization, and Sino-American Conflict, 1947-1958*, Princeton University Press, Princeton.

Chudowsky, V. & Kuzio, T., 2003: "Does Public Opinion Matter in Ukraine? The Case of Foreign Policy", *Communist and Post-Communist Studies*, Vol. 36, No. 3, pp. 273-290.

Cladi, L. & Locatelli, A., 2016: "Structural Realism: Balancing, Bandwagoning Or What?", in Cladi, L. & Locatelli, A., (eds.) *International Relations Theory and European Security: We Thought We Knew*, Routledge, Oxon and New York, pp. 11-27.

Clem, S., R., 2011: "Going It Alone: Belarus as the Non-European European State", *Eurasian Geography and Economics*, Vol. 52, No. 6, pp. 780-798.

CNN, 2014: "Transcripts", available at: http://transcripts.cnn.com/TRANSCRIPTS/1405/25/fzgps.01.html (accessed: 17 June 2017).

Cooper, S., 2003: "State-Centric Balance-Of-Threat Theory", *Security Studies*, Vol. 13, No. 2, pp. 306-349.

Cornell, S. 2009. "Pipeline Power: The War in Georgia and the Future of the Caucasian Energy Corridor", *Georgetown Journal of International Affairs*, Vol. 10, No. 1, pp. 131-9.

DAAD, 2017: "Internationalization Agency", available at: https://www.daad.de/der-daad/ueber-den-daad/portrait/en/29143-the-internationalisation-agency/ (accessed: 17 June 2017).

D'Anieri, P. & Kuzio, T., 2017: "Public Opinion and Ukrainian Foreign Policy", in Cheng, T., J. & Lee, W., (eds.) *National Security, Public Opinion and Regime Asymmetry: A Six-Country Study*, World Scientific Publishing, Singapore, pp. 115-146.

Dannreuther, R., 2004: "Introduction: Setting the Framework", in Dannreuther, R., (ed.) *European Union Foreign and Security Policy: Towards a Neighbourhood Strategy*, pp. 1-11, Routledge, New York.

Dempsey, J., 2015: "The European Endowment for Democracy Goes Russian", *Carnegie Europe*, available at: https://carnegieeurope.eu/strategiceurope/?fa=59377 (accessed: 17 June 2017).

Dobreva, A., 2015: "How the EU Budget Is Spent: European Instrument for Democracy and Human Rights", *European Parliament Research Service Blog*, available at: https://epthinktank.eu/2015/10/09/european-instrument-for-democracy-and-human-rights/ (accessed: 17 June 2017).

Domaradzki, S., 2014: "The role of NATO and the EU in the Ukrainian Crisis", in Bachmann, K. & Lyubashenko, I., (eds.) *The Maidan Uprising, Separatism and Foreign Intervention: Ukraine's Complex Transition*, pp. 267-298, Peter Lang, Frankfurt am Main.

Doyle, M., W., 1983: "Kant, Liberal Legacies, and Foreign Affairs, Part 1", *Philosophy & Public Affairs*, Vol. 12, No. 3, pp. 205-35.

Drent, M., Hendriks, R. & Zandee, D., 2015: "New Threats, New EU and NATO Responses", *The Netherlands Institute of International Relations 'Clingendael'*, The Hague, available at: https://www.clingendael.nl/sites/default/files/New%20Threats_New%20EU_Nato%20Responses_Clingendael_July2015.pdf (accessed:25 September 2016).

Duncan, P., J., 2000: *Russian Messianism: Third Rome, Revolution, Communism and after*, Routledge, London.

Eap-csf.eu, 2014: "Moldovan National Platform Annual Report", Eastern Partnership Civil Society Forum, available at: http://eap-csf.eu/assets/files/moldova_annual%20report.pdf (accessed: 17 June 2017).

Ellul, J., 1973: *Propaganda: The Formation of Men's Attitudes*, Random House (Vintage Press), New York.

Elman, M., F., 1997: "The Need for a Qualitative Test of the Democratic Peace Theory", in Elman, M., F., (ed.) *Paths to Peace: Is Democracy the Answer?*, pp. 1-57, The MIT Press, Cambridge, Massachusetts.

Enpi-info.eu, 2014: "EU Neighbourhood Barometer Eastern Partnership", available at: http://www.enpi-info.eu/library/sites/default/files/attachments/ENPI%20Wave%206%20-%20Report%20East_EN.pdf (accessed: 17 January 2016).

Esipova, N. & English, C., 2008: "Belarusians Favor Close Ties with Russia Over EU, US", *Gallup*, available at: http://www.gallup.com/poll/106558/belarusians-favor-close-ties-russia-over-eu-us.aspx (accessed: 8 February 2017).

Esipova, N. & Ray, J., 2010: "Ukrainians Likely Support Move Away From NATO", *Gallup*, available at: http://www.gallup.com/poll/127094/ukrainians-likely-support-move-away-nato.aspx (accessed: 15 May 2017).

Esipova, N. & Ray, J., 2013, "Former Soviet Countries See More Harm from Breakup", *Gallup*, available at: http://www.gallup.com/poll/166538/former-soviet-countries-harm-breakup.aspx (accessed: 29 December 2016).

Esipova, N. & Ray, J., 2016: "Eastern Europeans, CIS Residents See Russia, US as Threats", *Gallup*, available at: http://www.gallup.com/poll/190415/eastern-europeans-cis-residents-russia-threats.aspx?g_source=greatest%20threat&g_medium=search&g_campaign=tiles (accessed:25 September 2016).

European Commission, 2002a: "Romano Prodi, President of the European Commission: A Wider Europe — A Proximity Policy as the Key to Stability", available at: http://europa.eu/rapid/press-release_SPEECH-02-619_en.htm (accessed: 16 June 2017).

European Commission, 2002b: "SPEECH/02/619 by Romano Prodi, President of the European Commission, 'A Wider Europe—A Proximity Policy as the Key to Stability'", available at: http://europa.eu/rapid/press-release_SPEECH-02-619_en.htm (accessed: 18 May 2017).

European Commission, 2011: "Action Fiche for Neighbourhood Civil Society Facility 2011", available at: https://ec.europa.eu/europe aid/sites/devco/files/aap-financing-neighbourhood-spe-general-budget-af-20110920_en.pdf (accessed: 17 June 2017).

European Commission, 2014: "Support Package for Ukraine", available at: http://ec.europa.eu/archives/commission_2010-2014/president /news/archives/2014/03/pdf/20140306-ukraine-package_en.pdf (accessed: 17 June 2017).

European Parliament, 2014: "Parliamentary Questions: "Answer Given by Mr Füle on Behalf of the Commission", available at: http://www.eu roparl.europa.eu/sides/getAllAnswers.do?reference=E-2014-00639 4&language=EN (accessed: 16 June 2017).

European Parliament, 2016: "EU Strategic Communications: With a View to Counteracting Propaganda", available at: http://www.europarl.europa.eu/RegData/etudes/IDAN/2016/578008/EXPO_IDA (2016)578008_EN.pdf (accessed: 16 June 2017).

Eurasia Partnership Foundation, 2014: "Roundtable Discussion Held on Implication of Crisis in Ukraine on the Nagorno-Garabagh Process", available at: http://www.epfound.org/news-events/announcements /roundtable-discussion-held-on-implication-of-crisis-in-ukraine-on-the-nagorno-garabagh-process.html (accessed: 17 June 2017).

Eurasia Partnership Foundation, 2017: "Organizational History", available at: http://www.epfound.org/about-us/organizational-history.html (accessed: 17 June 2017).

Federal Statistics Service of Russia, 2017: Statistical data has been retrieved from the official website of the organization, available at: http://www.gks.ru/ (accessed: 16 June 2017).

Fedirka, A., 2016: "Belarus: Between a Rock and a Hard Place", *Geopolitical Futures*, available at: https://geopoliticalfutures.com/belarus-between-a-rock-and-a-hard-place/ (accessed: 4 February 2017).

Fesenko, V., 2015: "Ukraine: Between Europe and Eurasia", in Dutkiewicz, P. & Sakwa, R., *Eurasian Integration—the View from Within*, Routledge, Oxon and New York, pp.126-149.

Filimonov, G., 2010: "Russia's Soft Power Potential", *Russia in Global Affairs*, available at: http://eng.globalaffairs.ru/number/Russias-Soft-Power-Potential-15086 (accessed: 18 January 2016).

Fischer, S., 2011: "Foreword", in Delcour, L., *Shaping the Post-Soviet Space? EU Policies and Approaches to Region-Building*, Asghate, Farnham, Surrey.

Fominykh, A., 2016: "Russia's Public Diplomacy in Central Asia and the Caucasus: The Role of the Universities", *The Hague Journal of Diplomacy*, Vol. 12, pp. 1-30.

Foyle, D., C., 1999: *Counting the Public in: Presidents, Public Opinion, and Foreign Policy*, Cambridge University Press, New York.

Freedom House, 2006: "Ukraine", available at: https://freedomhouse.org/report/freedom-world/2006/ukraine (accessed: 17 March 2017).

Freedom House, 2011: "Ukraine", available at: https://freedomhouse.org/report/freedom-world/2011/ukraine (accessed: 17 March 2017).

Freedom House, 2014: "Nations in Transit 2014: Ratings and Democracy Score Summary", available at: https://freedomhouse.org/sites/default/files/Data%20tables.pdf (accessed: 25 March 2017).

Freedom House, 2016: "Country Report: Russia", available at: https://freedomhouse.org/report/freedom-world/2016/russia (accessed: 28 April 2016).

Furman, E. & Libman, A., 2015: "Europeanization and the Eurasian Economic Union", in Dutkiewicz, P. & Sakwa, R., *Eurasian Integration — the View from Within*, Routledge, pp. 173-192, Oxon and New York.

Galeotti, M., 2016: "No, Russia is not preparing for all-out war", *OpenDemocracy*, available at: https://opendemocracy.net/od-russia/mark-galeotti/no-russia-is-not-preparing-for-all-out-war (accessed: 22 June 2016).

Gallarotti, G., M., 2010: *Cosmopolitan Power in International Relations: A Synthesis of Realism, Neoliberalism, and Constructivism*, Cambridge University Press, New York.

Gallarotti, G., M., 2011: "Soft power: What it is, why it's Important, and the conditions under which it can be effectively used", *Division II Faculty Publications*, Paper 57, available at: http://wesscholar.wesleyan.edu/div2facpubs/57 (accessed: 05 February 2016).

Garmazhapova, A., 2013: "Gde zhivut trolli. I kto ikh kormit", Novaya Gazeta, available at: http://www.novayagazeta.ru/politics/59889.html (accessed:7 December 2016).

Gelpi, C., F. & Griesdorf, M., 2001: "Winners or Losers? Democracies in International Crisis, 1918–94", *American Political Science Review*, Vol. 95, No. 3, pp. 633-47.

Gerasimov, V., 2013: "Tsennost' nauki v predvidenii", *Voyenno Promyshlennyy Kur'yer*, available at: http://www.vpknews.ru/articles/14632 (accessed: 18 June 2017).

Gershman, C., 2013: "Former Soviet States Stand up to Russia. Will the US?" *The Washington Post*, available at: https://www.washingtonpost.com/opinions/former-soviet-states-stand-up-to-russia-will-the-us/2013/09/26/b5ad2be4-246a-11e3-b75d-5b7f66349852_story.html?utm_term=.bf9848a3e1c5 (accessed: 25 March 2017).

Ghosh, M., 2014: "In Search of Sustainability: Civil Society in Ukraine", *Friedrich Ebert Stiftung, Berlin*, available at: http://library.fes.de/pdf-files/id-moe/10862.pdf (accessed: 4 May 2017).

Gorenburg, D., 2010: "Russia's State Armaments Program 2020: Is the Third Time the Charm for Military Modernization?" *PONARS Eurasia Policy*, Memo No. 125, CNA Strategic Studies.

Götz, E., 2015: "It's Geopolitics, Stupid: Explaining Russia's Ukraine Policy", *Global Affairs*, Vol. 1, No. 1, pp. 3-10.

Gramsci, A., 1971: *Selections from the Prison Notebooks*, Translated & Edited: Hoare, Q. & Smith, G., N., International Publishers, New York.

Gray, C., S., 2011: *Hard Power and Soft Power: The Utility of Military Force as an Instrument of Policy in 21st Century*, Strategic Studies Institute, US Army War College, Carlisle, PA.

Gretskiy, I., 2007: "The Orange Revolution: A Challenge for the Russian Orthodox Church", Paper presented for the 6th Pan-European International Relations Conference, Turin, Italy.

Grove, T., 2011: "Analysis: Russia Feeds Arms Addiction as Soft Power Fails", *Reuters*, Available at: http://www.reuters.com/article/2011/10/11/us-russia-military-idUSTRE79A2CB20111011 (accessed: 26 October 2015).

Guardian, 2013: "John McCain tells Ukraine protesters: 'We are here to support your just cause,'" available at: https://www.theguardian.com/world/2013/dec/15/john-mccain-ukraine-protests-support-just-cause (accessed: 22 February 2017).

Gvalia, G., Siroky, D., Lebanidze, B. & Iashvili, Z., 2013: "Thinking Outside the Bloc: Explaining the Foreign Policies of Small States", *Security Studies*, Vol. 22, No. 1, pp. 98-131.

Haas, M., 2007: "Current Geostrategy in the South Caucasus", *Eurasianet*, available at: https://eurasianet.org/current-geostrategy-in-the-south-caucasus (accessed: 16 October 2016).

Hagan, J., D., 1987: "Regimes, Political Oppositions, and the Comparative Analysis of Foreign Policy" in Hermann, C., F., Kegley, C., W. & Rosenau, J., N., *New Directions in the Study of Foreign Policy*, Allen and Unwin, Boston, pp. 339-365.

Hagemann, C., 2013: "External Governance on the Terms of the Partner? The EU, Russia and the Republic of Moldova in the European Neighbourhood Policy", *Journal of European Integration*, Vol. 35, No. 7, pp. 767-783.

Hayden, C., 2012: Rhetoric of Soft Power: *Public Diplomacy in Global Contexts*, Lexington, Lanham, MD.

Hill, F., 2006: "Moscow Discovers Soft Power", *Current History*, available at: https://www.brookings.edu/articles/moscow-discovers-soft-power/ (accessed: 19 November).

Holsti, O., R., 1992: "Public Opinion and Foreign Policy: Challenges to the Almond-Lippmann Consensus Mershon Series: Research Programs and Debates", *International Studies Quarterly*, Vol. 36, No. 4, pp. 439-466.

Huseynov, V., 2015: "Post-Soviet Georgia's Foreign Policy: Strategic Idealism and the Russian Challenge", *Caucasus International*, Vol. 5, No. 3, pp. 117-131.

Huseynov, V., 2016: "Soft Power Geopolitics: How Does the Diminishing Utility of Military Power Affect the Russia — West Confrontation over the "Common Neighbourhood", *Eastern Journal of European Studies*, Vol. 7, No. 2, pp. 71-90.

Hyde-Price, A., 2007: *European Security in the Twenty-First Century: The Challenge of Multipolarity*, Routledge, Abingdon.

ICPS, 2010: "Inside Ukraine", available at: http://old.icps.com.ua/files/articles/57/96/Inside_Ukraine_ENG_8.pdf (accessed: 18 January 2016).

IFAD (International Fund for Agricultural Development), 2015: "Sending Money Home: European flows and markets", available at: https://www.ifad.org/documents/10180/3594696/money_europe.pdf/5ac7733f-39e6-4b1b-a1dc-f7038b5caa0b?version=1.2 (accessed: 11 May 2017),

Igumnova, L., O., 2014: "Imperskaya Identichnost' Yevropeyskogo Soyuza i Rossii", *Bulletin of the Tomsk State University, History*, Vol. 6, No. 32, pp. 45-55.

IISEPS, 2015: "The Most Important Results of the Public Opinion Poll in December 2015", available at: http://www.iiseps.org/?p=3865&lang=en (accessed: 13 February 2017).

IISEPS, 2016: "The Most Important Results of the Public Opinion Poll in June 2016", available at: http://www.iiseps.org/?p=4699&lang=en (accessed: 12 February 2017).

Interfax-religion, 2007: "Putin regards the nation's traditional religions and nuclear shield equally important for its security", available at: http://www.interfax-religion.com/?act=news&div=2550 (accessed: 29 October 2015.)

Interfax, 2015a: "Shoigu: Information Becomes Another Armed Forces Component", available at: http://www.interfax.com/newsinf.asp?id=581851 (accessed 2 October 2016).

Interfax, 2015b: "Armeniya lidiruyet sredi postsovetskikh stran po dole russkoyazychnykh emigrantov" available at: http://www.interfax.ru/presscenter/484894 (accessed: 17 January 2016).

Interfax-Ukraine, 2014: "Poroshenko: Information Ministry's main task is to repel information attacks against Ukraine", available at: http://en.interfax.com.ua/news/economic/238615.html (accessed: 30 June 2017).

Interfax-Ukraine, 2017: "Ukrainian army will switch to NATO standards by 2020 and get new logistics system", available at: http://en.interfax.com.ua/news/general/394507.html (accessed: 13 March 2017).

Ioffe, G., 2004: "Understanding Belarus: Economy and Political Landscape", *Europe-Asia Studies*, Vol. 56, No. 1, pp. 85–118.

Ioffe, G., 2007: "Unfinished Nation-Building in Belarus and the 2006 Presidential Election", *Eurasian Geography and Economics*, Vol. 48, No. 1, pp. 37-58.

Ioffe, G., 2011: "Belarus and the West: From Estrangement to Honeymoon", *Journal of Communist Studies and Transition Politics*, Vol. 27, No. 2, pp. 217-240.

Ioffe, G., 2013: "Geostrategic Interest and Democracy Promotion: Evidence from Post-Soviet Space", *Europe-Asia Studies*, Vol. 65, No. 7, pp. 1255–1274.

Ioffe, G., 2014: "Language Is National Security in Belarus", *Eurasia Daily Monitor*, Vol. 11, No. 193.

Ioffe, G., 2015: "Belarus: An Unlikely Beneficiary of Crisis in Ukraine", *Tractus Aevorum*, Vol. 2, No. 2, pp. 226-231.

IRI, 2014: "Public Opinion Survey: Residents of Ukraine", available at: http://www.iri.org/sites/default/files/2014%20April%205%20IRI%20Public%20Opinion%20Survey%20of%20Ukraine,%20March%202014-26,%202014.pdf (accessed: 16 May 2017);

IRI, 2015: "Public Opinion Survey: Residents of Ukraine", available at: http://www.iri.org/sites/default/files/wysiwyg/2015-08-24_survey_of_residents_of_ukraine_july_16-30_2015.pdf (accessed: 17 May 2017).

IRI, 2016: "Public Opinion Survey Residents of Ukraine: September 28 – October 7, 2016", available at: http://www.iri.org/sites/default /files/iri_ukraine_poll_-_october_2016.pdf (accessed: 3 June 2017).

IRI, 2017: "Survey of Public Opinion in Georgia: February 22 – March 8, 2017", available at: http://www.iri.org/sites/default/files/iri_poll _presentation_georgia_2017.03-general.pdf (accessed: 3 June 2017).

Ivanter, V., Geets, V., Yasinskiy, V., Shirov, A. & Anisimov, A., 2012: "The Economic Effects of the Creation of the Single Economic Space and Potential Accession of Ukraine", *Eurasian Development Bank*, available at: http://www.eabr.org/general/upload/CII%20-%20izdania/Yer book-2012/a_n5_2012_06.pdf (accessed: 18 March 2017).

Jackson, N., 2003: *Russian Foreign Policy and the CIS: Theories, Debates and Actions*, Routledge, London.

Jackson, N., 2010: "The Role of External Factors in Advancing Non-Liberal Democratic Forms of Political Rule: A Case Study of Russia's Influence on Central Asian Regimes", *Contemporary Politics*, Vol. 16, No. 1, pp. 101–118.

Jarabik, B., 2006: "International Democracy Assistance to Belarus: An Effective Tool", in Forbig, J., Marples, R., D., Demes, P., (eds.) *Prospects for Democracy in Belarus*, The German Marshall Fund of the United States, Washington DC, pp. 85-94.

Levada Centre, 2011: "Religioznaya Vera v Rossii", available at: http://www.levada.ru/2011/09/26/religioznaya-vera-v-rossii/ (accessed: 2 June 2017).

Kacprzyk, A., 2015: "US Military Presence in Central and Eastern Europe: Consequences for NATO Strategic Adaptation, Deterrence and Allied Solidarity", *The Polish Institute of International Affairs*, Warsaw.

Karaganov, S., 2012: "Security Strategy: Why Arms?" *Russia in Global Affairs*, available at: http://eng.globalaffairs.ru/pubcol/Security-Strat egy-Why-Arms-15716 (accessed: 27 October 2016).

Kaźmierkiewicz, P., 2008: "Eastern Promises and Achievements: Poland's Democracy Assistance Policies and Priorities", in Kucharczyk, J. & Lovitt, J., (eds.) *Democracy's New Champions: European Democracy Assistance After EU Enlargement*, PASOS, Prague, pp. 81-113.

Khimshiashvili, P., 2014: "V krizis v razy povysilas' poseshchayemost' kursov baleta», – Konstantin Kosachev, rukovoditel' Rossotrudnichestva", *Vedomosti*, available at: http://www.vedomosti.ru/newspa per/articles/2014/03/13/v-krizis-v-razy-povysilas-poseschaemost-kursov-baleta (accessed: 11 May 2017).

King, R., Findlay, A. & Ahrens, J., 2010: "International Student Mobility Literature Review, Report to HEFCE, co-funded by the British Council and UK National Agency for Erasmus", *British Council*, London.

Kissinger, H., 2014: "Henry Kissinger: To Settle the Ukraine Crisis, Start at The End", *The Washington Post*, available at: https://www.washingtonpost.com/opinions/henry-kissinger-to-settle-the-ukraine-crisis-start-at-the-end/2014/03/05/46dad868-a496-11e3-8466-d34c451760b9_story.html (accessed: 08 July 2016).

Kochan, N., 2016: "Shaping Ukrainian Identity: The Churches in the Socio-Political Crisis", in Krawchuk, A. & Bremer, T., (eds.) *Churches in the Ukrainian Crisis*, Palgrave Macmillan, Houndsmills, pp.105-121.

Kommersant.ru, 2005: "Vladimir Putin Naznachil Barkhatnogo Kontrrevolyutsionera", available at: http://www.kommersant.ru/doc/556859 (accessed: 1 June 2017).

Kosachev, K., 2012: "*Rossotrudnichestvo Kak Instrument 'Myagkoy Sily'*", *Bel'giyskaya Federatsiya Russkoyazychnykh Organizatsiy*, available at: http://www.bfro.be/ru/k.kosachev.-rossotrudnichestvo-kak-instrument-mjagkoj-sily.html?cmp_id=108&news_id=5334 (accessed: 27 November 2016).

Korab-Karpowicz, W. J., 2010: "A History of Political Philosophy", *Global Scholarly Publication*, New York.

Koshkin, P., 2014: "The Kremlin is Inflexible with FLEX Educational Program", *Russia Direct*, available at: https://russia-direct.org/analysis/kremlin-inflexible-flex-educational-program (accessed: 29 May 2016).

Koshkin, P. & Smertina, K., 2014: "Russia's Soft Power Shouldn't Add up to Propaganda", *Russia Direct*, available at: http://www.russia-direct.org/qa/russias-soft-power-shouldnt-add-propaganda (accessed: 1 June 2017).

Kottasova, I., 2015: "Ukraine Recruits Internet Army to Fight Russian Trolls", *CNN*, available at: http://money.cnn.com/2015/02/25/technology/ukraine-russia-internet-army/ (accessed: 2 June 2017).

Kowalski, M., 2008: "Next Generation Democracy: Democracy Assistance Policies of the Visegrad Four Countries: Belarus", in Kucharczyk, J. & Lovitt, J., (eds.) *Democracy's New Champions: European Democracy Assistance After EU Enlargement*, PASOS, Prague, pp. 189-212.

Krawchuk, A., 2016: "Redefining Orthodox Identity in Ukraine after the Euromaidan", in Krawchuk, A. & Bremer, T., (eds.) *Churches in the Ukrainian Crisis*, Palgrave Macmillan, Houndsmills, pp. 175-202.

Kucharczyk, J. & Lovitt, J., 2008: "Re-energising Europe to Champion Democracy: The Visegrad Four Bring Fresh Transition Experience to the Donors' Side of the Table", in Kucharczyk, J. & Lovitt, J., (eds.) *Democracy's New Champions: European Democracy Assistance After EU Enlargement*, PASOS, Prague, pp. 15-27.

Kudors, A., 2010: "'Russian World' – Russia's Soft Power Approach to Compatriots Policy", *Russian Analytical Digest*, No. 81, available at: http://www.css.ethz.ch/publications/pdfs/RAD-81.pdf (accessed: 25 September 2016).

Kudrytski, A. & Markusheuski, D., 2004: "Belarus: Referen-doom", *Columbia International Affairs Online*, available at: http://www.ciaonet.org/pbei-2/tol-1/tol_2004/oct19-25/oct19-25b.html (accessed: 10 February 2017).

Kuzio, T., 2000: "Geopolitical pluralism in the CIS: The emergence of GUUAM", *European Security*, Vol. 9, No. 2, pp. 81-114.

Kuzio, T., 2011: "Political Culture and Democracy: Ukraine as an Immobile State", *East European Politics and Societies*, Vol. 25, No. 1, pp. 88–113.

Kyivpost, 2016: "Survey shows Poroshenko not supported by 73% of Ukrainians, Cabinet – by 79%, Parliament – by 87%", available at: https://www.kyivpost.com/ukraine-politics/survey-shows-poroshenko-not-supported-73-ukrainians-cabinet-79-parliament-87.html (accessed: 14 May 2017).

Labs, E., J., 1992: "Do Weak States Bandwagon?" *Security Studies*, Vol. 1, No. 3, pp. 383-416.

Lai, H., 2012: "Introduction: The Soft Power Concept and a Rising China", in Lai, H. & Lu, Y, (eds.) *China's Soft Power and International Relations*, Routledge, New York, pp. 1-21.

Landry, T., 2011: "The Colour Revolutions in the Rearview Mirror: Closer Than They Appear", *Canadian Slavonic Papers*, Vol. 53, No. 1, pp. 1-24.

Lane, D., 2009: "Coloured Revolution' as a Political Phenomenon", *Journal of Communist Studies and Transition Politics*, Vol. 25, No. 2-3, pp. 113-135.

Lang, K., 2015: "Their Gentle Force in the European Neighbourhood – A Comparison of Two Soft Power Engines", in Rostoks, T. & Spruds, A., (eds.) *The Different Faces of "Soft power": The Baltic States and Eastern Neighbourhood between Russia and the EU*, Latvian Institute of International Affairs, pp. 30-63.

Lankina, T. & Niemczyk, K., 2015: "Russia's Foreign Policy and Soft Power", in Cadier, D. & Light, M., (eds.) *Russia's Foreign Policy: Ideas, Domestic Politics and External Relations*, Palgrave Macmillan, New York, pp. 97-113.

Laruelle, M., 2015: "The "Russian World" Russia's Soft Power and Geopolitical Imagination", *Center on Global Interests*, Washington.

Lavenex, S. & Schimmelfennig, F., 2009: "EU rules beyond EU borders: theorizing external governance in European politics", *Journal of European Public Policy*, Vol. 16, No. 6, pp. 791–812.

Lawson, C., 2003: "Path-Dependence and the Economy of Belarus: The Consequences of Late Reforms", in Korosteleva, E., Lawson, C. & Marsh, R. (eds.) *Contemporary Belarus: Between Democracy and Dictatorship*, Routledge, London, pp. 125-136.

Layne, C. 2010: "The Unbearable Lightness of Soft Power" in Parmar, I. & Cox, M., (eds.) *Soft Power and US Foreign Policy: Theoretical, Historical and Contemporary Perspective*, Routledge, New York, pp. 51-82.

Lb.ua, 2017: "Ukraine-Russia trade drops by $30bn over three years", available at: https://en.lb.ua/news/2017/02/14/3118_ukrainerussia_trade_drops_30bn.html (accessed: 13 March 2017).

Lebow, N. & Kelly, R., 2001: "Thucydides and hegemony: Athens and the United States", *Review of International Studies*, Vol. 27, No. 4, pp. 593–609.

Lenta.ru, 2007: "Kolichestvo russkoyazychnykh ukraintsev za posledniy god sokratilos'", available at: http://lenta.ru/news/2007/12/17/language (accessed: 27 March 2017).

Lewis, D., 2016: "The 'Moscow Consensus': Constructing Autocracy in Post-Soviet Eurasia", *OpenDemocracy*, available at: https://www.opendemocracy.net/od-russia/david-lewis/moscow-consensus-constructing-autocracy-in-post-soviet-eurasia (accessed: 2 January 2017).

Li, M., 2009a: "Domestic Sources of China's Soft Power Approach", *China Security*, Vol. 5, No. 2, pp. 55-70.

Li, M. 2009b: "Soft Power in Chinese Discourse: Popularity and Prospect", in Li, M., (ed.) *Soft Power: China's Emerging Strategy in International Politics*, Lexington Books, Plymouth, UK, pp. 21-43.

Livingston, S., G., 1992: "The Politics of International Agenda-Setting: Reagan and North-South Relations", *International Studies Quarterly*, Vol. 36, No. 3, pp. 313-329.

Lobell, S., E., 2009: "Threat Assessment, the State, and Foreign Policy: A Neoclassical Realist Model", in Lobell, S., Ripsman, N. & Taliaferro, J., (eds.) *Neoclassical Realism, the State, and Foreign Policy*, Cambridge University Press, New York, pp. 42-74.

Lough, J., Lutsevych O., Pomerantsev P., Secrieru S. & Shekhovtsov A. 2014: "Russian Influence Abroad: Non-state Actors and Propaganda", *Chatham House*, available at: https://www.chathamhouse.org/sites/files/chathamhouse/field/field_document/20141024RussianInfluenceAbroad.pdf (accessed: 23 September 2016).

Luther, C. & Raab, K., 2015: "Wir Zählen Uns zur 'Soft Power'", *Zeit*, available at: http://www.zeit.de/reisen/2015-04/deutsche-welle-peter-limbourg-russland (accessed: 16 June 2017).

Lutsevych, O., 2016: "Agents of the Russian World Proxy Groups in the Contested Neighbourhood", *Chatham House*, available at: https://www.chathamhouse.org/sites/files/chathamhouse/public cations/research/2016-04-14-agents-russian-world-lutsevych.pdf (accessed: 28 November 2016).

Lynch, D., 2005: "Introduction" in Lynch, D. (ed.) *Changing Belarus*, Institute for Security Studies, European Union, Chaillot Paper N° 85, pp. 7-12.

MacDougall, C., J., 2009: "Post-Soviet Strategic Alignment: The Weight of History in the South Caucasus", Ph.D. Dissertation, Georgetown University.

Makarychev, A., 2011: "Hard Questions About Soft Power: A Normative Outlook at Russia's Foreign Policy", *DGAPanalyse kompakt*, Nr. 7, available at: https://dgap.org/de/article/getFullPDF/19605 (accessed: 2 June 2017).

Makarychev, A. & Deviatkov, A., 2012: "Eastern Partnership: Still a missing link in EU strategy?" *Centre for European Policy Studies*, available at: http://aei.pitt.edu/33335/1/Makarychev_&_Deviatkov_on_Eas tern_Partnership.pdf (accessed: 7 November 2016).

Makarychev, A., 2013: "Regionalism and Identities in the Common Neighbourhood: European and Russian Discourses", CEURUS EU-Russia Papers, No. 10.

Makarychev, A. & Kornilov, A., 2015: "Russia's Soft Power in the South Caucasus: Discourses, Communication, Hegemony", in A. Agadjanian, A. Jödicke & E. van der Zweerde (eds.) *Religion, Nation and Democracy in the South Caucasus*, Routledge, Oxon and New York, pp. 238-254.

Makili-Aliyev, K., 2013: "Azerbaijan's Foreign Policy: Between East and West", *Istituto Affari Internazionali*, available at: http://www.iai.it/sites/default/files/iaiwp1305.pdf (accessed: 5 June 2017).

Maliukevičius, N., 2013: "(Re)Constructing Russian Soft Power in Post-Soviet Region", *Baltic Security & Defence Review*, Vol. 15, No. 2, pp. 70-97.

Manaev, O., 2006: "Recent Trends in Belarusian Public Opinion", in Forbig, J., Marples, R., D. & Demes, P., (eds.) *Prospects for Democracy in Belarus*, The German Marshall Fund of the United States, Washington DC, pp. 37-46.

Mansfield, E., D. & Snyder, J., 2005: *Electing to Fight: Why Emerging Democracies Go to War*, Cambridge, MIT Press, Massachusetts.

March, L. & Herd, G., P., 2006: "Moldova Between Europe and Russia: Inoculating Against the Coloured Contagion?" *Post-Soviet Affairs*, Vol. 22, No. 4, pp. 349-379.

Marples, R., D., 2005: "Europe's Last Dictatorship: The Roots and Perspectives of Authoritarianism in 'White Russia'", *Europe-Asia Studies*, Vol. 57, No. 6, pp. 895–908.

Marples, R., D., 2009: "Outpost of Tyranny? The Failure of Democratization in Belarus", *Democratization*, Vol. 16, No. 4, pp. 756-776.

Marples, R., D., 2015: "Ethnic and Social Composition of Ukraine's Regions and Voting Patterns", in Pikulicka-Wilczewska, A. & Sakwa, R., (eds.) *Ukraine and Russia: People, Politics, Propaganda and Perspectives*, E-international Relations, Bristol, pp. 1-7.

Martel, F. 2010: *Mainstream. Enquête Surcette Culture Quiplaità Tout Lemonde*, Flammarion, Paris.

Marszal, A., 2013: "EU will not accept Russian veto, says Barroso", *The Telegraph*, available at: http://www.telegraph.co.uk/news/worldnews/europe/ukraine/10482680/EU-will-not-accept-Russian-veto-says-Barroso.html (accessed: 15 October 2017).

Mattern, J., B., 2007: "Why 'Soft Power' isn't so Soft: Representational Force and Attraction in World Politics", in Berenskoetter, F. & M. J. Williams, (eds.) *Power in World Politics*, Routledge, USA & Canada, pp. 98-119.

Maudave, B., 2010: "Frederic Martel's 'Mainstream'", *European Institute*, available at: https://www.europeaninstitute.org/index.php/98-european-affairs/april-may-2010/995-frederic-martels-qmainstreamq (accessed: 6 January 2017).

McDermott, R. 2015: "Slavic Brotherhood 2015 Rehearses Anti-Colour Revolution Operations", *Eurasia Daily Monitor*, Vol. 12, No. 160.

McDermott, R., 2016: "Gerasimov Calls for New Strategy to Counter Colour Revolution" *Eurasia Daily Monitor Volume*, Vol. 13, No. 46.

Mearsheimer, J., J., 1990: "Back to the Future: Instability in Europe after the Cold War", *International Security*, Vol. 15, No. 1, pp. 5-56.

Mearsheimer, J., J., 2001: *The Tragedy of Great Power Politics*, Norton, USA.

Mearsheimer, J., J., 2014: "Why the Ukraine Crisis Is the West's Fault: The Liberal Delusions That Provoked Putin", *Foreign Affairs*, available at: https://www.foreignaffairs.com/articles/russia-fsu/2014-08-18/why-ukraine-crisis-west-s-fault (accessed: 21 January 2016).

Medvedev, D., 2009: "President Dmitry Medvedev, "Go, Russia!" *The Official Website of President of Russia*, available at: http://en.kremlin.ru/events/president/news/5413 (accessed:22 December 2016).

Melissen, J., 2005: "The New Public Diplomacy: Between Theory and Practice", in Melissen, J., (ed.) *The New Public Diplomacy: Soft Power in International Relations*, Palgrave Macmillan, New York, pp. 3-27.

Melnykovska, I., Plamper, H. & Schweickert, R., 2012: "Do Russia and China promote autocracy in Central Asia?" Asia Europe Journal, Vol 10, No. 1, pp 75–89.

Mickelson, S., 1983: *America's Other Voice: The Story of Radio Free Europe and Radio Liberty*, Praeger Publishers, New York.

Miller, D. & Dinan, W., 2010: "Introduction", in Klaehn, J. (ed.) *The Political Economy of Media and Power*, Peter Lang, New York, pp. 1-5.

Missiroli, A., 2004: "The EU and its Changing Neighbourhood: Stabilization, Integration and Partnership", in Dannreuther, R. (ed.) *European Union Foreign and Security Policy: Towards a Neighbourhood Strategy*, Routledge, London, pp. 12-26.

Monaghan, A., 2013: "The New Russian Foreign Policy Concept: Evolving Continuity", *Chatham House*, available at: https://www.chathamhouse.org/sites/files/chathamhouse/public/Research/Russia%20 and%20Eurasia/0413pp_monaghan.pdf (accessed: 18 November 2016).

Monocle, 2015: "Monocle Soft Power Survey (2015)", available at: http://monocle.com/film/affairs/soft-power-survey-2015-16/ (accessed: 14 October 2016).

Morgenthau, H., J., 1965a: Politics among Nations, Alfred A. Knopf, New York.

Morgenthau, H., J., 1965b: Scientific Man versus Power Politics, Phoenix Books, Chicago

Morgenthau, H., J., 1967: Politics among Nations, Alfred Knopf, New York.

Morrison, D., 2014: "How William Hague Deceived the House of Commons on Ukraine", *Huffington Post*, available at: http://www.huffingtonpost.co.uk/david-morrison/ukraine-willliam-hague_b_4933 177.html (accessed: 22 February 2017).

Moscow Times, 2013: "Rogozin Warns Moldova on Relations", available at: http://www.themoscowtimes.com/business/article/rogozin-warns-moldova-on-relations/485526.html (accessed 18 January 2016).

Movchan, V. & Giucci, R., 2011: "Quantitative Assessment of Ukraine's Regional Integration Options: DCFTA with European Union vs. Customs Union with Russia, Belarus and Kazakhstan", Policy Paper 05/2011 (November), Institute for Economic Research and Policy Consulting, Kyiv.

Munro, N., 2007: "Which Way Does Ukraine Face? Popular Orientations Toward Russia and Western Europe", *Problems of Post-Communism*, Vol. 54, No. 6, pp. 43-58.

Muskhelishvili, M. & Jorjoliani, G., 2009: "Georgia's Ongoing Struggle for a Better Future Continued: Democracy Promotion Through Civil Society Development", *Democratization*, Vol. 16, No. 4, pp. 682-708.

Musiyaka,V., 2014: "Yanukovich sam lishil sebya zvaniya legitimnogo prezidenta", *Gazeta*, available at: http://gazeta.zn.ua/LAW/yanukovich-sam-lishil-sebya-zvaniya-legitimnogo-prezidenta-_.html (accessed: 25 February 2017).

Müllerson, R., 2014: "Ukraine: Victim of Geopolitics", *Chinese Journal of International Law*, pp. 133-145.

Myers, L., S., 2006: "Bringing Down Europe's Last Ex-Soviet Dictator", *The New York Times*, available at: http://www.nytimes.com/2006/02/26/magazine/26belarus.html (accessed: 6 February 2017).

National Statistical Committee of the Republic of Belarus, 2017: "Foreign Trade of the Republic of Belarus, 2017", available at: http://www.belstat.gov.by/en/ofitsialnaya-statistika/publications/statistical-publications-data-books-bulletins/public_compilation/index_80 10/ (accessed: 10 October 2017).

NATO, 1997: "Founding Act on Mutual Relations, Cooperation and Security between NATO and the Russian Federation signed in Paris, France", available at: https://www.nato.int/cps/en/natohq/official_texts_25468.htm (accessed: 18 May 2017).

NATO, 2014: "Wales Summit Declaration: Issued by the Heads of State and Government participating in the meeting of the North Atlantic Council in Wales", available at: http://www.nato.int/cps/en/natohq/official_texts_112964.htm (accessed: 18 May 2017).

NATO, 2015: "Press conference by the NATO Secretary General, Jens Stoltenberg, for the launch of the Annual Report 2014, NATO HQ, Brussels", available at: http://www.nato.int/cps/en/natohq/opinions_117022.htm (accessed: 10 February 2016).

NATO, 2017: "Readiness Action Plan", available at: https://www.nato.int/cps/en/natohq/topics_119353.htm (accessed: 18 May 2017).

NED, 2016: "Frequently Asked Question", available at: http://www.ned.org/about/faqs/ (accessed: 10 June 2016).

Nelson, M., 1997: *War of the Black Heavens: The Battles of Western Broadcasting in the Cold War*, Syracuse University Press, USA.

Newsru.com, 2014: "Glava FSB Vnov' Rasskazal ob 'Olimpiyskikh Teraktakh' i Poobeshchal Zhestko Reagirovat' na Popytki Gosperevorotov v Stranakh SNG", available at: http://www.newsru.com /russia/06jun2014/bortnikov.html (accessed: 6 June 2017).

Nice, A. 2012: "Playing Both Sides: Belarus between Russia and the EU", *German Council on Foreign Relations*, available at: https://dgap.org /de/article/getFullPDF/20843 (accessed: 13 January 2017).

Nielsen, L., K. & Vilson, M., 2013: "The Eastern Partnership—Soft Power Strategy or Policy Failure?" Paper prepared for the EURINT International Conference, "The EU as a Model of Soft Power in the Eastern Neighbourhood" Iasi, Romania.

Nordlinger, E., A., 1981: *On the Autonomy of the Democratic State*, Harvard University Press, Cambridge, Mass.

Nye, J., 2003: "Propaganda Isn't the Way: Soft Power", *International Herald Tribune*, available at: http://belfercenter.ksg.harvard.edu/publica tion/1240/propaganda_isnt_the_way.html (accessed: 05 February 2016).

Nye, J., 2004: *Soft power: The Means to Success in World Politics*, Public Affairs, New York.

Nye, J., 2007: "Notes on a Soft-Power Research Agenda", in Berenskoetter, F. & M. J. Williams, (eds.) *Power in World Politics*, Routledge, USA & Canada, pp. 162-172.

Nye, J., 2008a: "Toward a Liberal Realist Foreign Policy: A Memo for the Next President", *Harvard Magazine*, available at: http://harvardmag azine.com/2008/03/toward-a-liberal-realist.html (accessed:05 February 2016).

Nye, J., 2008b: "Public Diplomacy and Soft Power", *Annals of the American Academy of Political and Social Science*, Vol. 616, pp. 94-109.

Nye, J., 2008c: "Foreword", in Yasushi, W. & McConnell, D., L., (eds.) *Soft Power Superpowers: Cultural and National Assets of Japan and the United States*, M. E. Sharpe, New York, pp. ix-xiv.

Nye, J. 2010: "Responding to My Critics and Concluding Thoughts" in Parmar, I. & Cox, M., (eds.) *Soft Power and US Foreign Policy: Theoretical, Historical and Contemporary Perspective*, Routledge, New York, pp. 215-227.

Nye, J., 2011: *The Future of Power*, Public Affairs, New York.

Nye, J., 2012: "Why China Is Weak on Soft Power", *The New York Times*, available at: http://www.nytimes.com/2012/01/18/opinion/why-china-is-weak-on-soft-power.html (accessed: 08 February 2016).

Nye, J., 2013a: "What China and Russia Don't Get about Soft Power", *Foreign Policy Magazine*, available at: http://foreignpolicy.com/2013/04/29/what-china-and-russia-dont-get-about-soft-power/ (accessed: 25 January 2016).

Nye, J., 2013b: "Transcript of witness testimony to the House of Lords Select Committee on Soft Power and UK Influence", available at: http://www.parliament.uk/documents/lords-committees/soft-power-uk-influence/uc151013Ev10.pdf (accessed:24 January 2016).

Nye, J., 2014: "The Information Revolution and Soft Power", *Current History*, Vol. 113, No. 759, pp. 19-22.

Ó Beacháin, D., 2009: "Roses and Tulips: Dynamics of Regime Change in Georgia and Kyrgyzstan", *Journal of Communist Studies and Transition Politics*, Vol.25, No. 2–3, pp.199–226.

Office of the Under Secretary of Defense, 2016: "European Reassurance Initiative: Department of Defense Budget Fiscal Year (FY) 2017", available at: http://comptroller.defense.gov/Portals/45/Documents/defbudget/fy2017/FY2017_ERI_J-Book.pdf (accessed: 18 May 2017).

Official Website of Russia's Ministry of Foreign Affairs, 2007: "Obzor vneshney politiki Rossiyskoy Federatsii", available at: http://www.mid.ru/brp_4.nsf/0/3647DA97748A106BC32572AB002AC4DD (accessed: 26 October 2015).

Official Website of Russia's Ministry of Foreign Affairs, 2011: "Statement by Russian Foreign Minister Sergey Lavrov at the Opening of the Roundtable Session on "Public Diplomacy as an Instrument of Foreign Policy and Civil Society Development,'" available at: http://www.mid.ru/en/vistupleniya_ministra/-/asset_publisher/MCZ7HQuMdqBY/content/id/178346 (accessed: 26 April 2016).

Official Website of Russia's Ministry of Foreign Affairs, 2013: "Concept of the Foreign Policy of the Russian Federation Approved by President of the Russian Federation V. Putin on 12 February 2013", available at: http://www.mid.ru/en/foreign_policy/official_documents/-/asset_publisher/CptICkB6BZ29/content/id/122186 (accessed: 26 October 2018).

Official Website of Russian Orthodox Church's Department for External Church Relations, 2000: "Report by Metropolitan Kirill of Smolensk and Kaliningrad at the 'Orthodoxy on the Threshold of the Third Millennium' Theological Conference", available at: https://mospat.ru/archive/en/2000/03/ne003161/ (accessed: 2 December 2015).

Official Website of Russkiy Mir Foundation, 2012: "Vyacheslav Nikonov: Russia is Better than its Image in the West", available at: https://www.russkiymir.ru/en/publications/140317/ (accessed: 7 January 2017).

Official Website of the Gorchakov Foundation, 2015: "Executive Director's Address", available at: http://gorchakovfund.ru/en/about/ (accessed: 29 October 2015).

Official Website of the US Congress, 2016: "114th Congress; H.R.5094– STAND for Ukraine Act", available at: https://www.congress.gov/bill/114th-congress/house-bill/5094/text#toc-H62A026388BE B4523B38DE26290186DC1 (accessed: 1 October 2016).

Oldberg, I., 2011: "Aims and Means in Russian Foreign Policy", in Kanet, R., E., (ed.) *Russian Foreign Policy in the 21st Century*, Palgrave Macmillan, Houndmills, Basingstoke, Hampshire and New York, pp. 30-58.

Olszański, A., T., 2014: "The Ukrainian Orthodox Church's Stance on the Revolution and War", OSW Commentary No. 151, Centre for Eastern Studies (OSW), available at: https://www.osw.waw.pl/sites/default/files/commentary_151.pdf (accessed: 28 March 2017).

Onuch, O., 2014: "Who Were the Protesters?" *Journal of Democracy*, Vol. 25, No. 3, pp. 44-51.

Osgood, A., K., 2002: "Hearts and Minds: Unconventional Cold War", *Journal of Cold War Studies*, Vol. 4, No. 2, pp. 85-107.

Ostrovs'kyj, P., 2014: "EuroMaidan in Lviv: a View From the Inside", in Scheide, C. & Schmid, U., (eds) *The EuroMaidan in Ukraine November 2013 till February 2014*, Online Journal of the Center for Governance and Culture in Europe, University of St. Gallen, St. Gallen,. pp. 20-25

Padhol, U., M. & Marples, D., R., 2011: "The 2010 Presidential Election in Belarus", *Problems of Post-Communism*, Vol. 58, No. 1, pp. 3-16.

Panarin, I., 2010: *Pervaya Mirovaya Informatsionnaya Voyna: Razval SSSR*, Piter, Moscow.

Panarin, I., 2014: *Informatsionnaya Voyna, PR i mirovaya politika*, Goryachaya Liniya, Moscow.

Pankovski, A., 2016: "Belarus and Russia: From Brotherhood to Alliance", in Pankovsky, A. & Kostyugova, V., (eds.) *Belarusian Yearbook*, pp. 61-71, Lohvinaŭ, Vilnius.

Panova, V., V., 2015: "Russia's 'Soft' Policies towards the Baltic States", in Rostoks, T. & Spruds, A., (eds.) *The Different Faces of "Soft power": The Baltic States and Eastern Neighbourhood between Russia and the EU*, Latvian Institute of International Affairs, pp. 80-99.

Pantucci, R., 2015: "China's and Russia's Soft Competition in Central Asia", *Current History*, Vol. 114, No. 774, pp. 272-277.

Papayoanou, P., A., 1997: "Economic Interdependence and the Balance of Power", *International Studies Quarterly*, Vol. 41, No. 1, pp. 113-40.

Peisakhin, L., 2014: "Euromaidan Revisited: Causes of Regime Change in Ukraine One Year On", *Wilson Center*, available at: https://www.wilsoncenter.org/sites/default/files/5-kennan%20cable-Peisakhin.pdf (accessed: 26 March 2017).

Petro, N., N., 2014: "Ukraine's Ongoing Struggle with its Russian identity', *World Politics Review*, available at: http://www.worldpoliticsreview.com.sci-hub.cc/articles/13758/ukraine-s-ongoing-struggle-with-its-russian-identity (accessed: 27 March 2017).

Petro, N., N., 2015: "Understanding the Other Ukraine: Identity and Allegiance in Russophone Ukraine", in Pikulicka-Wilczewska, A. & Sakwa, R., (eds.) *Ukraine and Russia: People, Politics, Propaganda and Perspectives*, E-international Relations, Bristol, pp. 18-34.

Petrova, T., 2014: "Polish Democracy Promotion in Ukraine", *Carnegie Endowment for International Peace*, available at: http://carnegieendowment.org/2014/10/16/polish-democracy-promotion-in-ukraine-pub-56907 (accessed: 29 March 2017).

Petuxov, V., V., 2004: "Rossiya, Belarussia i Ukraina: Chto nas sblijaet i chto razedinyaet", Monitoring obshetvennoqo mnenia, Vol 2, No. 70, pp. 3-16.

Pew Research Centre, 2014: Russia's Global Image Negative amid Crisis in Ukraine. Available at: http://www.pewglobal.org/2014/07/09/russias-global-image-negative-amid-crisis-in-ukraine/ (accessed: 18 January 2016).

Pogorelskaja, S., W., 2002: "Die parteinahen Stiftungen als Akteure und Instrumente der deutschen Aussenpolitik", *Aus Politik und Zeitgeschichte*, Vol. 6, No. 7, pp. 29-38.

Polese, A., 2009: "Ukraine 2004: Informal Networks, Transformation of Social Capital and Coloured Revolutions", *Journal of Communist Studies and Transition Politics*, Vol. 25, No. 2-3, pp. 255-277.

Polit.ru, 2010: "YAzykovaya politika Ukrainy: deystviya vlasti, mneniya grazhdan", available at: http://www.polit.ru/article/2010/11/09/language/ (accessed: 28 March 2017).

Poluneev, Y., 2014: "Desyat' shokív Ukraíni. Chastina persha", Yekonomíchna Pravda, available at: http://www.epravda.com.ua/publications/2014/12/12/512627/view_print/&usg=ALkJrhizeiv1mTxjFgfZ3IW20aP_Wjjirw/ (accessed: 27 March 2017).

Pomerantsev, P. & Weiss, M., 2014: "The Menace of Unreality: How the Kremlin Weaponizes Information, Culture and Money", *Institute of Modern Russia*, available at: http://imrussia.org/media/pdf/Research/Michael_Weiss_and_Peter_Pomerantsev__The_Menace_of_Unreality.pdf (accessed: 22 September 2016).

Pomerantsev, P. 2015, "How to Beat Vladimir Putin in the Battle for Hearts and Eyeballs", *Financial Times*, available at: http://www.ft.com/intl/cms/s/0/1680e214-35f6-11e5-bdbb-35e55cbae175.html#axzz3qKhCJpte (accessed: 02 November 2015).

Popescu, N., 2006: "Russia's Soft Power Ambitions", *Centre for European Policy Studies*, Policy Brief, No. 115, available at: https://www.ceps.eu/system/files/book/1388.pdf (accessed: 2 June 2017).

Popescu, N. & Wilson, A., 2009a: "Russian and European Neighbourhood Policies Compared", *Southeast European and Black Sea Studies*, Vol. 9, No. 3, pp. 317-331.

Popescu, N. & Wilson, A., 2009b: "The Limits of Enlargement-Lite: European and Russian Power in the Troubled Neighbourhood", Policy Report, European Council on Foreign Relations, London.

Portnov, A., 2014: "EuroMaidan: Context and Meanings", in Scheide, C. & Schmid, U., (eds), *The EuroMaidan in Ukraine November 2013 till February 2014*, Online Journal of the Center for Governance and Culture in Europe, University of St. Gallen, St. Gallen, pp. 9-13.

Powell, R., 1991: "Absolute and Relative Gains in International Relations Theory", *the American Political Science Review*, Vol. 85, No. 4, pp. 1303-1320.

Priess, D., 1996: "Balance-of-Threat Theory and the Genesis of the Gulf Cooperation Council", *Security Studies*, Vol. 5, No. 4, pp. 143-71.

Przelomiec, M., 2014: "Poland on the Euromaidan", in Bachmann, K. & Lyubashenko, I., (eds.) *The Maidan Uprising, Separatism and Foreign Intervention: Ukraine's Complex Transition*, Peter Lang, Frankfurt am Main, pp. 299-320.

Puglisi, R., 2015: "A People's Army: Civil Society as a Security Actor in Post-Maidan Ukraine", *Istituto Affari Internazionali*, Working Papers 15.

Putin, V., 2001: "Vystuplenie Prezidenta Rossiiskoi Federatsii V. V. Putina na Kongresse sootechest-vennikov", *Nasledie.ru*, http://old.nasledie.ru/politvnt/19_44/article.php?art=24 (accessed: 1 July 2017).

Putin, V., 2012: "Rossiya i menyayushchiysya mir", available at: http://www.mn.ru/politics/78738 (accessed: 11 May 2017).

Qasimov, C., 2016a: "Disintegration Crisis in EU: A View from South Caucasus", *Meydan TV*, available at: https://www.meydan.tv/en/site/politics/15802/ (accessed: 13 July 2016).

Qasimov, C., 2016b: "Does the West Recognize the South Caucasus as a Fefacto Russian Sphere of Influence?" *Meydan TV*, available at: https://www.meydan.tv/en/site/politics/16885/ (accessed: 5 November 2016).

Radio Svoboda, 2013: "Vstup Ukraïni do NATO pídtrimuê lishe kozhen p'yatiy ukraïnets' — opituvannya", available at: https://www.radiosvoboda.org/a/25138975.html (accessed: 14 May 2017).

Raik, K., 2006a: "The EU as a Regional Power: Extended Governance and Historical Responsibility", in Meyer H. & Vogt, H., (eds.) *A Responsible Europe? Ethical Foundations of EU External Affairs*, Palgrave Macmillan, Basingstoke, pp. 76-97.

Raik, K., 2006b: "Making Civil Society Support Central to EU Democracy Assistance", in Forbig, J., Marples, R., D. & Demes, P., (eds.) *Prospects for Democracy in Belarus*, The German Marshall Fund of the United States, Washington DC, pp.170-177.

Rankin, J., 2016: "EU Lifts Most Sanctions against Belarus Despite Human Rights Concerns", *The Guardian*, available at: https://www.theguardian.com/world/2016/feb/15/eu-lifts-most-sanctions-against-belarus-despite-human-rights-concerns (accessed: 7 February 2017).

Rapoza, K., 2017: "Russia's Baltic Sea Pipeline Scares the Life Out of Ukraine", *Forbes*, available at: http://www.forbes.com/sites/kenrapoza/2017/02/09/russias-baltic-sea-pipeline-scares-the-life-out-of-ukraine/#2d56c70b336b (accessed: 20 February 2017).

Rathbun, B., 2008: "A Rose by Any Other Name: Neoclassical Realism as the Logical and Necessary Extension of Structural Realism", *Security Studies*, Vol. 17, No. 2, pp. 294-321.

Ray, J., 2011: "Russia's Leadership Not Popular Worldwide", available at: https://news.gallup.com/poll/148862/russia-leadership-not-popular-worldwide.aspx (accessed: 20 March 2017).

Ray, J., 2015: "Ukrainians Disillusioned with Leadership", available at: https://news.gallup.com/poll/187931/ukrainians-disillusioned-leadership.aspx (accessed: 20 March 2017).

Raybman, N., 2014: "Finansirovaniye Russia Today iz Gosbyudzheta Uvelichitsya na 41% v 2015 Godu — RBK", *Vedomosti*, available at: http://www.vedomosti.ru/politics/articles/2014/09/23/finansirovanie (accessed: 2 October 2016).

Reuters, 2008: "US says warned Georgia against Russia fight", available at: http://www.reuters.com/article/2008/08/19/us-georgia-ossetia-usa-idUSN1947796120080819 (accessed: 22 August 2015).

Reuters, 2017: "Ukraine's Poroshenko plans referendum on NATO membership: German media", available at: http://www.reuters.com/article/us-ukraine-nato-idUSKBN15H05K (accessed: 14 May 2017).

RFE/RL, 2012: "Clinton Calls Eurasian Integration an Effort to 'Re-Sovietize'", available at: http://www.rferl.org/a/clinton-calls-eurasian-integration-effort-to-resovietize/24791921.html (accessed: 17 May 2017).

RFE/RL, 2016: "Jobs", available at: http://www.rferl.org/jobs/detail/Dig1843-1501.html (accessed: 16 June 2017).

RFE/RL, 2017a: "Yanukovych Still Wants EU Accord", available at: http://www.rferl.org/a/ukraine-eu-/25183983.html (accessed: 11 May 2017).

RFE/RL, 2017b: "Poroshenko Restricts Access to Russian Websites, Social Networks", available at: https://www.rferl.org/a/ukraine-poroshenko-restricts-access-yandex-vkontakte/28490951.html (accessed: 17 May 2017).

RFE/RL, 2017c: "RFE/RL's Ukrainian Service: Radio Svoboda", available at: https://pressroom.rferl.org/p/6139.html (accessed: 11 May 2017).

Richmond, Y., 2003: *Cultural Exchange and the Cold War: Raising the Iron Curtain*, The Pennsylvania State University, University Park, PA.

Rimple, P., 2015: "How Strong Is Russia's Soft Power in Georgia?", *Eurasianet.org*, available at: http://www.eurasianet.org/node/72671 (accessed: 23 June 2017).

Rinnert, D., 2011: "The Eastern Partnership in Georgia: Increasing Efficiency of EU Neighbourhood Policies in the South Caucasus", Working Paper, German Institute for International and Security Affairs, Berlin, Germany.

Ripsman, N., M., 2009: "Neoclassical realism and domestic interest groups" in Lobell, S., Ripsman, N. & Taliaferro, J., (eds.) *Neoclassical Realism, the State, and Foreign Policy*, Cambridge University Press, New York, pp. 170-193.

Ripsman, N., M., Taliaferro, J., W. & Lobell, S., E., 2009: "Conclusion: The State of Neoclassical Realism", in Lobell, S., Ripsman, N. & Taliaferro, J., (eds.) *Neoclassical Realism, the State, and Foreign Policy*, Cambridge University Press, New York, pp. 280-299.

Rondeli, A., 2001: "The Choice of Independent Georgia", in Chufrin, S., (ed.) *The Security of the Caspian Sea Region*, Oxford University Press, Oxford, pp .195-211.

Rontoyanni, C., 2005: "Belarusian Foreign Policy", Lynch, D. (ed.) *Changing Belarus*, pp. 47-66, Institute for Security Studies, European Union, Chaillot Paper N° 85.

Roselle, L., Miskimmon, A. & O'Loughlin, B., 2014: "Strategic Narrative: A New Means to Understand Soft Power", *Media, War and Conflict*, Vol. 7, No. 1, pp. 70–84.

Rose, G., 1998: "Neoclassical Realism and Theories of Foreign Policy", *World Politics*, Vol. 51, No. 1, pp. 144-172.

Rostoks, T. & Potjomkina, D., 2015: "Soft power of the EU and Russia in Eastern Europe: Soft Power vs (not so) Soft Manipulation?" in Rostoks, T. & Spruds, A., (eds.) *The Different Faces of "Soft power": The Baltic States and Eastern Neighbourhood between Russia and the EU*, Latvian Institute of International Affairs, pp. 243-255.

RT, 2009: "Everything's ready for Customs Union" — Medvedev", available at: https://www.rt.com/politics/official-word/medvedev-belarus-media/ (accessed: 16 January 2017).

RT, 2015: "Want more RT? Tune in for French and German", available at: https://www.rt.com/news/232455-rt-french-german-news/ (accessed: 28 October 2015).

RT, 2016: "Ukraine bans all Russian movies released since 2014", available at: https://www.rt.com/news/337728-ukraine-bans-russian-movies/ (accessed: 5 May 2017).

Rukhadze, V., 2016, "Russia's Soft Power in Georgia: How Does It Work?" *Eurasia Daily Monitor*, Vol. 13, No. 34, available at: https://jamestown.org/program/russias-soft-power-in-georgia-how-does-it-work/ (accessed: 23 June 2017).

Russett, B., 1993: *Grasping the Democratic Peace: Principles for a Post-Cold War World*, Princeton, Princeton University Press, New Jersey.

Russett, B., 2009: "Democracy, War and Expansion through Historical Lenses", *European Journal of International Relations*, Vol. 5, No. 9, pp. 9-36.

Rutland, P., 2015: "An Unnecessary War: The Geopolitical Roots of the Ukraine Crisis", in Pikulicka-Wilczewska, A. & Sakwa, R., (eds.) *Ukraine and Russia: People, Politics, Propaganda and Perspectives*, E-International Relations, Bristol, pp. 122-133.

Rutland, P. & Kazantsev, A., 2016: "The limits of Russia's 'soft power'", *Journal of Political Power*, Vol. 9, No. 3, pp.395-413.

Ryabchuk, A., 2014: "Right Revolution? Hopes and Perils of the Euromaidan Protests in Ukraine", *Journal of Contemporary Central and Eastern Europe*, Vol. 22, No. 1, pp. 127-134.

Ryder, A., 2002: "History", in Bell, I., (ed.) *Eastern Europe, Russia and Central Asia 2003*, The Gresham Press, London, pp. 136-142.

Rywkin, M., 2014: "Ukraine: Between Russia and the West", *American Foreign Policy Interests: The Journal of the National Committee on American Foreign Policy*, Vol. 36, No. 2, pp. 119-126.

Saari, S., 2014: "Russia's Post-Orange Revolution Strategies to Increase its Influence in Former Soviet Republics: Public Diplomacy po russkii", *Europe-Asia Studies*, Vol. 66, No. 1, pp. 50-66.

Sadowski, R., 2015: "Poland's Sof Power in Eastern Europe", in Rostoks, T. & Spruds, A., (eds.) *The Different Faces of "Soft power": The Baltic States and Eastern Neighbourhood between Russia and the EU*, Latvian Institute of International Affairs, pp. 64-79.

Sakwa, R., 2011a: "Russia's Identity: Between the 'Domestic' and the 'International'", *Europe-Asia Studies*, Vol. 63, No. 6, pp. 957–975.

Sakwa, R., 2011b: "Russia and Europe: Whose Society?", *European Integration*, Vol. 33, No. 2, 197–214.

Sakwa, R., 2015: *Frontline Ukraine: Crisis in the Borderland*, I.B. Tauris, London.

Samokhvalov, V., 2015: "Ukraine between Russia and the European Union: Triangle Revisited", *Europe-Asia Studies*, Vol. 67, No. 9, pp. 1371-1393.

Sasse, G., 2012: "Linkages and the Promotion of Democracy: the EU's Eastern Neighbourhood", *Democratization*, Vol. 20, No. 4, pp. 553-591.

Savin, K., 2014: "Maidan 2013 in Kiev: Revolution in People's Heads", in Scheide, C. & Schmid, U., (eds) *The EuroMaidan in Ukraine November 2013 till February 2014*, Online Journal of the Center for Governance and Culture in Europe, University of St. Gallen, St. Gallen, pp. 5-8.

Schadler, R., 2013: "Hillary Clinton's Unfinished Business at the Broadcasting Board of Governors", *US News*, Available at: https://www.us news.com/opinion/blogs/world-report/2013/02/26/hillary-clin tons-unfinished-business-at-the-broadcasting-board-of-governors (accessed: 22 September 2016).

Schweller, R., L., 1994: "Bandwagoning for Profit: Bringing the Revisionist State Back In", *International Security*, Vol. 19, No. 1, pp. 72–107.

Schweller, R., L., 1997: "New Realist Research on Alliances: Refining, Not Refuting, Waltz's Balancing Proposition", *The American Political Science Review*, Vol. 91, No. 4, pp. 927-930.

Schweller, R., L, 2004: "Unanswered Threats: A Neoclassical Realist Theory of Underbalancing", International Security, Vol. 29, No. 2, pp.159-201.

Semonov, M., 2016: "Myagkaya Sila Rossii na Ukraine", *Center for Support and Development Public Initiatives "Creative Diplomacy"*, available at: http://www.picreadi.ru/myagkaya-sila-rossii-na-ukraine/ (accessed: 5 May 2017).

Shapovalova, N., 2010: "Assessing Democracy Assistance: Ukraine", *FRIDE*, available at: http://fride.org/descarga/IP_WMD_Ucrania_ ENG_jul10.pdf (accessed: 29 March 2017).

Shapovalova, N., 2014: "The Role of Crime in Ukraine—Russia Relations", in Bachmann, K. & Lyubashenko, I., (eds.) *The Maidan Uprising, Separatism and Foreign Intervention: Ukraine's Complex Transition*, Peter Lang, Frankfurt am Main, pp. 227-266.

Sharp, P., 2005: "Revolutionary States, Outlaw Regimes and the Techniques of Public Diplomacy", in Melissen, J., (ed.) *The New Public Diplomacy: Soft Power in International Relations*, Palgrave Macmillan, New York, pp. 106-123.

Shearman, P., 2010: "History, Russia and the West, and Cold Wars", Kanet, R., E. (ed.) *Russian Foreign Policy in the 21st Century*, Palgrave Macmillan, New York, pp. 11-29.

Shepherd, R., 2006: "The United States and Europe's Last Dictatorship", in Forbig, J., Marples, R., D., Demes, P., (eds.) *Prospects for Democracy in Belarus*, The German Marshall Fund of the United States, Washington DC, pp.71-78.

Sherr, J., 2013: *Hard Diplomacy and Soft Coercion: Russia's Influence Abroad*, Chatham House, London.

Sherr, J., 2015: "A War of Narratives and Arms", in: Giles, K., Hanson, P., Lyne, R., Nixey, J., Sherr, J. & Wood, A., *The Russian Challenge*, pp. 23-32, the Chatham House Report, available at: https://www.chathamhouse.org/sites/files/chathamhouse/field/field_document/20150605RussianChallengeGilesHansonLyneNixeySherrWoodUpdate.pdf (accessed: 28 November 2016).

Shilov, V., H., 2014: "Moskovskiy Maydan Avgusta 1991 Goda: Predposylki i Posledstviya", Nauchnyye Vedomosti, Vol. 31, No. 15(186), pp. 183-189.

Shlapak, D. & Johnson, M., W., 2016: "Outnumbered, Outranged, and Outgunned: How Russia Defeats NATO", *War on the Rocks*, available at: https://warontherocks.com/2016/04/outnumbered-outranged-and-outgunned-how-russia-defeats-nato/ (accessed: 22 June 2016).

Shubin, V., 2004: "Russia and Africa: moving in the Right Direction?" in Taylor, I. & Williams, P., (eds.) *Africa in International Politics: External Involvement on the Continent*, Routledge, London, pp. 102-105.

Siddi, M. & Gaweda, B., 2012: "Bystander in its Neighbourhood? The European Union's Involvement in Protracted Conflicts in the Post-Soviet Space", *IEP Policy Papers on Eastern Europe and Central Asia*, No. 1.

Silitski, V., 2005: "Internal Developments in Belarus", in Lynch, D. (ed.) *Changing Belarus*, Institute for Security Studies, European Union, Chaillot Paper N° 85, pp.25-46.

Skålnes, S., L., 2005: "Geopolitics and the Eastern Enlargement of the European Union", in Shimmelfennig, F. & Sedelmeier, U., *The Politics of European Union Enlargement: Theoretical Approaches*, Routledge, London and New York, pp. 213-233.

Skak, M., 2010: "Russia's New 'Monroe Doctrine'" in Kanet, R., E. (ed.) *Russian Foreign Policy in the 21st Century*, Palgrave Macmillan, New York, pp. 138-154.

Smith, M., J., 1993a: *Pressure, Power, and Policy: State Autonomy and Policy Networks in Britain and the United States*, University of Pittsburgh Press, Pittsburgh.

Smith, M., 1993b: *Pax Russica: Russia's Monroe Doctrine*, The Royal United Services Institute for Defence Studies, London.

Smith, N., R., 2015: "The EU and Russia's Conflicting Regime Preferences in Ukraine: Assessing Regime Promotion Strategies in the Scope of the Ukraine Crisis", *European Security*, Vol. 24, No. 4, pp. 1-16.

Smith, N. R., 2016: "The EU under a Realist Scope: Employing a Neoclassical Realist Framework for the Analysis of the EU's Deep and Comprehensive Free Trade Agreement Offer to Ukraine", *International Relations*, Vol. 30, No. 1, pp. 29–48.

Smith, M., 2017: "Most NATO Members in Eastern Europe See It as Protection", available at: http://www.gallup.com/poll/203819/nato-members-eastern-europe-protection.aspx (accessed: 13 February 2017).

Socor, V., 2005: "Kremlin Redefining Policy in "Post-Soviet Space", *Eurasia Daily Monitor*, Vol. 2, No. 27, available at: https://Jamestown.org/program/kremlin-redefining-policy-in-post-soviet-space/ (accessed: 27 March 2017).

Solonenko, I., 2014: "Ukrainian Civil Society from the Orange Revolution to Euromaidan: Striving for a New Social Contract", in IFSH (ed.) *OSCE Yearbook 2014*, Baden-Baden, pp. 219-235.

Sparrow, T., 2014: "From Maidan to Moscow: Washington's response to the crisis in Ukraine", in Bachmann, K. & Lyubashenko, I., (eds.) *The Maidan Uprising, Separatism and Foreign Intervention: Ukraine's Complex Transition*, Peter Lang, Frankfurt am Main, pp. 321-348.

Speedie, C., D., 2015: "Soft Power: The Values that Shape Russian Foreign Policy", *Carnegie Council for Ethics in International Affairs*, available at: https://www.carnegiecouncil.org/publications/articles_papers_reports/740 (accessed: 23 December 2016).

Spiegel, 2010: "Terrible losses overnight: cables track US diplomatic efforts to avert Russian-Georgian conflict", available at: http://www.spiegel.de/international/world/terrible-loses-overnightcables-track-us-diplomatic-efforts-to-avert-russian-georgian-conflict-a-732294.html (accessed: 22 August 2015).

Splidsboel-Hansen, F., 2000: "GUUAM and the Future of CIS Military Cooperation", *European Security*, Vol. 9, No. 4, pp.92-110.

Sprehe, K., H., 2010: "Ukraine Says 'No' to NATO", *Pew Research Center*, available at: http://www.pewglobal.org/2010/03/29/ukraine-says-no-to-nato/ (accessed: 15 May 2017).

SIPRI, 2016: "Military Expenditure Database", available at: http://www.sipri.org/research/armaments/milex/milex_database (accessed: 14 April 2016).

Sputniknews, 2009: "'Eastern Partnership': EU Trying to Split CIS", available at: http://sputniknews.com/voiceofrussia/2009/02/27/245157.html (accessed: 15 April 2016).

Sputniknews, 2012: "Russia to strengthen ties with Diaspora, expats", available at: http://sputniknews.com/voiceofrussia/2012_06_27/79525664/ (accessed: 29 October 2015).

Sputniknews, 2016a: "Nuland: US Spends $100Mln to Counter Russian Propaganda Since 2014", available at: https://sputniknews.com/politics/201606081040963385-us-russian-propaganda-nuland/ (accessed: 16 June 2017).

Sputniknews, 2016b: "Russian Military Experts to Develop 'Soft Power' Concept—Reports", available at: https://sputniknews.com/russia/20160301/1035564527/russia-softpower-hybrid-warfare.html (accessed: 18 June 2017)

Sputniknews, 2016c: "Residents of 11 Countries Compare Life Before and After Collapse of Soviet Union", available at: https://sptnkne.ws/c4XH (accessed: 28 June 2017).

Starchak, V., M., 2009: 'Rossiyskoe obrazovanie na russkom yazyke kak factor vliyaniya Rossii v Tsentralnoy Azii: chto proiskhodit I chto delat', Russkiy Mir Foundation, available at: http://www.russkiymir.ru/analytics/tables/news/119895/ (accessed: 22 December 2016).

State Statistics Committee of Ukraine, 2001: "National Composition of Population", available at: http://2001.ukrcensus.gov.ua/eng/results/general/nationality/ (accessed: 27 March 2017).

State Statistics Service of Ukraine, 2013: "External Economic Activity", available at: http://ukrstat.org/en/druk/publicat/kat_e/publ6_e.htm (accessed: 10 October 2017).

Stegniy, O., 2011: "Ukraine and the Eastern Partnership: 'Lost in Translation'?" *Journal of Communist Studies and Transition Politics*, Vol. 27, No. 1, pp.50-72.

Stepanenko, V., 2006: "Civil Society in Post-Soviet Ukraine: Civic Ethos in the Framework of Corrupted Sociality?" *East European Politics and Societies*, 20, pp. 571-597.

Stewart, S. 2009: "The Interplay of Domestic Contexts and External Democracy Promotion: Lessons from Eastern Europe and the South Caucasus", *Democratization*, Vol. 16, No. 4, pp. 804-824.

Stopfake.org, 2017: "About us", available at: http://www.stopfake.org/en/about-us/ (accessed: 11 May 2017).

Stratcomcoe, 2016: "Social Media as a Tool of Hybrid Warfare", NATO Strategic Communications Centre of Excellence available at: http://www.stratcomcoe.org/social-media-tool-hybrid-warfare (accessed: 2 June 2017).

Strobel, W., 2015: "US Losing 'Information war' to Russia, Other Rivals—study", *Reuters*, available at: http://www.reuters.com/article/usa-broadcasting-idUSL2N0WP23620150325 (accessed: 16 June 2017).

Surkov, V., 2006: "Suverenitet—Eto Politicheskiy Sinonim Konkurentosposobnosti" in Garadzha, N. (ed.) *Suverenitet*, Evropa Publishers, Moscow, pp. 63-119.

Surzhko-Harned, L. & Zahuranec, J., A., 2017: "Framing the Revolution: The Role of Social Media in Ukraine's Euromaidan Movement", *Nationalities Papers*, Vol. 45, No. 5, pp. 758-779.

Suslov, M., 2016: "The Russian Orthodox Church and the Crisis in Ukraine", in Krawchuk, A. & Bremer, T., (eds.) *Churches in the Ukrainian Crisis*, Palgrave Macmillan, Houndsmills, pp. 133-162.

Sussman, G., 2010: *Branding Democracy: US Regime Change in Post-Soviet Eastern Europe*, Peter Lang, New York.

Szeptycki, A., 2014: "Independent Ukraine", in Bachmann, K. & Lyubashenko, I., (eds.) *The Maidan Uprising, Separatism and Foreign Intervention: Ukraine's Complex Transition*, Peter Lang, Frankfurt am Main, pp. 19-42.

Szostek, J., 2014: "Russia and the News Media in Ukraine: A Case of "Soft Power"?", *East European Politics and Societies*, Vol. 28, No. 3, pp. 463-486.

Szostek, J., 2015: "Russian Influence on News Media in Belarus", *Communist and Post-Communist Studies*, Vol. 48, pp. 1-13.

Tafuro, E., 2014: "Fatal Attraction? Russia's Soft Power in its Neighbourhood—Analysis", *FRIDE*, available at: http://fride.org/descarga/29.05.2014_EurasiaReview_US_ET.pdf (accessed: 25 September 2016).

Tagesschau.de, 2015: "Russischsprachiges TV-Programm in Estland: 'Wichtiger als Panzer'", available at: https://www.tagesschau.de/ausland/estland-russland-101.html (accessed: 16 June 2017).

Taliaferro, W., J., 2009: "Neoclassical Realism and Resource Extraction: State Building for Future War", in Lobell, S., Ripsman, N. & Taliaferro, J., (eds.) *Neoclassical Realism, the State, and Foreign Policy*, Cambridge University Press, New York, pp. 194-226.

Taliaferro, W., J., Lobell, S., E. & Ripsman, N., M., 2009: "Introduction: Neoclassical Realism, the State, and Foreign Policy", in Lobell, S., Ripsman, N. & Taliaferro, J., (eds.) *Neoclassical Realism, the State, and Foreign Policy*, Cambridge University Press, New York, pp. 1-41.

Tansey, O., 2015: "The Problem with Autocracy Promotion", *Democratization*, Vol. 23, No. 1, pp. 141-163.

Tarnoff, C., 2007: "US Assistance to the Former Soviet Union. Conressional Research Service Report for Congress", *Federation of American Scientists*, available at www.fas.org/sgp/crs/row/RL32866.pdf (accessed: 3 June 2016).

TASS, 2014: "Patriarch Kirill hopes Russian-Ukrainian spiritual unity is preserved", available at: http://tass.com/russia/720955/amp (accessed: 28 March 2017).

TASS, 2016a: "Russia's Rearmament 50% Ahead of Plan—Official", available at: http://tass.ru/en/defense/859099 (accessed: 16 June 2017).

TASS, 2016b: "Signs having the word 'Russia' banned in Ukraine's Chernovtsy", available at: http://tass.com/world/867237 (accessed: 5 May 2017).

Taylor, R., 1979: *Film Propaganda: Soviet Russia and Nazi Germany*, I.B. Tauris, London.

Telegraph, 2016: "US to Station Armoured Brigade in Eastern Europe from 2017", available at: http://www.telegraph.co.uk/news/2016/03/30/us-to-station-armoured-brigade-in-eastern-europe-from-2017/ (accessed: 18 May 2017).

Teleradio Moldova, 2014: "Almost 70% of remittances arrived in Moldova in 2013, originate in Russia", available at: https://www.trm.md/en/economic/aproape-70-din-transferurile-din-strainatate-au-pro venit-din-rusia-in-2013/ (accessed: 11 May 2017).

Tolstrup, J., 2009: "Studying a Negative External Actor: Russia's Management of Stability and Instability in the 'Near Abroad,'" *Democratization*, Vol. 16, No. 5, pp. 922–944.

Torkunov, A., 2013: "Education as a Soft Power Instrument of Russia's Foreign Policy", *Russia International Affairs Council*, available at: http://russiancouncil.ru/en/analytics-and-comments/analytics/education-as-a-soft-power-instrument-of-russia-s-foreign-pol/ (accessed: 2 June 2017).

Traynor, I. & Grytsenko, O., 2013: "Ukraine Suspends Talks on EU Trade Pact as Putin Wins Tug of War", *The Guardian*, available at: http://www.theguardian.com/world/2013/nov/21/ukraine-suspends-preparations-eu-trade-pact (accessed: 20 January 2016).

Trenin, D., 2011: *Post-Imperium: A Eurasian Story*, Carnegie Endowment for International Peace, Washington, DC.

Tsygankov, A., P., 2005: "Vladimir Putin's Vision of Russia as a Normal Great Power", *Post-Soviet Affairs*, Vol. 21, No. 2, pp. 132–158.

Ukraynskaya Pravda, 2015a: "Poroshenko pidpisav zakoni pro dekomunizatsiyu", available at: http://www.pravda.com.ua/news/2015/05/15/7068057/ (accessed: 27 March 2017).

Ukraynskaya Pravda, 2015b: "V Ukraïni pereymenuyut' 22 mista i 44 selishcha", available at: http://www.pravda.com.ua/news/2015/06/4/7070191/ (accessed: 27 March 2017).

UNESCO, 2016: "Global Flow of Tertiary Students", available at: http://uis.unesco.org/en/uis-student-flow#slideoutmenu (accessed: 30 March 2017).

UNESCO, 2017: "Statistics" available at: http://data.uis.unesco.org/# (accessed: 30 March 2017).

UNIAN, 2014a: "Segodnya vecherom v Ukraine vyklyuchat neskol'ko rossiyskikh kanalov", available at: https://www.unian.net/politics/895188-segodnya-vecherom-v-ukraine-vyiklyuchat-neskolko-rossiyskih-kanalov.html (accessed: 25 March 2017).

UNIAN, 2014b: "Since 1991 US has invested $5 billion to promote democracy in Ukraine, but they did not finance Maidan – Nuland", available at: https://www.unian.info/politics/910206-since-1991-us-has-invested-5-billion-to-promote-democracy-in-ukraine-but-they-did-not-finance-maidan-nuland.html (accessed: 11 May 2017).

UNIAN, 2016a: "Poll: Nearly two-thirds of Russians support Kremlin's policy toward Ukraine", available at: https://www.unian.info/world/1253904-poll-nearly-two-thirds-of-russians-support-kremlins-policy-toward-ukraine.html (accessed: 16 May 2017).

UNIAN, 2016b: "Ukrainians less support European integration – poll", available at: https://www.unian.info/society/1287694-ukrainians-less-support-european-integration-poll.html (accessed: 17 May 2017).

USAID, 2016: "Civil Society Development", available at: https://www.usaid.gov/where-we-work/europe-and-eurasia/belarus/civil-society-development (accessed: 17 June 2017).

Van Evera, S., 1990–1991: "Primed for Peace: Europe after the Cold War", *International Security*, Vol. 15, No. 3, pp. 7–57.

Van der Togt, T., 2017: "The "Belarus factor" From balancing to bridging geopolitical dividing lines in Europe?", *The Netherlands Institute of International Relations 'Clingendael'*, The Hague, available at: https://www.clingendael.nl/sites/default/files/Report_The_Belarus_factor.pdf (accessed: 20 May 2017).

Van Herpen, M., H., 2014: *Putin's Wars: The Rise of Russia's New Imperialism*, Rowman & Littlefield, Lanham, MD.

Van Herpen, M., H., 2015: *Putin's Propaganda Machine: Soft Power and Russian Foreign Policy*, Rowman & Littlefield, Lanham, MD.

Vanderhill, R., 2014: "Promoting Democracy and Promoting Authoritarianism: Comparing the Cases of Belarus and Slovakia", *Europe-Asia Studies*, Vol. 66, No. 2, pp. 255-283.

Vardanyan, A., 2015: "Russia's Policy in Armenia and its Impact Tools", *"Aravot" Daily*, available at: http://en.aravot.am/2015/11/19/173046/ (accessed: 1 June 2017).

Vasilevich, N., 2014: "The Belarusian Orthodox Church in the Shadow of the State", *Russian Politics and Law*, Vol. 52, No. 5, pp. 7-31.

Vasilevich, N., 2016: "Religious Sphere: Prayer for Belarus, Prayer for Lukashenko?", in Pankovsky, A. & Kostyugova, V., (eds.) *Belarusian Yearbook*, Lohvinaŭ, Vilnius, pp. 171-178.

Vieira, A., V., G., 2014a: "The Politico-Military Alliance of Russia and Belarus: Re-Examining the Role of NATO and the EU in Light of the Intra-Alliance Security Dilemma", *Europe-Asia Studies*, Vol. 66, No. 4, pp. 557-577.

Vieira, A., V., G., 2014b: "Ukraine's Crisis and Russia's Closest Allies: A Reinforced Intra-Alliance Security Dilemma at Work", *The International Spectator: Italian Journal of International Affairs*, Vol. 49, No. 4, pp. 97-111.

Vilpišauskas, R.,Ališauskas, R., Kasčiūnas, L., Dambrauskaitė, Ž., Sinica, V., Levchenko, I. & Chirila, V., 2012: "Eurasian Union: A Challenge for the European Union and Eastern Partnership Countries", *Eastern European Studies Centre*, Vilnius, Lithuania.

Vincent, R., C., 2007: "Global Communication and Propaganda" in Kamalipour, Y., R., (ed.) *Global Communication*, Cengage Learning, Wadsworth, pp. 232-270.

Vorobiov, I., 2015a: "Why Ukrainians Are Speaking More Ukrainian", *Foreign Policy Magazine*, available at: http://foreignpolicy.com/2015/06/26/why-ukrainians-are-speaking-more-ukrainian/ (accessed: 14 May 2017).

Vorobiov, I., 2015b: "Surprise! Ukraine Loves NATO", *Foreign Policy Magazine*, http://foreignpolicy.com/2015/08/13/surprise-ukraine-loves-nato/ (accessed: 14 May 2017).

Vuving, A., 2009: "How Soft Power Works", Paper presented at the panel "Soft Power and Smart Power", *American Political Science Association annual meeting*, available at: http://apcss.org/Publications/Vuving%20How%20soft%20power%20works%20APSA%202009.pdf (accessed: 05 February 2016).

Walker, S., 2013: "Ukraine's EU Trade Deal will be Catastrophic, Says Russia", *The Guardian*, available at: http://www.theguardian.com/world/2013/sep/22/ukraine-european-union-trade-russia (accessed: 18 January 2016).

Walker, C., 2016: "The Hijacking of 'Soft Power'", *Journal of Democracy*, Vol. 27, No. 1, pp. 49-53.

Waller, J., M., 2007: *The Public Diplomacy Reader*, The Institute of World Politics Press, Washington, DC.

Walt, M., S., 1987: *The Origins of Alliances*, Cornell University Press, Ithaca and London.

Walt, S., 2002: "The Enduring Relevance of the Realist Tradition", in Katznelson, I. & Milner, H., V., (eds.) *Political Science: The State of the Discipline*, Norton, New York, pp. 197-230.

Waltz, K., 2001: *Man, the State and War: A Theoretical Analysis*, Columbia University Press, New York.

Waltz, K., 1979: *Theory of International Politics*, Addison-Wesley, Reading, MA.

Walsh, I., J., 2005: "Persuasion in International Politics: A Rationalist Account", *Politics & Policy*, Vol. 33, No. 4, pp. 642-670.

Wapinski, M., 2014: "The Orange Revolution and its aftermath", in Bachmann, K. & Lyubashenko, I., (eds.) *The Maidan Uprising, Separatism and Foreign Intervention: Ukraine's Complex Transition*, Peter Lang, Frankfurt am Main, pp. 43-60.

Warrick, J., 2011: "Clinton: US Losing Global Public-Relations Battle—to 'Baywatch' and Wrestling", *The Washington Post*, available at: http://www.washingtonpost.com/wp-dyn/content/article/2011/03/02/AR2011030206898.html (accessed:22 September 2016).

Weber, M. 1978: *Economy and Society, vol. II*, eds. Roth, G. & Wittich, C., University of California Press, Berkeley.

Welch, D., 2003: "Introduction: Propaganda in Historical Perspective", in Cull, N., J., Culbert, D. & Welch, D., (eds.) *Propaganda and Mass Persuasion: A Historical Encyclopaedia, 1500 to the Present*, Oxford and Santa Barbara CA: ABC-Clio, pp. xv-xxi.

Welt, C., 2010: "Georgia's Rose Revolution: From Regime Weakness to Regime Collapse" in Bunce, V., McFaul, M. & Stoner-Weiss, K. (eds.) *Democracy and Authoritarianism in the Postcommunist World*, Cambridge University Press, Cambridge, pp. 155-188.

Wesolowsky. T., 2015: "Kaliningrad, Moscow's Military Trump Card", *Radio Free Europe/Radio Liberty*, available at: https://www.rferl.org/a/kaliningrad-russia-nato-west-strategic/27079655.html (accessed: 16 June 2017).

White, S., Korosteleva, J. & Allison, R., 2006: "NATO: The View from the East", *European Security*, Vol. 15, No. 2, pp. 165-190.

White, S., McAllister, I. & Feklyunina, V., 2010: "Belarus, Ukraine, and Russia: East or West?", *British Journal of Politics and International Relations*, Vol. 12, No. 3, pp. 344-367.

White, S., Biletskaya, T. & McAllister, I., 2014: "Belarusians between East and West", *Post-Soviet Affairs*, Vol. 32, No. 1, pp. 1-27.

Whitmore, B., 2013: "Vladimir Putin, Conservative Icon", *The Atlantic*, available at: http://www.theatlantic.com/international/archive/2013/12/vladimir-putin-conservative-icon/282572/ (accessed: 2 January 2017).

Willis, A., 2012: "Mitt Romney: Russia is America's 'number one geopolitical foe'", *The Telegraph*, available at: https://www.telegraph.co.uk/news/worldnews/us-election/9168533/Mitt-Romney-Russia-is-Americas-number-one-geopolitical-foe.html (accessed: 17 May 2017).

Wilson, A., 2005: *Ukraine's Orange Revolution*, Yale University Press, New Haven, CT.

Wilson, A., 2011: *Belarus: The Last Dictatorship in Europe*, Yale University Press, London.

Wilson, A., 2014: *Ukraine Crisis: What It Means for the West*, Yale University Press, London and New Haven, CT.

Wilson, J., L., 2015: "Russia and China Respond to Soft Power: Interpretation and Readaptation of a Western Construct", *Politics*, Vol. 35, No. 3/4, pp. 287-300.

Wohlforth, W., C., 1993: *The Elusive Balance*, Cornell University Press, Ithaca, NY.

Wohlforth, W., C., 2004: "Revisiting Balance of Power Theory in Central Eurasia", in Paul, T., V., Wirtz, J. & Fortmann, M., (eds.) *Balance of Power: Theory and Practice in the 21st Century*, Stanford University Press, Stanford, pp. 214-238.

Wolczuk, R., 2002: *Ukraine's Foreign and Security Policy 1991–2000*, Basees/Curzon Series on Russian and East European Studies, RoutledgeCurzon, New York.

World Bank, 2014: "Remittances to Developing Countries to Grow by 5 Percent This Year, While Conflict-Related Forced Migration is at All-Time High, Says WB Report", available at: http://www.worldbank.org/en/news/press-release/2014/10/06/remittances-developing-countries-five-percent-conflict-related-migration-all-time-high-wb-report (accessed: 11 May 2017).

World Bank, 2017a: "GDP (current US$): World Bank national accounts data, and OECD National Accounts data files", http://data.worldbank.org/indicator/NY.GDP.MKTP.CD?locations=EU-US-1W (accessed: 16 June 2017).

World Bank, 2017b: Statistics sourced from the World Bank, available at: http://data.worldbank.org/region/EUU, (accessed 16 June 2017).

Yaffa, J., 2014: "Dmitry Kiselev is Redefining the Art of Russian Propaganda", *New Republic*, available at: https://newrepublic.com/article/118438/dmitry-kiselev-putins-favorite-tv-host-russias-top-propogandist (accessed: 2 October 2016).

Yanukovych, V., 2010: "Ukraine will be a Bridge between East and West", available at: https://www.wsj.com/articles/SB10001424052748704804204575069251843839386 (accessed: 12 March 2017).

Yarashevich, V., 2014: "Political Economy of Modern Belarus: Going Against Mainstream?" *Europe-Asia Studies*, Vol. 66, No. 10, pp. 1703-1734.

Zahran, G. & Ramos, L., 2010: "From Hegemony to Soft Power: Implications of a Conceptual Change", in Parmar, I. & Cox, M., (eds.) *Soft Power and US Foreign Policy: Theoretical, Historical and Contemporary Perspective*, Routledge, New York, pp. 12-31.

Zevelev, I., 2008: "Russia's Policy Toward Compatriots in the Former Soviet Union", *Russia In Global Affairs*, Vol. 6, No. 1, pp. 49-62.

Zheng, Y. & Zhang, C., 2012: "'Soft power' and Chinese soft power" in Lai, H. & Lu, Y., (eds.) *China's Soft Power and International Relations*, Routledge, New York, pp. 21-38.

Zimmermann, H., 2007: "Realist Power Europe? The EU in the Negotiations about China's and Russia's WTO Accession", *Journal of Common Market Studies*, Vol. 45, No. 4, pp. 813-832.

SOVIET AND POST-SOVIET POLITICS AND SOCIETY
Edited by Dr. Andreas Umland | ISSN 1614-3515

1   Андреас Умланд (ред.) | Воплощение Европейской конвенции по правам человека в России. Философские, юридические и эмпирические исследования | ISBN 3-89821-387-0

2   Christian Wipperfürth | Russland – ein vertrauenswürdiger Partner? Grundlagen, Hintergründe und Praxis gegenwärtiger russischer Außenpolitik | Mit einem Vorwort von Heinz Timmermann | ISBN 3-89821-401-X

3   Manja Hussner | Die Übernahme internationalen Rechts in die russische und deutsche Rechtsordnung. Eine vergleichende Analyse zur Völkerrechtsfreundlichkeit der Verfassungen der Russländischen Föderation und der Bundesrepublik Deutschland | Mit einem Vorwort von Rainer Arnold | ISBN 3-89821-438-9

4   Matthew Tejada | Bulgaria's Democratic Consolidation and the Kozloduy Nuclear Power Plant (KNPP). The Unattainability of Closure | With a foreword by Richard J. Crampton | ISBN 3-89821-439-7

5   Марк Григорьевич Меерович | Квадратные метры, определяющие сознание. Государственная жилищная политика в СССР. 1921 – 1941 гг | ISBN 3-89821-474-5

6   Andrei P. Tsygankov, Pavel A. Tsygankov (Eds.) | New Directions in Russian International Studies | ISBN 3-89821-422-2

7   Марк Григорьевич Меерович | Как власть народ к труду приучала. Жилище в СССР – средство управления людьми. 1917 – 1941 гг. | С предисловием Елены Осокиной | ISBN 3-89821-495-8

8   David J. Galbreath | Nation-Building and Minority Politics in Post-Socialist States. Interests, Influence and Identities in Estonia and Latvia | With a foreword by David J. Smith | ISBN 3-89821-467-2

9   Алексей Юрьевич Безугольный | Народы Кавказа в Вооруженных силах СССР в годы Великой Отечественной войны 1941-1945 гг. | С предисловием Николая Бугая | ISBN 3-89821-475-3

10 Вячеслав Лихачев и Владимир Прибыловский (ред.) | Русское Национальное Единство, 1990-2000. В 2-х томах | ISBN 3-89821-523-7

11 Николай Бугай (ред.) | Народы стран Балтии в условиях сталинизма (1940-е – 1950-е годы). Документированная история | ISBN 3-89821-525-3

12 Ingmar Bredies (Hrsg.) | Zur Anatomie der Orange Revolution in der Ukraine. Wechsel des Elitenregimes oder Triumph des Parlamentarismus? | ISBN 3-89821-524-5

13 Anastasia V. Mitrofanova | The Politicization of Russian Orthodoxy. Actors and Ideas | With a foreword by William C. Gay | ISBN 3-89821-481-8

14 Nathan D. Larson | Alexander Solzhenitsyn and the Russo-Jewish Question | ISBN 3-89821-483-4

15 Guido Houben | Kulturpolitik und Ethnizität. Staatliche Kunstförderung im Russland der neunziger Jahre | Mit einem Vorwort von Gert Weisskirchen | ISBN 3-89821-542-3

16 Leonid Luks | Der russische „Sonderweg"? Aufsätze zur neuesten Geschichte Russlands im europäischen Kontext | ISBN 3-89821-496-6

17 Евгений Мороз | История «Мёртвой воды» – от страшной сказки к большой политике. Политическое неоязычество в постсоветской России | ISBN 3-89821-551-2

18 Александр Верховский и Галина Кожевникова (ред.) | Этническая и религиозная интолерантность в российских СМИ. Результаты мониторинга 2001-2004 гг. | ISBN 3-89821-569-5

19 Christian Ganzer | Sowjetisches Erbe und ukrainische Nation. Das Museum der Geschichte des Zaporoger Kosakentums auf der Insel Chortycja | Mit einem Vorwort von Frank Golczewski | ISBN 3-89821-504-0

20 Эльза-Баир Гучинова | Помнить нельзя забыть. Антропология депортационной травмы калмыков | С предисловием Кэролайн Хамфри | ISBN 3-89821-506-7

21 Юлия Лидерман | Мотивы «проверки» и «испытания» в постсоветской культуре. Советское прошлое в российском кинематографе 1990-х годов | С предисловием Евгения Марголита | ISBN 3-89821-511-3

22 Tanya Lokshina, Ray Thomas, Mary Mayer (Eds.) | The Imposition of a Fake Political Settlement in the Northern Caucasus. The 2003 Chechen Presidential Election | ISBN 3-89821-436-2

23 Timothy McCajor Hall, Rosie Read (Eds.) | Changes in the Heart of Europe. Recent Ethnographies of Czechs, Slovaks, Roma, and Sorbs | With an afterword by Zdeněk Salzmann | ISBN 3-89821-606-3

24 *Christian Autengruber* | Die politischen Parteien in Bulgarien und Rumänien. Eine vergleichende Analyse seit Beginn der 90er Jahre | Mit einem Vorwort von Dorothée de Nève | ISBN 3-89821-476-1

25 *Annette Freyberg-Inan with Radu Cristescu* | The Ghosts in Our Classrooms, or: John Dewey Meets Ceauşescu. The Promise and the Failures of Civic Education in Romania | ISBN 3-89821-416-8

26 *John B. Dunlop* | The 2002 Dubrovka and 2004 Beslan Hostage Crises. A Critique of Russian Counter-Terrorism | With a foreword by Donald N. Jensen | ISBN 3-89821-608-X

27 *Peter Koller* | Das touristische Potenzial von Kam''janec'–Podil's'kyj. Eine fremdenverkehrsgeographische Untersuchung der Zukunftsperspektiven und Maßnahmenplanung zur Destinationsentwicklung des „ukrainischen Rothenburg" | Mit einem Vorwort von Kristiane Klemm | ISBN 3-89821-640-3

28 *Françoise Daucé, Elisabeth Sieca-Kozlowski (Eds.)* | Dedovshchina in the Post-Soviet Military. Hazing of Russian Army Conscripts in a Comparative Perspective | With a foreword by Dale Herspring | ISBN 3-89821-616-0

29 *Florian Strasser* | Zivilgesellschaftliche Einflüsse auf die Orange Revolution. Die gewaltlose Massenbewegung und die ukrainische Wahlkrise 2004 | Mit einem Vorwort von Egbert Jahn | ISBN 3-89821-648-9

30 *Rebecca S. Katz* | The Georgian Regime Crisis of 2003-2004. A Case Study in Post-Soviet Media Representation of Politics, Crime and Corruption | ISBN 3-89821-413-3

31 *Vladimir Kantor* | Willkür oder Freiheit. Beiträge zur russischen Geschichtsphilosophie | Ediert von Dagmar Herrmann sowie mit einem Vorwort versehen von Leonid Luks | ISBN 3-89821-589-X

32 *Laura A. Victoir* | The Russian Land Estate Today. A Case Study of Cultural Politics in Post-Soviet Russia | With a foreword by Priscilla Roosevelt | ISBN 3-89821-426-5

33 *Ivan Katchanovski* | Cleft Countries. Regional Political Divisions and Cultures in Post-Soviet Ukraine and Moldova | With a foreword by Francis Fukuyama | ISBN 3-89821-558-X

34 *Florian Mühlfried* | Postsowjetische Feiern. Das Georgische Bankett im Wandel | Mit einem Vorwort von Kevin Tuite | ISBN 3-89821-601-2

35 *Roger Griffin, Werner Loh, Andreas Umland (Eds.)* | Fascism Past and Present, West and East. An International Debate on Concepts and Cases in the Comparative Study of the Extreme Right | With an afterword by Walter Laqueur | ISBN 3-89821-674-8

36 *Sebastian Schlegel* | Der „Weiße Archipel". Sowjetische Atomstädte 1945-1991 | Mit einem Geleitwort von Thomas Bohn | ISBN 3-89821-679-9

37 *Vyacheslav Likhachev* | Political Anti-Semitism in Post-Soviet Russia. Actors and Ideas in 1991-2003 | Edited and translated from Russian by Eugene Veklerov | ISBN 3-89821-529-6

38 *Josette Baer (Ed.)* | Preparing Liberty in Central Europe. Political Texts from the Spring of Nations 1848 to the Spring of Prague 1968 | With a foreword by Zdeněk V. David | ISBN 3-89821-546-6

39 *Михаил Лукьянов* | Российский консерватизм и реформа, 1907-1914 | С предисловием Марка Д. Стейнберга | ISBN 3-89821-503-2

40 *Nicola Melloni* | Market Without Economy. The 1998 Russian Financial Crisis | With a foreword by Eiji Furukawa | ISBN 3-89821-407-9

41 *Dmitrij Chmelnizki* | Die Architektur Stalins | Bd. 1: Studien zu Ideologie und Stil | Bd. 2: Bilddokumentation | Mit einem Vorwort von Bruno Flierl | ISBN 3-89821-515-6

42 *Katja Yafimava* | Post-Soviet Russian-Belarussian Relationships. The Role of Gas Transit Pipelines | With a foreword by Jonathan P. Stern | ISBN 3-89821-655-1

43 *Boris Chavkin* | Verflechtungen der deutschen und russischen Zeitgeschichte. Aufsätze und Archivfunde zu den Beziehungen Deutschlands und der Sowjetunion von 1917 bis 1991 | Ediert von Markus Edlinger sowie mit einem Vorwort versehen von Leonid Luks | ISBN 3-89821-756-6

44 *Anastasija Grynenko in Zusammenarbeit mit Claudia Dathe* | Die Terminologie des Gerichtswesens der Ukraine und Deutschlands im Vergleich. Eine übersetzungswissenschaftliche Analyse juristischer Fachbegriffe im Deutschen, Ukrainischen und Russischen | Mit einem Vorwort von Ulrich Hartmann | ISBN 3-89821-691-8

45 *Anton Burkov* | The Impact of the European Convention on Human Rights on Russian Law. Legislation and Application in 1996-2006 | With a foreword by Françoise Hampson | ISBN 978-3-89821-639-5

46 *Stina Torjesen, Indra Overland (Eds.)* | International Election Observers in Post-Soviet Azerbaijan. Geopolitical Pawns or Agents of Change? | ISBN 978-3-89821-743-9

47 *Taras Kuzio* | Ukraine – Crimea – Russia. Triangle of Conflict | ISBN 978-3-89821-761-3

48 *Claudia Šabić* | "Ich erinnere mich nicht, aber L'viv!" Zur Funktion kultureller Faktoren für die Institutionalisierung und Entwicklung einer ukrainischen Region | Mit einem Vorwort von Melanie Tatur | ISBN 978-3-89821-752-1

49 *Marlies Bilz* | Tatarstan in der Transformation. Nationaler Diskurs und Politische Praxis 1988-1994 | Mit einem Vorwort von Frank Golczewski | ISBN 978-3-89821-722-4

50 *Марлен Ларюэль (ред.)* | Современные интерпретации русского национализма | ISBN 978-3-89821-795-8

51 *Sonja Schüler* | Die ethnische Dimension der Armut. Roma im postsozialistischen Rumänien | Mit einem Vorwort von Anton Sterbling | ISBN 978-3-89821-776-7

52 *Галина Кожевникова* | Радикальный национализм в России и противодействие ему. Сборник докладов Центра «Сова» за 2004-2007 гг. | С предисловием Александра Верховского | ISBN 978-3-89821-721-7

53 *Галина Кожевникова и Владимир Прибыловский* | Российская власть в биографиях I. Высшие должностные лица РФ в 2004 г. | ISBN 978-3-89821-796-5

54 *Галина Кожевникова и Владимир Прибыловский* | Российская власть в биографиях II. Члены Правительства РФ в 2004 г. | ISBN 978-3-89821-797-2

55 *Галина Кожевникова и Владимир Прибыловский* | Российская власть в биографиях III. Руководители федеральных служб и агентств РФ в 2004 г.| ISBN 978-3-89821-798-9

56 *Ileana Petroniu* | Privatisierung in Transformationsökonomien. Determinanten der Restrukturierungs-Bereitschaft am Beispiel Polens, Rumäniens und der Ukraine | Mit einem Vorwort von Rainer W. Schäfer | ISBN 978-3-89821-790-3

57 *Christian Wipperfürth* | Russland und seine GUS-Nachbarn. Hintergründe, aktuelle Entwicklungen und Konflikte in einer ressourcenreichen Region| ISBN 978-3-89821-801-6

58 *Togzhan Kassenova* | From Antagonism to Partnership. The Uneasy Path of the U.S.-Russian Cooperative Threat Reduction | With a foreword by Christoph Bluth | ISBN 978-3-89821-707-1

59 *Alexander Höllwerth* | Das sakrale eurasische Imperium des Aleksandr Dugin. Eine Diskursanalyse zum postsowjetischen russischen Rechtsextremismus | Mit einem Vorwort von Dirk Uffelmann | ISBN 978-3-89821-813-9

60 *Олег Рябов* | «Россия-Матушка». Национализм, гендер и война в России XX века | С предисловием Елены Гощило | ISBN 978-3-89821-487-2

61 *Ivan Maistrenko* | Borot'bism. A Chapter in the History of the Ukrainian Revolution | With a new Introduction by Chris Ford | Translated by George S. N. Luckyj with the assistance of Ivan L. Rudnytsky | Second, Revised and Expanded Edition ISBN 978-3-8382-1107-7

62 *Maryna Romanets* | Anamorphosic Texts and Reconfigured Visions. Improvised Traditions in Contemporary Ukrainian and Irish Literature | ISBN 978-3-89821-576-3

63 *Paul D'Anieri and Taras Kuzio (Eds.)* | Aspects of the Orange Revolution I. Democratization and Elections in Post-Communist Ukraine | ISBN 978-3-89821-698-2

64 *Bohdan Harasymiw in collaboration with Oleh S. Ilnytzkyj (Eds.)* | Aspects of the Orange Revolution II. Information and Manipulation Strategies in the 2004 Ukrainian Presidential Elections | ISBN 978-3-89821-699-9

65 *Ingmar Bredies, Andreas Umland and Valentin Yakushik (Eds.)* | Aspects of the Orange Revolution III. The Context and Dynamics of the 2004 Ukrainian Presidential Elections | ISBN 978-3-89821-803-0

66 *Ingmar Bredies, Andreas Umland and Valentin Yakushik (Eds.)* | Aspects of the Orange Revolution IV. Foreign Assistance and Civic Action in the 2004 Ukrainian Presidential Elections | ISBN 978-3-89821-808-5

67 *Ingmar Bredies, Andreas Umland and Valentin Yakushik (Eds.)* | Aspects of the Orange Revolution V. Institutional Observation Reports on the 2004 Ukrainian Presidential Elections | ISBN 978-3-89821-809-2

68 *Taras Kuzio (Ed.)* | Aspects of the Orange Revolution VI. Post-Communist Democratic Revolutions in Comparative Perspective | ISBN 978-3-89821-820-7

69 *Tim Bohse* | Autoritarismus statt Selbstverwaltung. Die Transformation der kommunalen Politik in der Stadt Kaliningrad 1990-2005 | Mit einem Geleitwort von Stefan Troebst | ISBN 978-3-89821-782-8

70 *David Rupp* | Die Rußländische Föderation und die russischsprachige Minderheit in Lettland. Eine Fallstudie zur Anwaltspolitik Moskaus gegenüber den russophonen Minderheiten im „Nahen Ausland" von 1991 bis 2002 | Mit einem Vorwort von Helmut Wagner | ISBN 978-3-89821-778-1

71 *Taras Kuzio* | Theoretical and Comparative Perspectives on Nationalism. New Directions in Cross-Cultural and Post-Communist Studies | With a foreword by Paul Robert Magocsi | ISBN 978-3-89821-815-3

72 *Christine Teichmann* | Die Hochschultransformation im heutigen Osteuropa. Kontinuität und Wandel bei der Entwicklung des postkommunistischen Universitätswesens | Mit einem Vorwort von Oskar Anweiler | ISBN 978-3-89821-842-9

73 *Julia Kusznir* | Der politische Einfluss von Wirtschaftseliten in russischen Regionen. Eine Analyse am Beispiel der Erdöl- und Erdgasindustrie, 1992-2005 | Mit einem Vorwort von Wolfgang Eichwede | ISBN 978-3-89821-821-4

74 Alena Vysotskaya | Russland, Belarus und die EU-Osterweiterung. Zur Minderheitenfrage und zum Problem der Freizügigkeit des Personenverkehrs | Mit einem Vorwort von Katlijn Malfliet | ISBN 978-3-89821-822-1

75 Heiko Pleines (Hrsg.) | Corporate Governance in post-sozialistischen Volkswirtschaften | ISBN 978-3-89821-766-8

76 Stefan Ihrig | Wer sind die Moldawier? Rumänismus versus Moldowanismus in Historiographie und Schulbüchern der Republik Moldova, 1991-2006 | Mit einem Vorwort von Holm Sundhaussen | ISBN 978-3-89821-466-7

77 Galina Kozhevnikova in collaboration with Alexander Verkhovsky and Eugene Veklerov | Ultra-Nationalism and Hate Crimes in Contemporary Russia. The 2004-2006 Annual Reports of Moscow's SOVA Center | With a foreword by Stephen D. Shenfield | ISBN 978-3-89821-868-9

78 Florian Küchler | The Role of the European Union in Moldova's Transnistria Conflict | With a foreword by Christopher Hill | ISBN 978-3-89821-850-4

79 Bernd Rechel | The Long Way Back to Europe. Minority Protection in Bulgaria | With a foreword by Richard Crampton | ISBN 978-3-89821-863-4

80 Peter W. Rodgers | Nation, Region and History in Post-Communist Transitions. Identity Politics in Ukraine, 1991-2006 | With a foreword by Vera Tolz | ISBN 978-3-89821-903-7

81 Stephanie Solywoda | The Life and Work of Semen L. Frank. A Study of Russian Religious Philosophy | With a foreword by Philip Walters | ISBN 978-3-89821-457-5

82 Vera Sokolova | Cultural Politics of Ethnicity. Discourses on Roma in Communist Czechoslovakia | ISBN 978-3-89821-864-1

83 Natalya Shevchik Ketenci | Kazakhstani Enterprises in Transition. The Role of Historical Regional Development in Kazakhstan's Post-Soviet Economic Transformation | ISBN 978-3-89821-831-3

84 Martin Malek, Anna Schor-Tschudnowskaja (Hgg.) | Europa im Tschetschenienkrieg. Zwischen politischer Ohnmacht und Gleichgültigkeit | Mit einem Vorwort von Lipchan Basajewa | ISBN 978-3-89821-676-0

85 Stefan Meister | Das postsowjetische Universitätswesen zwischen nationalem und internationalem Wandel. Die Entwicklung der regionalen Hochschule in Russland als Gradmesser der Systemtransformation | Mit einem Vorwort von Joan DeBardeleben | ISBN 978-3-89821-891-7

86 Konstantin Sheiko in collaboration with Stephen Brown | Nationalist Imaginings of the Russian Past. Anatolii Fomenko and the Rise of Alternative History in Post-Communist Russia | With a foreword by Donald Ostrowski | ISBN 978-3-89821-915-0

87 Sabine Jenni | Wie stark ist das „Einige Russland"? Zur Parteibindung der Eliten und zum Wahlerfolg der Machtpartei im Dezember 2007 | Mit einem Vorwort von Klaus Armingeon | ISBN 978-3-89821-961-7

88 Thomas Borén | Meeting-Places of Transformation. Urban Identity, Spatial Representations and Local Politics in Post-Soviet St Petersburg | ISBN 978-3-89821-739-2

89 Aygul Ashirova | Stalinismus und Stalin-Kult in Zentralasien. Turkmenistan 1924-1953 | Mit einem Vorwort von Leonid Luks | ISBN 978-3-89821-987-7

90 Leonid Luks | Freiheit oder imperiale Größe? Essays zu einem russischen Dilemma | ISBN 978-3-8382-0011-8

91 Christopher Gilley | The 'Change of Signposts' in the Ukrainian Emigration. A Contribution to the History of Sovietophilism in the 1920s | With a foreword by Frank Golczewski | ISBN 978-3-89821-965-5

92 Philipp Casula, Jeronim Perovic (Eds.) | Identities and Politics During the Putin Presidency. The Discursive Foundations of Russia's Stability | With a foreword by Heiko Haumann | ISBN 978-3-8382-0015-6

93 Marcel Viëtor | Europa und die Frage nach seinen Grenzen im Osten. Zur Konstruktion ‚europäischer Identität' in Geschichte und Gegenwart | Mit einem Vorwort von Albrecht Lehmann | ISBN 978-3-8382-0045-3

94 Ben Hellman, Andrei Rogachevskii | Filming the Unfilmable. Casper Wrede's 'One Day in the Life of Ivan Denisovich' | Second, Revised and Expanded Edition | ISBN 978-3-8382-0044-6

95 Eva Fuchslocher | Vaterland, Sprache, Glaube. Orthodoxie und Nationenbildung am Beispiel Georgiens | Mit einem Vorwort von Christina von Braun | ISBN 978-3-89821-884-9

96 Vladimir Kantor | Das Westlertum und der Weg Russlands. Zur Entwicklung der russischen Literatur und Philosophie | Ediert von Dagmar Herrmann | Mit einem Beitrag von Nikolaus Lobkowicz | ISBN 978-3-8382-0102-3

97 Kamran Musayev | Die postsowjetische Transformation im Baltikum und Südkaukasus. Eine vergleichende Untersuchung der politischen Entwicklung Lettlands und Aserbaidschans 1985-2009 | Mit einem Vorwort von Leonid Luks | Ediert von Sandro Henschel | ISBN 978-3-8382-0103-0

98 Tatiana Zhurzhenko | Borderlands into Bordered Lands. Geopolitics of Identity in Post-Soviet Ukraine | With a foreword by Dieter Segert | ISBN 978-3-8382-0042-2

99 *Кирилл Галушко, Лидия Смола (ред.)* | Пределы падения – варианты украинского будущего. Аналитико-прогностические исследования | ISBN 978-3-8382-0148-1

100 *Michael Minkenberg (Ed.)* | Historical Legacies and the Radical Right in Post-Cold War Central and Eastern Europe | With an afterword by Sabrina P. Ramet | ISBN 978-3-8382-0124-5

101 *David-Emil Wickström* | Rocking St. Petersburg. Transcultural Flows and Identity Politics in the St. Petersburg Popular Music Scene | With a foreword by Yngvar B. Steinholt | Second, Revised and Expanded Edition | ISBN 978-3-8382-0100-9

102 *Eva Zabka* | Eine neue „Zeit der Wirren"? Der spät- und postsowjetische Systemwandel 1985-2000 im Spiegel russischer gesellschaftspolitischer Diskurse | Mit einem Vorwort von Margareta Mommsen | ISBN 978-3-8382-0161-0

103 *Ulrike Ziemer* | Ethnic Belonging, Gender and Cultural Practices. Youth Identitites in Contemporary Russia | With a foreword by Anoop Nayak | ISBN 978-3-8382-0152-8

104 *Ksenia Chepikova* | ‚Einiges Russland' - eine zweite KPdSU? Aspekte der Identitätskonstruktion einer postsowjetischen „Partei der Macht" | Mit einem Vorwort von Torsten Oppelland | ISBN 978-3-8382-0311-9

105 *Леонид Люкс* | Западничество или евразийство? Демократия или идеократия? Сборник статей об исторических дилеммах России | С предисловием Владимира Кантора | ISBN 978-3-8382-0211-2

106 *Anna Dost* | Das russische Verfassungsrecht auf dem Weg zum Föderalismus und zurück. Zum Konflikt von Rechtsnormen und -wirklichkeit in der Russländischen Föderation von 1991 bis 2009 | Mit einem Vorwort von Alexander Blankenagel | ISBN 978-3-8382-0292-1

107 *Philipp Herzog* | Sozialistische Völkerfreundschaft, nationaler Widerstand oder harmloser Zeitvertreib? Zur politischen Funktion der Volkskunst im sowjetischen Estland | Mit einem Vorwort von Andreas Kappeler | ISBN 978-3-8382-0216-7

108 *Marlène Laruelle (Ed.)* | Russian Nationalism, Foreign Policy, and Identity Debates in Putin's Russia. New Ideological Patterns after the Orange Revolution | ISBN 978-3-8382-0325-6

109 *Michail Logvinov* | Russlands Kampf gegen den internationalen Terrorismus. Eine kritische Bestandsaufnahme des Bekämpfungsansatzes | Mit einem Geleitwort von Hans-Henning Schröder und einem Vorwort von Eckhard Jesse | ISBN 978-3-8382-0329-4

110 *John B. Dunlop* | The Moscow Bombings of September 1999. Examinations of Russian Terrorist Attacks at the Onset of Vladimir Putin's Rule | Second, Revised and Expanded Edition | ISBN 978-3-8382-0388-1

111 *Андрей А. Ковалёв* | Свидетельство из-за кулис российской политики I. Можно ли делать добро из зла? (Воспоминания и размышления о последних советских и первых послесоветских годах) | With a foreword by Peter Reddaway | ISBN 978-3-8382-0302-7

112 *Андрей А. Ковалёв* | Свидетельство из-за кулис российской политики II. Угроза для себя и окружающих (Наблюдения и предостережения относительно происходящего после 2000 г.) | ISBN 978-3-8382-0303-4

113 *Bernd Kappenberg* | Zeichen setzen für Europa. Der Gebrauch europäischer lateinischer Sonderzeichen in der deutschen Öffentlichkeit | Mit einem Vorwort von Peter Schlobinski | ISBN 978-3-89821-749-1

114 *Ivo Mijnssen* | The Quest for an Ideal Youth in Putin's Russia I. Back to Our Future! History, Modernity, and Patriotism according to Nashi, 2005-2013 | With a foreword by Jeronim Perović | Second, Revised and Expanded Edition | ISBN 978-3-8382-0368-3

115 *Jussi Lassila* | The Quest for an Ideal Youth in Putin's Russia II. The Search for Distinctive Conformism in the Political Communication of Nashi, 2005-2009 | With a foreword by Kirill Postoutenko | Second, Revised and Expanded Edition | ISBN 978-3-8382-0415-4

116 *Valerio Trabandt* | Neue Nachbarn, gute Nachbarschaft? Die EU als internationaler Akteur am Beispiel ihrer Demokratieförderung in Belarus und der Ukraine 2004-2009 | Mit einem Vorwort von Jutta Joachim | ISBN 978-3-8382-0437-6

117 *Fabian Pfeiffer* | Estlands Außen- und Sicherheitspolitik I. Der estnische Atlantizismus nach der wiedererlangten Unabhängigkeit 1991-2004 | Mit einem Vorwort von Helmut Hubel | ISBN 978-3-8382-0127-6

118 *Jana Podßuweit* | Estlands Außen- und Sicherheitspolitik II. Handlungsoptionen eines Kleinstaates im Rahmen seiner EU-Mitgliedschaft (2004-2008) | Mit einem Vorwort von Helmut Hubel | ISBN 978-3-8382-0440-6

119 *Karin Pointner* | Estlands Außen- und Sicherheitspolitik III. Eine gedächtnispolitische Analyse estnischer Entwicklungskooperation 2006-2010 | Mit einem Vorwort von Karin Liebhart | ISBN 978-3-8382-0435-2

120 *Ruslana Vovk* | Die Offenheit der ukrainischen Verfassung für das Völkerrecht und die europäische Integration | Mit einem Vorwort von Alexander Blankenagel | ISBN 978-3-8382-0481-9

121 *Mykhaylo Banakh* | Die Relevanz der Zivilgesellschaft bei den postkommunistischen Transformationsprozessen in mittel- und osteuropäischen Ländern. Das Beispiel der spät- und postsowjetischen Ukraine 1986-2009 | Mit einem Vorwort von Gerhard Simon | ISBN 978-3-8382-0499-4

122 *Michael Moser* | Language Policy and the Discourse on Languages in Ukraine under President Viktor Yanukovych (25 February 2010–28 October 2012) | ISBN 978-3-8382-0497-0 (Paperback edition) | ISBN 978-3-8382-0507-6 (Hardcover edition)

123 *Nicole Krome* | Russischer Netzwerkkapitalismus Restrukturierungsprozesse in der Russischen Föderation am Beispiel des Luftfahrtunternehmens "Aviastar" | Mit einem Vorwort von Petra Stykow | ISBN 978-3-8382-0534-2

124 *David R. Marples* | 'Our Glorious Past'. Lukashenka's Belarus and the Great Patriotic War | ISBN 978-3-8382-0574-8 (Paperback edition) | ISBN 978-3-8382-0675-2 (Hardcover edition)

125 *Ulf Walther* | Russlands "neuer Adel". Die Macht des Geheimdienstes von Gorbatschow bis Putin | Mit einem Vorwort von Hans-Georg Wieck | ISBN 978-3-8382-0584-7

126 *Simon Geissbühler (Hrsg.)* | Kiew – Revolution 3.0. Der Euromaidan 2013/14 und die Zukunftsperspektiven der Ukraine | ISBN 978-3-8382-0581-6 (Paperback edition) | ISBN 978-3-8382-0681-3 (Hardcover edition)

127 *Andrey Makarychev* | Russia and the EU in a Multipolar World. Discourses, Identities, Norms | With a foreword by Klaus Segbers | ISBN 978-3-8382-0629-5

128 *Roland Scharff* | Kasachstan als postsowjetischer Wohlfahrtsstaat. Die Transformation des sozialen Schutzsystems | Mit einem Vorwort von Joachim Ahrens | ISBN 978-3-8382-0622-6

129 *Katja Grupp* | Bild Lücke Deutschland. Kaliningrader Studierende sprechen über Deutschland | Mit einem Vorwort von Martin Schulz | ISBN 978-3-8382-0552-6

130 *Konstantin Sheiko, Stephen Brown* | History as Therapy. Alternative History and Nationalist Imaginings in Russia, 1991-2014 | ISBN 978-3-8382-0665-3

131 *Elisa Kriza* | Alexander Solzhenitsyn: Cold War Icon, Gulag Author, Russian Nationalist? A Study of the Western Reception of his Literary Writings, Historical Interpretations, and Political Ideas | With a foreword by Andrei Rogatchevski | ISBN 978-3-8382-0589-2 (Paperback edition) | ISBN 978-3-8382-0690-5 (Hardcover edition)

132 *Serghei Golunov* | The Elephant in the Room. Corruption and Cheating in Russian Universities | ISBN 978-3-8382-0570-0

133 *Manja Hussner, Rainer Arnold (Hgg.)* | Verfassungsgerichtsbarkeit in Zentralasien I. Sammlung von Verfassungstexten | ISBN 978-3-8382-0595-3

134 *Nikolay Mitrokhin* | Die "Russische Partei". Die Bewegung der russischen Nationalisten in der UdSSR 1953-1985 | Aus dem Russischen übertragen von einem Übersetzerteam unter der Leitung von Larisa Schippel | ISBN 978-3-8382-0024-8

135 *Manja Hussner, Rainer Arnold (Hgg.)* | Verfassungsgerichtsbarkeit in Zentralasien II. Sammlung von Verfassungstexten | ISBN 978-3-8382-0597-7

136 *Manfred Zeller* | Das sowjetische Fieber. Fußballfans im poststalinistischen Vielvölkerreich | Mit einem Vorwort von Nikolaus Katzer | ISBN 978-3-8382-0757-5

137 *Kristin Schreiter* | Stellung und Entwicklungspotential zivilgesellschaftlicher Gruppen in Russland. Menschenrechtsorganisationen im Vergleich | ISBN 978-3-8382-0673-8

138 *David R. Marples, Frederick V. Mills (Eds.)* | Ukraine's Euromaidan. Analyses of a Civil Revolution | ISBN 978-3-8382-0660-8

139 *Bernd Kappenberg* | Setting Signs for Europe. Why Diacritics Matter for European Integration | With a foreword by Peter Schlobinski | ISBN 978-3-8382-0663-9

140 *René Lenz* | Internationalisierung, Kooperation und Transfer. Externe bildungspolitische Akteure in der Russischen Föderation | Mit einem Vorwort von Frank Ettrich | ISBN 978-3-8382-0751-3

141 *Juri Plusnin, Yana Zausaeva, Natalia Zhidkevich, Artemy Pozanenko* | Wandering Workers. Mores, Behavior, Way of Life, and Political Status of Domestic Russian Labor Migrants | Translated by Julia Kazantseva | ISBN 978-3-8382-0653-0

142 *David J. Smith (Eds.)* | Latvia – A Work in Progress? 100 Years of State- and Nation-Building | ISBN 978-3-8382-0648-6

143 *Инна Чувычкина (ред.)* | Экспортные нефте- и газопроводы на постсоветском пространстве. Анализ трубопроводной политики в свете теории международных отношений | ISBN 978-3-8382-0822-0

144 *Johann Zajaczkowski* | Russland – eine pragmatische Großmacht? Eine rollentheoretische Untersuchung russischer Außenpolitik am Beispiel der Zusammenarbeit mit den USA nach 9/11 und des Georgienkrieges von 2008 | Mit einem Vorwort von Siegfried Schieder | ISBN 978-3-8382-0837-4

145 *Boris Popivanov* | Changing Images of the Left in Bulgaria. The Challenge of Post-Communism in the Early 21st Century | ISBN 978-3-8382-0667-7

146 *Lenka Krátká* | A History of the Czechoslovak Ocean Shipping Company 1948-1989. How a Small, Landlocked Country Ran Maritime Business During the Cold War | ISBN 978-3-8382-0666-0

147 *Alexander Sergunin* | Explaining Russian Foreign Policy Behavior. Theory and Practice | ISBN 978-3-8382-0752-0

148 *Darya Malyutina* | Migrant Friendships in a Super-Diverse City. Russian-Speakers and their Social Relationships in London in the 21st Century | With a foreword by Claire Dwyer | ISBN 978-3-8382-0652-3

149 *Alexander Sergunin, Valery Konyshev* | Russia in the Arctic. Hard or Soft Power? | ISBN 978-3-8382-0753-7

150 *John J. Maresca* | Helsinki Revisited. A Key U.S. Negotiator's Memoirs on the Development of the CSCE into the OSCE | With a foreword by Hafiz Pashayev | ISBN 978-3-8382-0852-7

151 *Jardar Østbø* | The New Third Rome. Readings of a Russian Nationalist Myth | With a foreword by Pål Kolstø | ISBN 978-3-8382-0870-1

152 *Simon Kordonsky* | Socio-Economic Foundations of the Russian Post-Soviet Regime. The Resource-Based Economy and Estate-Based Social Structure of Contemporary Russia | With a foreword by Svetlana Barsukova | ISBN 978-3-8382-0775-9

153 *Duncan Leitch* | Assisting Reform in Post-Communist Ukraine 2000–2012. The Illusions of Donors and the Disillusion of Beneficiaries | With a foreword by Kataryna Wolczuk | ISBN 978-3-8382-0844-2

154 *Abel Polese* | Limits of a Post-Soviet State. How Informality Replaces, Renegotiates, and Reshapes Governance in Contemporary Ukraine | With a foreword by Colin Williams | ISBN 978-3-8382-0845-9

155 *Mikhail Suslov (Ed.)* | Digital Orthodoxy in the Post-Soviet World. The Russian Orthodox Church and Web 2.0 | With a foreword by Father Cyril Hovorun | ISBN 978-3-8382-0871-8

156 *Leonid Luks* | Zwei „Sonderwege"? Russisch-deutsche Parallelen und Kontraste (1917-2014). Vergleichende Essays | ISBN 978-3-8382-0823-7

157 *Vladimir V. Karacharovskiy, Ovsey I. Shkaratan, Gordey A. Yastrebov* | Towards a New Russian Work Culture. Can Western Companies and Expatriates Change Russian Society? | With a foreword by Elena N. Danilova | Translated by Julia Kazantseva | ISBN 978-3-8382-0902-9

158 *Edmund Griffiths* | Aleksandr Prokhanov and Post-Soviet Esotericism | ISBN 978-3-8382-0903-6

159 *Timm Beichelt, Susann Worschech (Eds.)* | Transnational Ukraine? Networks and Ties that Influence(d) Contemporary Ukraine | ISBN 978-3-8382-0944-9

160 *Mieste Hotopp-Riecke* | Die Tataren der Krim zwischen Assimilation und Selbstbehauptung. Der Aufbau des krimtatarischen Bildungswesens nach Deportation und Heimkehr (1990-2005) | Mit einem Vorwort von Swetlana Czerwonnaja | ISBN 978-3-89821-940-2

161 *Olga Bertelsen (Ed.)* | Revolution and War in Contemporary Ukraine. The Challenge of Change | ISBN 978-3-8382-1016-2

162 *Natalya Ryabinska* | Ukraine's Post-Communist Mass Media. Between Capture and Commercialization | With a foreword by Marta Dyczok | ISBN 978-3-8382-1011-7

163 *Alexandra Cotofana, James M. Nyce (Eds.)* | Religion and Magic in Socialist and Post-Socialist Contexts. Historic and Ethnographic Case Studies of Orthodoxy, Heterodoxy, and Alternative Spirituality | With a foreword by Patrick L. Michelson | ISBN 978-3-8382-0989-0

164 *Nozima Akhrarkhodjaeva* | The Instrumentalisation of Mass Media in Electoral Authoritarian Regimes. Evidence from Russia's Presidential Election Campaigns of 2000 and 2008 | ISBN 978-3-8382-1013-1

165 *Yulia Krasheninnikova* | Informal Healthcare in Contemporary Russia. Sociographic Essays on the Post-Soviet Infrastructure for Alternative Healing Practices | ISBN 978-3-8382-0970-8

166 *Peter Kaiser* | Das Schachbrett der Macht. Die Handlungsspielräume eines sowjetischen Funktionärs unter Stalin am Beispiel des Generalsekretärs des Komsomol Aleksandr Kosarev (1929-1938) | Mit einem Vorwort von Dietmar Neutatz | ISBN 978-3-8382-1052-0

167 *Oksana Kim* | The Effects and Implications of Kazakhstan's Adoption of International Financial Reporting Standards. A Resource Dependence Perspective | With a foreword by Svetlana Vlady | ISBN 978-3-8382-0987-6

168 *Anna Sanina* | Patriotic Education in Contemporary Russia. Sociological Studies in the Making of the Post-Soviet Citizen | With a foreword by Anna Oldfield | ISBN 978-3-8382-0993-7

169 *Rudolf Wolters* | Spezialist in Sibirien Faksimile der 1933 erschienenen ersten Ausgabe | Mit einem Vorwort von Dmitrij Chmelnizki | ISBN 978-3-8382-0515-1

170 *Michal Vít, Magdalena M. Baran (Eds.)* | Transregional versus National Perspectives on Contemporary Central European History. Studies on the Building of Nation-States and Their Cooperation in the 20th and 21st Century | With a foreword by Petr Vágner | ISBN 978-3-8382-1015-5

171 *Philip Gamaghelyan* | Conflict Resolution Beyond the International Relations Paradigm. Evolving Designs as a Transformative Practice in Nagorno-Karabakh and Syria | With a foreword by Susan Allen | ISBN 978-3-8382-1057-5

172 *Maria Shagina* | Joining a Prestigious Club. Cooperation with Europarties and Its Impact on Party Development in Georgia, Moldova, and Ukraine 2004–2015 | With a foreword by Kataryna Wolczuk | ISBN 978-3-8382-1084-1

173 *Alexandra Cotofana, James M. Nyce (Eds.)* | Religion and Magic in Socialist and Post-Socialist Contexts II. Baltic, Eastern European, and Post-USSR Case Studies | With a foreword by Anita Stasulane | ISBN 978-3-8382-0990-6

174 *Barbara Kunz* | Kind Words, Cruise Missiles, and Everything in Between. The Use of Power Resources in U.S. Policies towards Poland, Ukraine, and Belarus 1989–2008 | With a foreword by William Hill | ISBN 978-3-8382-1065-0

175 *Eduard Klein* | Bildungskorruption in Russland und der Ukraine. Eine komparative Analyse der Performanz staatlicher Antikorruptionsmaßnahmen im Hochschulsektor am Beispiel universitärer Aufnahmeprüfungen | Mit einem Vorwort von Heiko Pleines | ISBN 978-3-8382-0995-1

176 *Markus Soldner* | Politischer Kapitalismus im postsowjetischen Russland. Die politische, wirtschaftliche und mediale Transformation in den 1990er Jahren | Mit einem Vorwort von Wolfgang Ismayr | ISBN 978-3-8382-1222-7

177 *Anton Oleinik* | Building Ukraine from Within. A Sociological, Institutional, and Economic Analysis of a Nation-State in the Making | ISBN 978-3-8382-1150-3

178 *Peter Rollberg, Marlene Laruelle (Eds.)* | Mass Media in the Post-Soviet World. Market Forces, State Actors, and Political Manipulation in the Informational Environment after Communism | ISBN 978-3-8382-1116-9

179 *Mikhail Minakov* | Development and Dystopia Studies in Post-Soviet Ukraine and Eastern Europe | With a foreword by Alexander Etkind | ISBN 978-3-8382-1112-1

180 *Aijan Sharshenova* | The European Union's Democracy Promotion in Central Asia A Study of Political Interests, Influence, and Development in Kazakhstan and Kyrgyzstan in 2007–2013 | With a foreword by Gordon Crawford | ISBN 978-3-8382-1151-0

181 *Andrey Makarychev, Alexandra Yatsyk (Eds.)* | Boris Nemtsov and Russian Politics. Power and Resistance | With a foreword by Zhanna Nemtsova | ISBN 978-3-8382-1122-0

182 *Sophie Falsini* | The Euromaidan's Effect on Civil Society. Why and How Ukrainian Social Capital Increased after the Revolution of Dignity | With a foreword by Susann Worschech | ISBN 978-3-8382-1131-2

183 *Andreas Umland (Ed.)* | Ukraine's Decentralization. Challenges and Implications of the Local Governance Reform after the Euromaidan Revolution | ISBN 978-3-8382-1162-6

184 *Leonid Luks* | A Fateful Triangle. Essays on Contemporary Russian, German and Polish History | ISBN 978-3-8382-1143-5

185 *John B. Dunlop* | The February 2015 Assassination of Boris Nemtsov and the Flawed Trial of his Alleged Killers. An Exploration of Russia's "Crime of the 21st Century" | ISBN 978-3-8382-1188-6

186 *Vasile Rotaru* | Russia, the EU, and the Eastern Partnership. Building Bridges or Digging Trenches? | ISBN 978-3-8382-1134-3

187 *Marina Lebedeva* | Russian Studies of International Relations. From the Soviet Past to the Post-Cold-War Present | With a foreword by Andrei P. Tsygankov | ISBN 978-3-8382-0851-0

188 *Tomasz Stępniewski, George Soroka (Eds.)* | Ukraine after Maidan. Revisiting Domestic and Regional Security | ISBN 978-3-8382-1075-9

189 *Petar Cholakov* | Ethnic Entrepreneurs Unmasked. Political Institutions and Ethnic Conflicts in Contemporary Bulgaria | ISBN 978-3-8382-1189-3

190 *A. Salem, G. Hazeldine, D. Morgan (Eds.)* | Higher Education in Post-Communist States. Comparative and Sociological Perspectives | ISBN 978-3-8382-1183-1

191 *Igor Torbakov* | After Empire. Nationalist Imagination and Symbolic Politics in Russia and Eurasia in the Twentieth and Twenty-First Century | With a foreword by Serhii Plokhy | ISBN 978-3-8382-1217-3

192 *Aleksandr Burakovskiy* | Jewish-Ukrainian Relations in Late and Post-Soviet Ukraine. Articles, Lectures and Essays from 1986 to 2016 | ISBN 978-3-8382-1210-4

193 *Natalia Shapovalova, Olga Burlyuk (Eds.)* | Civil Society in Post-Euromaidan Ukraine. From Revolution to Consolidation | With a foreword by Richard Youngs | ISBN 978-3-8382-1216-6

194 *Franz Preissler* | Positionsverteidigung, Imperialismus oder Irredentismus? Russland und die „Russischsprachigen", 1991–2015 | ISBN 978-3-8382-1262-3

195 *Marian Madeła* | Der Reformprozess in der Ukraine 2014-2017. Eine Fallstudie zur Reform der öffentlichen Verwaltung | Mit einem Vorwort von Martin Malek | ISBN 978-3-8382-1266-1

196 *Anke Giesen* | „Wie kann denn der Sieger ein Verbrecher sein?" Eine diskursanalytische Untersuchung der russlandweiten Debatte über Konzept und Verstaatlichungsprozess der Lagergedenkstätte „Perm'-36" im Ural | ISBN 978-3-8382-1284-5

197 *Alla Leukavets* | The Integration Policies of Belarus and Ukraine vis-à-vis the EU and Russia. A Comparative Case Study Through the Prism of a Two-Level Game Approach | ISBN 978-3-8382-1247-0

198 *Oksana Kim* | The Development and Challenges of Russian Corporate Governance I. The Roles and Functions of Boards of Directors | With a foreword by Sheila M. Puffer | ISBN 978-3-8382-1287-6

199 *Thomas D. Grant* | International Law and the Post-Soviet Space I. Essays on Chechnya and the Baltic States | With a foreword by Stephen M. Schwebel | ISBN 978-3-8382-1279-1

200 *Thomas D. Grant* | International Law and the Post-Soviet Space II. Essays on Ukraine, Intervention, and Non-Proliferation | ISBN 978-3-8382-1280-7

201 *Slavomír Michálek, Michal Štefansky* | The Age of Fear. The Cold War and Its Influence on Czechoslovakia 1945–1968 | ISBN 978-3-8382-1285-2

202 *Iulia-Sabina Joja* | Romania's Strategic Culture 1990–2014. Continuity and Change in a Post-Communist Country's Evolution of National Interests and Security Policies | With a foreword by Heiko Biehl | ISBN 978-3-8382-1286-9

203 *Andrei Rogatchevski, Yngvar B. Steinholt, Arve Hansen, David-Emil Wickström* | War of Songs. Popular Music and Recent Russia-Ukraine Relations | With a foreword by Artemy Troitsky | ISBN 978-3-8382-1173-2

204 *Maria Lipman (ed.)* | Russian Voices on Post-Crimea Russia. An Almanac of Counterpoint Essays from 2015–2018 | ISBN 978-3-8382-1251-7

205 *Ksenia Maksimovtsova* | Language Conflicts in Contemporary Estonia, Latvia, and Ukraine. A Comparative Exploration of Discourses in Post-Soviet Russian-Language Digital Media | With a foreword by Ammon Cheskin | ISBN 978-3-8382-1282-1

206 *Michal Vít* | The EU's Impact on Identity Formation in East-Central Europe between 2004 and 2013. Perceptions of the Nation and Europe in Political Parties of the Czech Republic, Poland, and Slovakia | With a foreword by Andrea Pető | ISBN 978-3-8382-1275-3

207 *Per A. Rudling* | Tarnished Heroes. The Organization of Ukrainian Nationalists in the Memory Politics of Post-Soviet Ukraine | ISBN 978-3-8382-0999-9

208 *Kaja Gadowska, Peter Solomon (Eds.)* | Legal Change in Post-Communist States. Progress, Reversions, Explanations | ISBN 978-3-8382-1312-5

209 *Paweł Kowal, Georges Mink, Iwona Reichardt (Eds.)* | Three Revolutions: Mobilization and Change in Contemporary Ukraine I. Theoretical Aspects and Analyses on Religion, Memory, and Identity | ISBN 978-3-8382-1321-7

210 *Paweł Kowal, Georges Mink, Adam Reichardt, Iwona Reichardt (Eds.)* | Three Revolutions: Mobilization and Change in Contemporary Ukraine II. An Oral History of the Revolution on Granite, Orange Revolution, and Revolution of Dignity | ISBN 978-3-8382-1323-1

211 *Li Bennich-Björkman, Sergiy Kurbatov (Eds.)* | When the Future Came: The Collapse of the USSR and the Emergence of National Memory in Post-Soviet History Textbooks | ISBN 978-3-8382-1335-4

212 *Olga R. Gulina* | Migration as a (Geo-)Political Challenge in the Post-Soviet Space. Border Regimes, Policy Choices, Visa Agendas | With a foreword by Nils Muižnieks | ISBN 978-3-8382-1338-5

213 *Turoma, Sanna; Aitamurto, Kaarina; Vladiv-Glover, Slobodanka* | Essays on Post-Soviet Society and the State. ISBN 978-3-8382-1346-0

ibidem.eu